Political Sociology

Political Sociology

READINGS ON POWER, POLITICS, STATE, AND SOCIETY

FIRST EDITION

Edited by Sebahattin Ziyanak

SAN DIEGO

Bassim Hamadeh, CEO and Publisher
John Remington,Executive Editor
Gem Rabanera, Senior Project Editor
Celeste Paed, Associate Production Editor
Jess Estrella, Senior Graphic Designer
Trey Soto, Licensing Coordinator
Natalie Piccotti, Director of Marketing
Kassie Graves, Vice President of Editorial
Jamie Giganti, Director of Academic Publishing

Printed in the United States of America.

CONTENTS

INTRODUCTION

My experience as a social science professor and my continuous search for effective sources with which to teach have lead me to create this book, which focuses on the sociological context of political activities through controversial global and domestic political issues. During my time teaching, I have asked my students questions such as: "What do you anticipate to learn in this course?" From their answers, I realized some students were nervous to enroll in a political sociology course. Some of them had never heard of the subject before. An additional few were excited to learn more about political sociology during an election year. A final group thought it was just a course about voting.

I evaluated numerous articles in order to provide the reader, no matter their preconceptions about the course, with a sense of the richness and comprehensive resources that inform political sociology. In doing so, I found the most captivating readings, selected from recognized scholars in the field of political sociology. My aim was to focus on global and domestic, as well as past and present, political and social issues to provide broad illustrations for how to understand political sociology itself.

This book is primarily intended for sociology students. However, it will be relevant for students in political science, public policy and administration, gender studies, and diversity studies. The political sociology textbook examines the association between society, the state, and the foundations of politics. It will provide students the tools with which they can understand the nature of society and seek solutions to solving social political problems, including

- civic culture
- political power
- the role of women
- how power is legitimized in capitalism
- control in news coverage and agency
- the relationship between states and women
- how large-scale technological systems became symbols of state power

The textbook contains eight chapters.

Chapter 1: Good Citizens of a World Power: Postwar Reconfigurations of the Obligation to Give. This chapter is an overview that explores how citizens support a strong civic culture in which giving, loaning, and volunteering become cornerstones of the social fabric.

Chapter 2: Elites and Class Structures. This chapter introduces the discussion on elites by outlining the processes of elite formation in the major industrialized countries of the United States, Germany, France, Britain, and Japan.

Chapter 3: Agency Design, the Mass Media, and the Blame for Agency Scandals. Here, the reader learns about formal presidential control in news coverage. It seeks to examine whether presidents are held responsible for the mistakes of their agencies and what the media's role is in shaping that responsibility.

Chapter 4: Women, Democracy, and the State. The authors address the relationship between states and women from the sociological perspectives of democracy and development. They also consider how states are fundamentally gendered institutions, and how states both create and reproduce gender biases.

Chapter 5: The Power of Hope Through Community. This chapter is filled with information regarding the destruction of the primarily African American town of Pinhook, Missouri, located in the Birds Point–New Madrid Floodway. This chapter explains racial politics in the Missouri Bootheel region and how race may have factored into the decision to flood the spillway.

Chapter 6: Big Artifacts: Technological Symbolism and State Power. The author focuses on big technology and how it serves as a symbol of state power, wealth, and political authority. This chapter provides a glimpse into significant examples from both historical and contemporary worlds to demonstrate symbols of state power throughout the centuries.

Chapter 7: Vicious Circles: The Structure of Power and the Culture of Judgment. This chapter is an account of the rise of broad political movements in North America and Europe. It provides a basic understanding of *false consciousness* and its impact upon the lives of individuals.

Chapter 8: The Investment Theory of Politics. The author analyzes the *median voter theorem* and the *investment theory of politics* and turns our attention to the history of voter inequality, the continuing concerns of voter suppression, and how oppression is related to the voter theorem.

Overall, this book presents an understanding of the political and social world. The expectation is that as a reader delves into this book, they will discover a broad spectrum of political sociological concepts. They will be happily surprised as they engage with these varied, interesting topics.

- How politics affect our daily lives
- Political social constructs
- The political motivation of groups
- How politics plays a role in sociology
- What sort of social factors influence the political ideologies of specific groups
- The circumstances shaping peoples' opinions and actions
- How society shapes politics and how politics shape society

This textbook will provide the reader with a basic understanding to examine events in the political and social world by identifying power structures and the distribution of power in our society.

Lastly, I hope this textbook will fill the gap in modern political sociology texts.

■ CHAPTER 1

The Nature of Political Sociology: Civic Political Culture

Editor's Introduction

This chapter examines the components of a strong civic culture. Clemens first describes citizen support through giving, loaning, and volunteering as powerful enactments of citizenship. Then, she goes on to discuss impactful political resources that include nationalization of economic activity, a strong sense of municipal membership, and frequent citizen engagement. One poignant example of exemplary civic culture occurs during wartime, when many Americans donate to nonprofit organizations in order to feel as if they are doing their part to support the fights for freedom. To examine the links between charity and citizenship and the scale of citizen support for national efforts, Clemens draws upon the example of President Franklin Delano Roosevelt's administration, during which a "national infrastructure of benevolence" had been constructed. Finally, she analyzes bureaucratic, autonomous, and public authority to further understanding about the dynamics of American governance and the development of political power to coordinate civil society.

READING 1 Good Citizens of a World Power: Postwar Reconfigurations of the Obligation to Give

Elisabeth S. Clemens

In 1943, more than 80 percent of Americans surveyed by George Gallup reported that they had donated to the American Red Cross during the past year.[1] Other war charities benefited from elevated levels of giving, and at the same time, citizens purchased war bonds in large numbers. Although all these contributions were understood as "voluntary," the pressures to give were often intense. The scale of citizen support for the war exemplified the consolidation of a strong civic culture in which giving, loaning, and volunteering were powerful enactments of citizenship. Linked to the nationalization of economic activity and the power of a revered wartime president, this pattern of citizen engagement was a formidable political resource.

But by 1946, this regime of wartime solidarity expressed through civic benevolence was already at risk. The American Red Cross commissioned another confidential poll from George Gallup. This time they found that support had fallen dramatically, particularly among those who had direct ties to someone serving overseas. Troubling as this discontent among veterans and their families was to the Red Cross, it represented only one dimension of the destabilization of the distinctive regime of national mobilization that had characterized the Second World War. In an extension of patterns evident for decades, and especially in the mobilization for the Great—not yet First—World War, military mobilization had driven the US government to expand in ways that depended massively on extended collaborations with private organizations to rally support, to produce war material, to provide aid to the troops, and to discipline the civilian population. Reliant as it was on local business leaders, corporate executives, and a nascent category of public relations experts, this model of governing through public-private collaboration expanded public power and delegated a portion of control to private individuals and organizations.

Under Franklin Delano Roosevelt, however, this delegation of control had been attached to a new demand—namely, that organized labor be given a seat at the civic "roundtables" that had played such an important role in the mobilization of resources and public support for national efforts during war, natural disaster, economic crisis, and renewed war. This demand represented a "nationalization" of associational governance in at least two senses of the term: an intensification of presidential direction of civic mobilization and a requirement that effective participation—as leaders as well as contributors—be extended beyond the business and community elites long central to the architecture of civic associations in the United States. This marked shift in the structure of control over civic efforts in support of the federal government set the terms for a postwar political struggle over the demobilization of the wartime state and the role of civic associations in American public life. The result of this competition would be a strange hybrid political regime that linked the celebration of voluntary participation in local politics to an expansive internationalism in support of the

Cold War national security state. This moment of national dominance, the high water mark of "the American Century," was marked by a puzzling combination of voluntarism and statism.

The Associational State in American Political Development

Viewed through the lens of comparative politics, the history of the American state has seemed anomalous, a deviation from the trajectories followed by governing arrangements in Europe and elsewhere. Instead of conforming to the model of centralized, bureaucratic, autonomous public authority often equated with the modern state, American governance has been organized through *both* public institutions and private organizations or individuals. This type of regime relies on what sociologist Michael Mann has called "infrastructural" strength, allowing for the development of "power to coordinate civil society" without a commensurate increase in the scale or visibility of formal public institutions.[2] The apparently "weak state" scholars of nineteenth-century American politics observed has been recharacterized as a system of governance that relied significantly on these "sinews of power" that extended far beyond the visible boundaries of official institutions.[3]

Attention to infrastructural power has been central to dispelling what historian William Novak has termed "the myth of the 'weak' American state." In terms of the capacity or resources available to the federal government, the existence of a rich network of collaboration with private individuals or organizations helps to explain how such a small government—measured in terms of its budget or personnel—could accomplish so much in terms of expanding across a continent and mobilizing for modern wars, both civil and overseas. But if infrastructural power helps to explain the capacity of the American state, this concept has been less effective at posing a related question: if governance is constituted through infrastructural networks, then who governs?[4] What determines the particular configuration of networks of governance and relations of power?

This question requires moving beyond the ratio of visible to submerged state capacities. In addition, there is a politics surrounding the specific configurations of associational involvement in governance and, by extension, conflicts over control of critical networks in these expansive state-linked collaborations. Over the course of the twentieth century, the "associational state" repeatedly morphed into new forms, at times more closely linked to the building of new federal agencies and capacities and at others more aligned with those opposed to the expansion of federal powers. Consequently, the recognition of the distinctive character of American state building is only a first step, framed as it is by the comparison with the more classically Weberian administrative state that cases drawn from continental Europe exemplify. Beyond the comparative analysis of state forms there lies the question of the distinctive politics of different associational configurations.

Different arrangements of infrastructural power advantaged different political actors and were consistent with different policy visions. One variant, celebrated as the "associative state," was championed by Herbert Hoover as secretary of commerce and then as president in the 1920s.[5] This vision has often been understood as an alternative to the expanded government of Franklin Delano Roosevelt's New Deal, with its array of new regulatory agencies, citizen entitlements, and social insurance programs. From this vantage point, party politics plays out as a contest over the extent of associational or collaborative government, with more conservative administrations expected to favor limiting the role and size of public agencies and programs.

Despite the undoubted hostility of many conservatives to the expansion of state intervention,[6] this standard account misses the important ways in which associational politics and governance have proved attractive regardless of an administration's ideological commitments. Roosevelt himself did not shy from harnessing civic and voluntary groups to public projects. Examples can be found in the policy responses to the depression years of the 1930s,[7] in his own signature project of civic benevolence, the March of Dimes, as well as the national mobilization in support of World War II. Rather than rejecting the associational methods linked to the conservative opposition to the New Deal, Roosevelt managed a transformation of purpose and control. His accomplishment did not escape leading public relations experts whose profession had developed out of the massive fund-raising efforts of the First World War:[8] "The present occupant of the White House is preeminent among all men in public life in his ability to think in selling terms and speak in advertising language."[9] Roosevelt had, in effect, stolen their methods and mastered an approach to civic mobilization long felt to be the distinctive property of business and community elites. If this moment of crisis can be understood as a political competition for loyalty and obligation,[10] Roosevelt appeared a clear winner, and in the process the president engineered a decisive shift in the control of civic benevolence and the ramified system of associational governance.

Although the New Deal had begun with the drawing of a bright line between federal programs and private, charitable relief efforts, this clean divide was soon blurred.[11] Roosevelt came to appreciate the power of charitable fund-raising in his personal campaign to put his polio facility at Warm Springs, Georgia, on a stable financial footing. What began as the Committee to Celebrate the President's Birthday soon grew into what we still know as the March of Dimes. Faced with the inevitable limits of federal revenue, Roosevelt also insisted on the continuing responsibility of private relief and local government contributions to aid for the unemployed and, particularly, the unemployable as the depression lingered on through much of the decade.

With respect to the delivery of social services, the result was not a return to Hoover's vision of smaller government and revived independent voluntarism, but rather a complex and attenuated web of relationships between formally private voluntary efforts and federal funds, mandates, and tax subsidies. As early as 1935, federal social security legislation had been amended to allow public funds to flow to private, not-for-profit social service agencies, specifically to residential and nursing homes for the elderly.[12] The result was the emergence and eventual consolidation of a field of what were now known as "nonprofit organizations." Although many of these organizations traced their origins to the Charity Organization Societies of the late nineteenth century or the progressive social reform efforts of the Progressive Era, these newly named nonprofit organizations were now managed by professional social workers and nested in networks that linked business-dominated centralized municipal fund-raising and local volunteer efforts that were structured in deference to professional authority.[13] Consequently, the flow of federal funding to at least some of these organizations did not necessarily result in a political alliance between local providers and the national state. Rather, this first infusion of federal funds into the domain of nonprofit organizations helped to strengthen what many conservatives believed to be a bulwark against further expansion of the national welfare state.[14] Thus the flow of federal funds alone was not sufficient to align civic organizations with national political projects. As the case of social service provision illustrates, federal financial support might well strengthen the hand of local municipal and business elites.

As the conflicts that would become a second world war gathered force, Roosevelt turned again to the American Red Cross as a vehicle for raising citizen contributions for war relief that could be sent where no federal assistance could go as a consequence of the power of isolationist forces in Congress. Federal agencies revived the impressive infrastructure of advertising and salesmanship of war bonds that had played such an important role in the First World War.[15] Many read these efforts through a political lens. Roosevelt's revival of "Red Cross patriotism" and the success of the March of Dimes represented, to at least some of his critics, a disturbing resemblance to the fascist societies just defeated in war.

By the end of the Second World War, the ties between charity and citizenship had been anchored in the person of President Franklin Delano Roosevelt for well over a decade. A part of his achievement consisted in recentering the emotional focus of civic benevolence on the presidency itself. But a second element involved translating civic benevolence into a more inclusive mode. While voluntary associations have long been an established feature of the social landscape for a wide range of ethnic, religious, occupational, recreational, improvement, and educational efforts, the fact of associating did not automatically translate into meaningful influence over public affairs.[16] Civic groups dominated by business had edged aside the membership-based voluntary associations of the nineteenth century: the Grange, the Alliance, the Knights of Labor, and all the women's clubs. These cliques of local notables now had to acknowledge the role of the national government and to provide a seat at the table for organized labor if they were to remain even partially in control of their own benevolent empires. This insistence on a more inclusive[17] organization of civic benevolence set the terms for a fierce competition over the same terrain in the years after the war.

Presidential Variants on Civic Benevolence

President Roosevelt's death removed a central pillar of this regime of nationalized reciprocity. Although the drive for the March of Dimes in the year after his death would set records as a national memorial for Roosevelt himself, thereafter the efforts became more problematic, revived only as the prospect of a successful polio vaccine came into view during the 1950s.[18] The configuration of civic voluntarism and expanded state activities that had been consolidated through the New Deal and the world war was up for grabs again.

Although calls for a single coordinated war fund drive had never been fully realized (in this, as in almost every administrative matter, FDR preferred to have multiple players in a single field), many groups had chafed at the partial centralization of control whether in the Red Cross or the War Chests. The result was a period of flux in which some groups defected from centralized fund-raising, others made plays to wrest control from the groups that had dominated the wartime organization of civic benevolence, still others turned from nationalizing benevolence to fund-raising that would strengthen institutions—particularly in health care and higher education—that would serve as bulwarks against state expansion and pillars of domains of private enterprise.

These efforts to deconstruct the specifically *presidential* focus of civic benevolence did not mean an abandonment of nation-building projects. In the emerging context of the Cold War, large-scale organized voluntarism and community democracy served important expressive purposes, demonstrating to the world the practices of civic membership and self-governance that exemplified liberal internationalism. The challenge, therefore, was to unwind the webs of reciprocity that had linked citizens throughout the nation to the charismatic figure of FDR himself while preserving the vitality of local forms of participation once economic crisis and international conflict had come to an end.

A Legacy Envisioned

Following the president's death and as wartime expectations of national unity faded, the postwar years brought efforts to redefine the linking of charity and citizenship. From the late 1940s through the 1950s, Roosevelt's longtime allies sought to perpetuate the connection of giving to a strong national identity, notably through the mechanism of national blood banking and the continuing war against polio. But other camps advocated a return to more local networks of civic responsibility. In some part, this was the "local" of the bowling leagues and Parent-Teacher Associations that were populated by returning veterans, their spouses, and burgeoning families.[19] But, perhaps more significantly, this was also the local of chambers of commerce and community hospital boards that occupied the center of networks boosting economic development.[20] All three—nationalized citizen philanthropy, local-civic, and local-business—of these configurations can be characterized as "infrastructural" or "associational," but they supported very different distributions of power and understandings of national membership and obligations.

The terms of conflict involved the level of voluntary giving as well as the locus of control. Economic elites came to understand giving by citizens as an obstacle to the expansion of a consumer economy at the same time that they recognized the potential of a newly conceptualized nonprofit sector as a site for setting boundaries on the expansion of public social provision. This potential for limiting explicitly public programs was underwritten by expanding streams of tax-subsidized contributions, enabled by the linking of a long-standing individual deduction for charitable contributions with the introduction of a mass income tax as well as the regularization of corporate charitable contributions in the Wealth Act of 1935. As federal spending programs increasingly recognized nonprofit organizations—whether social welfare agencies, community hospitals, or research universities—as legitimate recipients of public funds, the ingredients were in place for the distinctive brew of public and private efforts that has come to characterize American governance in the second half of the twentieth century.[21] Thus the postwar years provide an opportunity for exploring how political struggles operated to decouple cultural logics from one configuration of alliances and then embed them in different networks of reciprocity and responsibility.

Alternatives, however, were imaginable. The wartime experience worked powerfully on political imaginations, particularly of those who understood how extended networks of civic benevolence sustained the capacity and legitimacy of state action. Nowhere had this lesson been better learned than in the circles closest to President Roosevelt. Within those circles, perhaps no one understood the implications of this model of governance and solidarity more fully than Basil O'Connor, FDR's former law partner, founding president of the National Foundation for Infantile Paralysis (which received 50 percent of funds raised by the March of Dimes), and, as of 1944, president of the American Red Cross. Situated at the intersection of structures of civic organization and formal political institutions, O'Connor understood what might be accomplished by a peacetime alignment of nation and citizen through voluntary gifts.

O'Connor proposed a domestic substitute for wartime mobilization as a method of generating national solidarity. He argued that a national system of blood banking would provide a moral infrastructure for national unity:

> The goal of the National Blood Program is to provide blood and blood derivatives, without charge for the products, wherever needed throughout the nation.
>
> To accomplish the objectives of this new service to humanity, the Red Cross will have the advice and guidance of medical, health, and hospital, authorities ... with full realization that it is a program of, for, and by the people of this nation. ...
>
> The program is a cooperative project in which hospital and medical authorities, public health officials, and the American Red Cross will participate to ensure the soundest policies and the highest possible standards of operation.
>
> The most important participant, however, must be the citizenry. The *need* of the people *for* blood has been our motivating force in establishing this new program. And only the *generosity* of the *people* in *donating* their blood to the sick and injured will provide the power to drive this program forward with sustained momentum. ...
>
> The National Blood Program presents the opportunity to all our citizens to contribute directly to the saving of life and the prevention of suffering—not as an ideal but as a concrete act of generosity.
>
> What if the donor cannot actually trace, with his own eyes, the use of his blood to the beneficiary? Each gift of blood will have tangible value to someone in need. The picture is clear. It needs only to be made vivid in the minds of the American people.
>
> A pint of blood given by John Doe rests in the storage vault of a blood center. Not far away on a main highway, two cars come speeding toward each other and collide. Their occupants are torn by broken glass and twisted metal and suffer great loss of blood. John Doe's blood is rushed to the bedside of one of the victims, who has well-nigh bled to death, and is poured into his veins. John Doe's blood has helped to save a life.
>
> Another donor's blood has been processed into plasma and held for emergency use. Weeks later a fire breaks out in one of the city's large buildings. Dozens of residents suffer shock and terrible burns. This plasma is poured into the veins of one of the victims, even before there is time to transport her to the hospital. The donor's gift of blood has lessened shock and suffering. ...
>
> The blood of generous citizens, donated to the general welfare, will be the raw material out of which may come great discoveries in the amelioration of prevention of some of mankind's worst enemies. Men and women—the volunteers of America—could not give of themselves to a finer cause. Yes, this is truly a milepost for all the participating chapters. Likewise it is a milepost for the medical world.[22]

This passage, quoted at length, links themes of civic solidarity, preparedness, and progress. It is a textbook plan for generating national solidarity through an extended system of indirect exchange,[23] albeit a plan that elided the official policies of racial exclusion and segregation that had been retained despite vocal civil rights protests throughout the war and the remainder of the decade.[24] Through the practice of donating blood, so the model operated, citizens give gifts that then forge ties of gratitude among strangers (and, by extension, contribute to a vast system of mutual insurance against unexpected accidents and threats to health). These acts of generosity contribute to more than the repair of the damaged bodies of fellow citizens; they also sustain the progress of science and medicine that will contribute to the well-being of all, present and future generations alike.

For the five years that he led the organization, Basil O'Connor worked to realize this vision of a national infrastructure of benevolence consistent with democratic commitments and expansive participation. He pushed the first revisions of the Red Cross charter, adopted more than four decades earlier when Mabel Boardman and her allies had ousted Clara Barton in 1902. (Boardman herself died in 1946, only a year after stepping down from the position of Red Cross secretary that she had held for decades.) The revision shifted power to the local chapters which would now elect a clear majority of the board, the remaining seats to be filled either ex officio by representatives of the federal cabinet departments or by nominations from the current board.[25] At the tail end of a long Democratic administration, having provided relief to citizens and support to soldiers, the Red Cross stood on the verge of a stronger alignment with basic democratic principles. But, in many respects, the shift came too late to forestall criticism, defection, competition, and a slide from national influence.

O'Connor's attempt to transpose a model of nationalized civic benevolence from wartime to peaceable uses foundered in the face of opposition fueled both by a general suspicion of any extension of the Roosevelt–Truman political hegemony and by the specific fear of government expansion into a national health service. This latter point, after all, represented one of the lines drawn in the sand by critics of the New Deal in the late 1930s.[26] But the defeat of O'Connor's national blood-banking plan was only a first move in a broader effort to realign voluntary efforts with different structures of power and circuits of exchange. The business leaders and community elites who had long watched as Roosevelt gained leverage over local networks of voluntary associations were now poised to retake control.

A Legacy Undone

The possibility of constructing a national infrastructure of benevolence was undermined by political developments set in motion by the Roosevelt administration itself. With its roots in the tradition of civic deference that stretched back to the antebellum Whigs, organized benevolence did not necessarily mesh smoothly with the expansion of democratic rights and participation pushed by the New Deal and wartime mobilization. The friction surfaced early in relationships between the Red Cross and the Congress of Industrial Organizations (CIO). While the CIO had participated in multiple wartime drives led by the Red Cross, frustrations had mounted at the failure of the Red Cross to provide meaningful opportunities to participate in the volunteer services and decision making of the organization. Early in 1946, the CIO withdrew from joint fund-raising, asserting that "the Red Cross had not indicated any interest in the CIO's efforts to promote volunteer participation in home nursing, first aid, and other essential Red Cross volunteer work, and that 'our efforts to create a more wholesome understanding between Red Cross chapters and local labor groups were discouraged at every turn.'" Holding out the possibility of a rapprochement, the CIO expressed its hope "that under your [Basil O'Connor's] leadership the Red Cross will become a truly American Red Cross, democratized for full participation for everyone in the community."[27]

If the union members of the CIO felt that they had been excluded from full membership in the "community" as represented by the American Red Cross because of their politics, other organizations put themselves forward as more appropriate representatives of *local* rather than *national* community. The alternative was represented by the resurgence of federated fund-raising, once organized through the hundreds of "community chests" but increasingly now under the banner of "United Funds." This fund-raising model was pioneered in Detroit in 1949 and, from the perspective of the Red Cross, constituted a threat to its own understanding of national patriotism articulated through voluntarism. The Red Cross defense was presented in an official pamphlet that, according to newspaper reports, contended that the idea of united fund-raising was "being 'actively sold' to business leaders, large corporations and membership organizations, in Michigan by the United Health and Welfare Fund of Michigan, Inc., and on a nation-wide scale by the Michigan unit as well as by Community Chests and Councils, Inc., of New York." At the national meeting in 1949, the Red Cross "struck out … against 'coercive' attempts to federate all welfare fund drives in one annual appeal." Red Cross officials argued that "'compulsory federated fund-raising' would be federated and controlled first on a state-wide and eventually on a national basis. The system would produce one mammoth annual financial campaign carried on simultaneously throughout the country 'under the direction of this national authority,' according to the Red Cross."[28] In the alternation of "community" and "national," two different configurations of voluntarism are visible. The first, represented by the Red Cross, linked local chapters to the national organization with its presidential imprimatur. The second, exemplified by the Community Chests and Councils Inc., sought to span the nation geographically through a loose web of municipally centered organizations.[29]

As wartime mobilization receded, national organizations such as the American Red Cross once again found themselves competing for control of charitable citizenship with locally oriented efforts to harness networks of reciprocity and mutuality. The conflicts over the relationship of the Red Cross to the Community Chests that had flared in the 1920s resurfaced, pushing the leadership to issue a statement as to "Why the American National Red Cross Does Not Permit Participation in Any Joint Fund Raising Campaign."[30] This argument was couched in an extended analogy to world politics: "One argument against communism is the fact that under this system those who deserve to be better off *are not* and those who do not deserve to be better off *are.* To a considerable extent this has been the experience of Community Chest agencies. The weak and less needed organizations must ride in on the wake of the stronger ones. Without much question it can be said that the Red Cross, because of its very nature and purpose as a national and international force, deserves to be better off financially than possibly can be provided through any communized fund-raising device."[31]

These conflicts turned on money and power. Familiar complaints were recited, that local Red Cross chapters had joined Community Chests with the assurance of certain distributions from the united drives, yet those assurances were not honored. Revenues were slashed, memberships declined, and "most chapters identified with chests tended to become more and more localized in their point of view and to lose sight of the fact that they were the agents of a national organization governed by a Congressional Charter. Furthermore, in some instances, the chapter's identity in the local community faded almost to the vanishing point. … Chests tended to become dictatorial and to assume vested authority over chapters along with other member agencies." Apart from the implications for the amount of funds raised or needy persons served, each separate fund-raising effort sustained a particular network of influence and particular understanding of the relational quality of civic life. Thus the conflicts surrounding national charities and the civic role of philanthropy were not necessarily expressions of populist resentments but the mutual suspicion of distinctive subsets of the many different elite networks that organized life within and across the nation's communities.[32]

Eventually, the Red Cross succumbed to the pressure from a handful of powerful local chapters to allow participation in joint fund-raising in industrial plants that allowed only one fund-raising drive per year. This agreement was hedged about with conditions—that the Red Cross would determine its own budgetary means added into the total amount of the drive, that the Red Cross would retain the right to organize independent drives in the broader community—but the change of principle was clear. By-then-former Red Cross president Basil O'Connor blasted the policy change, arguing that payroll deductions "no matter how dressed up, are compulsory assessments on employes [*sic*] for health and welfare activities." This compulsion, O'Connor argued, undermined the pretense of voluntarism as a legitimate alternative to public social services:

> If funds for health and welfare are to be obtained by assessment, then the proper mechanism to use is obviously the power of taxation where the burden falls on all and not just on labor.
>
> If the public will not voluntarily support voluntary associations for health and welfare, the indication is that the public believes such associations should no longer exist and that health and welfare should be totally a matter of governmental operation. That seventy million people annually support the March of Dimes shows clearly that the public has reached no such decision.[33]

In the space of a few years, networks of corporate leaders had substantially retaken control over the organizational infrastructure of civic benevolence, leading critics to see "voluntary" fund-raising as a new form of economic dictatorship capable of coercing employees to donate funds to support services that could be funded more democratically through taxation. On this dimension, the postwar politics of civic benevolence shifted the balance between a charisma-driven nationalizing mode and a much more municipally centered, business-dominated form of mobilization.

As a consequence, the philanthropically sustained sense of common membership in a national community was increasingly frayed. Focusing his comments on the "ingrate crisis area" of Flint, Michigan, which had been struck by a tornado in 1954, Red Cross president E. Roland Harriman complained that "the pattern had been to wait until 'the Red Cross finished the job of meeting basic needs' and then to use the contributions from other sources 'to replace losses on a pro rata basis' without respect to the resources of the recipients and their ability to re-establish themselves.' … In the future, he said, 'communities that don't help themselves in the total responsibility of a disaster can hardly expect to be recipients of nation-wide generosity.'"[34]

In parallel with these shamings and scoldings, others attempted to revive the sense of national obligation and solidarity. As fund-raising efforts fell short in 1953, Mamie Eisenhower made a "personal appeal to the mothers of America," calling for them to donate both funds and blood. Attempting to explain the troubling shortfall, the First Lady speculated: "'What they perhaps do not realize is that the same pint of blood they contribute can be processed into gamma globulin and also into serum albumin, the blood derivative which our Korean combat wounded need so desperately.' Through the Red Cross, therefore, Mrs. Eisenhower stressed blood today did double duty. 'We can help children walk and wounded to live.'"[35] In these appeals, the faded spirit of wartime civic benevolence reappeared, but the results fell short of the national solidarity that was to have been generated by circuits of blood donation and receipt within a unified citizenry.

The shift from national networks of benevolence to more restricted circuits of mutual aid was evident across policy domains, including not only disaster relief but also medical care. The same tension between the inclusive "indirect exchange" envisioned in O'Connor's plan and the organizational features of the postwar health care system produced a schism within blood banking over issues that went to the heart of a Maussian model of gift exchange.[36] Whereas the Red Cross under O'Connor had envisioned a system in which blood would be donated without compensation and available to all those who needed it, the medical societies—at least in the vicinity of New York City—were interested in linking the provision of blood to the financial practices of private hospitals. Consequently, they promoted a system in which donors would receive "credits" for donations that would entitle them to a certain amount of blood for themselves if needed (at a ratio of up to four pints for every one pint donated) and, at a slightly less generous rate, to other family members. The Red Cross protested that if a system of credits was to function it needed to recognize that blood donation often happened in the context of group membership—in fraternal lodges, unions, churches, workplaces—rather than narrowly within the bounds of family.[37] Credits, they argued, needed to be transferable to comembers in these organizations. But these arguments did not persuade the leadership of professional medical societies, and their breach with the Red Cross widened further. Here, civic benevolence was not only denationalized, it also was increasingly individualized and disembedded from the variegated voluntary associations that had been a feature of the American landscape for more than a century.

Through the cumulative effects of these conflicts over the specific forms of associational voluntarism, the years following the end of World War II saw the landscape of civic benevolence fracture along multiple dimensions. The unified fund drives of wartime gave way to increased competition, dissent, and mutual recrimination as various groups and constituencies contested the right of any one group to represent and choreograph the generosity of the American people. This splintering among organizations committed to some encompassing civic vision was accompanied by a retreat into professionalism on the part of organizations that had once served as focal points for the mobilization of a sense of mutual obligation within the nation's towns and cities. As historian Andrew Morris has demonstrated, the Charity Organization Societies and relief boards that had provided a venue for recognition and coordination of benevolence prior to the New Deal emerged from the Second World War as entities dedicated to professional therapeutic work with a mix of paying and subsidized clients.[38] But even if the volume of civic benevolence had been turned down, these methods still operated within the nation's cities to provide relief and to activate relationships of civic membership and governance. Here too, however, the capacity of civic benevolence to mobilize political solidarity was on the wane.

A Transformed Organizational Landscape

In the years immediately after the war, social service organizations oscillated between these two understandings of their role, alternately acting as private charities or as professional nonprofit agencies. Thus the winter of 1947 brought appeals that would have seemed quite familiar a half century earlier: "For $15 one of these children will find a wealth of warmth in a bright new coat. $10 will fit his little sister into a sturdy snowsuit, and $5 will keep a youngster snug with a set of galoshes, mittens and stockings."[39] Yet by later that spring, one study committee of the same organization, the Community Service Society of New York (the product of a merger between the Association for Improving the Conditions of the Poor, established in the 1840s, and the New York Charity Organization Society, established in 1882) reported: "In the light of our study it would appear that in the process of growth and expansion the Family Service Department has been undergoing a gradual change in function, as evidenced by the greater emphasis on research and staff development and by a deepening of the content of case work, to the point where it has become more nearly a family-counseling and child-guidance service."[40] This organizational transformation involved multiple reconfigurations, not least the relationships between organization and donor as well as organization and client. Above all, the remnants of the traditional ties of benevolence between donors (or the organization as their representative) and clients had to be purged.

These organizational changes extended the new division of labor between government and private efforts that had begun to be articulated early in the New Deal. Whereas FDR had spoken about government's responsibility for "economic maladjustment" and charity's jurisdiction over "individual maladjustment," the language now referenced the relationship of those providing and receiving services. The key distinction conflated references to commerce and totalitarianism, drawing a line between "mass" services and "individuated" or "retail" services.[41] Urging support for the Community Service Society of New York, Frederick Sheffield wrote to Laurance Rockefeller:

> This new society is equipped to do all of the jobs that the prior organizations did and do them more effectively and more efficiently. Of course, you realize what this means to our community. My personal belief is that unless the right kinds of private charitable organizations are supported in these days, the future of each individual's relationship to his community will become more and more dependent upon government and less and less individualistic. The particular charity, moreover, reaches down into the very roots of the troubles which so many charities have to help and for which so much government expenditure is necessary.[42]

Whereas the nation-centered civic benevolence of wartime had emphasized how each small gift incorporated individuals into a national struggle, here the emphasis was on private charity as a limit on the intrusion of government service that was understood to be corrosive of democratic values. Thus the linking of mass citizen benevolence to national projects and patriotism eroded. And, as a consequence, circuits of reciprocity were reoriented.

With the struggle over government financial support for relief and social services now long settled in the affirmative, nonprofit organizations confronted the question of how to motivate supporters to make contributions above and beyond their mandated taxes. Absent the rallying force of a national crisis or presidential charisma, what was to persuade people to give freely in order to forestall the need to expand mandatory taxation to support those same community services? In the fund-raising drives of the 1950s, charitable motives were displaced by references to business calculation infused with political commitments: "This is a straightforward business appeal. The century-old Community Service Society is in the business of helping to keep sound the New York community in which you do business, to help protect the community's family life—the bedrock of democracy."[43]

Yet for all these changes, the mobilization of resources in the nonprofit sector continued to rely on networks of personal reciprocity.[44] These were recalibrated to accommodate the expansion of widespread, almost mass-market solicitation[45] and to convey respect for the individual choices made by donors rather than inherited family ties to a particular organization.[46] Fund-raisers understood the extra influence that came with an appeal embedded in a personal or business relationship. As the Community Service Society reported in December 1955:

> Every effort has been made in this campaign to increase the extent of personal solicitation of our more generous contributors. This means that instead of having one of the chief officers of the Society appeal for a renewal or an increased contribution, we have been able to enlist a good number of civic and business leaders who have taken responsibility for approaching certain individuals with whom they have influence.
>
> Since a great deal of our fund raising has to be by mail, the campaign organization has been built up with an aim to providing the most effective signatures on the mail solicitations, e.g. executives in Wall Street have been written to by fellow executives; lawyers have been approached through letters signed by one of several prominent lawyers serving on the campaign committee, etc."[47]

In this respect, the postwar pattern following the Second World War paralleled that after the First. While the Red Cross, the organization most closely identified with the national military effort, fizzled and fractured in peacetime, the municipal pieces of the fund-raising machinery were quickly repurposed and even strengthened. Circuits of giving built on and even strengthened relationships in the world of work, either through quasi-mandatory assessments of employees within a firm or the interpersonal persuasion (and pressure) of organized businessman-to-businessman solicitation. The resulting funds supported a wide range of activities ranging from the self-provisioning of an expansive middle class through scouting groups and the Y's (which, in turn, were increasingly orienting themselves to recreation rather than spiritual uplift[48]) to the support of the professionalized social service agencies that now dealt with "clients," some of whom paid for services, others of whom were subsidized by funds raised through federated campaigns.

As Basil O'Connor had argued with respect to joint fund-raising within industrial plants, this represented something very close to a system of taxation, but a system that was most "mandatory" for workers and over which business leaders exercised considerable control. The limits of this system would be revealed in the 1960s, as multiplying strains on the fabric of urban life would invite new federal interventions. Ironically, these interventions would be "contracted out" to the very system of nonprofit organizations that had been sustained as a bulwark against the expansion of tax-supported community services.

Civic Benevolence and State Building

In important respects, the resulting vision of civic participation reversed many of the important precepts of the model of benevolent patriotism that had been deployed by nation builders since the nation's founding. Local ties enacted in participation were embedded in the social imaginary of an extended system of national solidarity. Gifts circulated among strangers, linking diverse places and types of people without requiring direct social ties. Envisioned on this national scale, organized civic benevolence constituted a reinforcing armature for a political order ever-threatened with secession and group conflict.

By the 1950s, however, the continued efforts of private voluntary associations to contain the expansion of *domestic* public spending programs coexisted with a recognition of the role of a powerful national government, particularly one that would project its (putatively benevolent) power in a contested and dangerous world. This dual vision would mark the state-building strategies of the Kennedy administration, in which military strength was coupled with the "authentic" personal engagement of the Peace Corps or later Vista in American cities. It would emerge in yet another configuration during Johnson's Great Society, in which massively expanded federal funding for poverty relief and economic development would flow through community nonprofits, many of which traced their lineage back through the professionalized social service organizations of the 1950s to the reform-minded groups of the turn of the century.

Perversely, at least from the vantage point of those who had championed voluntary social service as a bulwark against state expansion, this configuration allowed for a continued escalation of federal spending combined with a diffusion of governmental control and accountability. Public funds were channeled to private organizations in an enormously complex web of contracts, grants, and subsidies that continues to defy efforts at regulation or even documentation. Thus the effort to dismantle the national configuration of civic benevolence out of concern that it would unduly enhance the power of the presidency has had the result of enhancing the scale of government while disguising and degrading the capacity of any political actor or institution to oversee the operations of this vast new system of associational governance.

This greatly expanded web of federal, state, and local grants to nonprofit organizations has had the additional effect of undercutting the power of community-level federated fund-raising to enact a strong sense of municipal membership. While the leaders of the community chest movement had presumed a set of common concerns to motivate contributions and direct the resulting funds, by the late 1950s and 1960s, newly mobilized groups increasingly charged that such centralized fund-raising and distributing models overlooked or misunderstood the needs of their particular community or cause.[49] Patterns of giving, like those of distributing funds, became increasingly fragmented and difficult to map clearly into civic identities. Although levels of giving and donating have continued to fluctuate, subjects of celebration and anxiety, these exchanges no longer effectively enact the model of civic benevolence that had been such a powerful force in mobilizing much—if never all—of the nation across a series of crises culminating in the Second World War.

Notes

1 The American Red Cross commissioned a series of "confidential" polls from George Gallup. "A Study of the Public's Attitude toward the

American Red Cross" (October 8, 1943); "A Study of the Public's Attitude toward the American Red Cross with a Supplement Dealing with World War II Veterans" (June 28, 1946; this report includes comparisons to the 1943 and 1944 surveys). Records of the American National Red Cross, 1935–46, RG 200, Box 764, 494.2; National Archives and Records Administration, College Park, Maryland.

2 Michael Mann, *The Sources of Social Power*, vol. 1, *A History of Power from the Beginning to A.D. 1760* (New York: Cambridge University Press, 1986), 477.

3 This characterization of the United States as governed by a "weak state" has a long history but is often linked to Stephen Skowronek's characterization of nineteenth-century government as a "state of courts and parties." *Building a New American State: The Expansion of National Administrative Capacities, 1877–1920* (New York: Cambridge University Press, 1982). On "infrastructural power," see Michael Mann, "The Autonomous Power of the State: Its Origins, Mechanisms, and Results," *European Journal of Sociology* 25, no. 2 (1984): 185–213. In the context of American political development, see Brian Balogh, *A Government Out of Sight: The Mystery of National Authority in Nineteenth-Century America* (New York: Cambridge University Press, 2009); Elisabeth S. Clemens, "Lineages of the Rube Goldberg State: Building and Blurring Public Programs, 1900–1940," in *The Art of the State: Rethinking Political Institutions*, ed. Ian Shapiro, Stephen Skowronek, and Daniel Galvin (New York: New York University Press, 2006); and William Novak, "The Myth of the 'Weak' American State," *American Historical Review* 113, no. 3 (2008): 752–72. The phrase "sinews of power" is taken from John Brewer, *The Sinews of Power: War, Money, and the English State, 1688–1783* (New York: Alfred A. Knopf, 1989).

4 The classic statement of this question comes from Robert A. Dahl, *Who Governs? Democracy and Power in an American City* (New Haven, CT: Yale University Press, 1963). Dahl's commitment to a pluralist analysis of American politics put him at odds with those who underscored the pervasive power of elite networks. For a review of this debate, see Shamus Khan, "The Sociology of Elites," *Annual Review of Sociology* 38 (2102): 364–65.

5 Ellis W. Hawley, "Herbert Hoover, the Commerce Secretariat, and the Vision of an 'Associative State,' 1921–1928," *Journal of American History* 61 (1974): 116–40. See also Guy Alchon, *The Invisible Hand of Planning: Capitalism, Social Science, and the State in the 1920s* (Princeton, NJ: Princeton University Press, 1985); Mark Frederickson, *New Capitalism in the New Era: American Labor and Economic Rights from World War I to the Great Depression* (New York: Cambridge University Press, forthcoming).

6 At least with respect to social provision and economic regulation; military mobilization and national security are different issues.

7 See Elisabeth S. Clemens, "In the Shadow of the New Deal: Reconfiguring the Roles of Government and Charity, 1928–1940," in *Politics and Partnerships: The Role of Voluntary Associations in America's Political Past and Present*, ed. Clemens and Doug Guthrie (Chicago: University of Chicago Press, 2010); Andrew J. F. Morris, *The Limits of Voluntarism: Charity and Welfare from the New Deal through the Great Society* (New York: Cambridge University Press, 2009).

8 Scott M. Cutlip, *Fund Raising in the United States: Its Role in American Philanthropy* (New Brunswick, NJ: Rutgers University Press, 1965), 128.

9 Bruce Barton quoted in Roland Marchand, *Creating the Corporate Soul: The Rise of Public*

Relations and Corporate Imagery in American Big Business (Berkeley: University of California Press).

10 For the development of this concept in the context of the First World War, see Christopher Capozzola, *Uncle Sam Wants You: World War I and the Making of the Modern American Citizen* (New York: Oxford University Press, 2008): "Looking at the history of a liberal society like the United States, it might seem that Americans have never really had to think much about their political obligations, let alone act on them. In the later wars of the twentieth and twenty-first centuries, liberal individualism, an economy of consumption, a nationalized culture, legally protected civil liberties, and an expanded federal state all played more prominent roles in public life. But even so, throughout American history, a citizenship of obligation has always coexisted with one of rights, as a patchwork of political cultures supported a hybrid state as jumbled as Uncle Sam's ill-fitting suit" (6).

11 Clemens, "In the Shadow of the New Deal."

12 David C. Hammack, "Failure and Resilience: Pushing the Limits in Depression and Wartime," in *Charity, Philanthropy, and Civility in American History*, ed. Lawrence Friedman and Mark McGarvie (New York: Cambridge University Press, 2003).

13 Morris, *Limits of Voluntarism.*

14 Ironically, however, the same changes that decoupled voluntary organizations from the presidential philanthropy of the Depression and world war would lay the foundations for a recoupling with national governance as a later Democratic president, Lyndon Baines Johnson, discovered a formula for state building through voluntary associations in peacetime. Steven Rathgeb Smith and Michael Lipsky, *Nonprofits for Hire: The Welfare State in the Age of Contracting* (Cambridge, MA: Harvard University Press, 1993).

15 James T. Sparrow, *Warfare State: World War II Americans and the Age of Big Government* (New York: Oxford University Press, 2011), 119–59. For the classic study of the underlying dynamics of such fund-raising efforts, see Robert K. Merton, with the assistance of Marjorie Fiske and Alberta Curtis, *Mass Persuasion: The Social Psychology of a War Bond Drive* (New York: Harper and Brothers, 1946).

16 Elisabeth S. Clemens, *The People's Lobby: Organizational Innovation and the Rise of Interest Group Politics in the United States, 1890–1925* (Chicago: University of Chicago Press, 1997).

17 The linkage of giving to civic inclusion was dramatized at its limits, where the Red Cross policy of refusing—and later segregating—blood donations from African Americans was paralleled by disproportionately low rates of cash contributions from blacks. Thomas A. Guglielmo, "'Red Cross, Double Cross': Race and America's World War II–Era Blood Donor Service," *Journal of American History* 97, no. 1 (2010): 63–90.

18 David L. Sills, *The Volunteers: Means and Ends in a National Organization* (Glencoe, IL: Free Press, 1957); David M. Oshinsky, *Polio: An American Story* (New York: Oxford University Press, 2005).

19 Suzanne Mettler, *Soldiers to Citizens: The G.I. Bill and the Making of the Greatest Generation* (New York: Oxford University Press, 2005); Robert D. Putnam, *Bowling Alone: The Collapse and Revival of American Community* (New York: Simon and Schuster, 2000).

20 Emily Barman, *Contesting Communities: The Transformation of Workplace Charity* (Stanford, CA: Stanford University Press, 2006); Elisabeth S. Clemens, "From City Club to Nation-State: Business Networks in American Political Development," *Theory and Society* 39 (2010): 377–96.

21 For examples of this large literature, see Jacob S. Hacker, *The Divided Welfare State: The Battle over Public and Private Social Benefits in the United*

States (New York: Cambridge University Press, 20002); Smith and Lipsky, *Nonprofits for Hire*; Jennifer R. Wolch, *The Shadow State: Government and Voluntary Sector in Transition* (New York: Foundation Center, 1990).

22 Rockefeller Archive Center, OMR, Welfare Interests General, RG III 2 P. Box 1, Folder 1. American Red Cross. Dedication Address by Basil O'Connor, President, The American National Red Cross. At the inauguration of THE NATIONAL BLOOD PROGRAM. Rochester, New York, January 12, 1948. After accepting O'Connor's resignation in 1949 (he was succeeded by General George Marshall), President Truman praised O'Connor for having "given your country a relief agency capable of efficient work through strictly democratic processes" and concurred "in your opinion that the Red Cross blood program may well become the greatest single health activity in history." "Truman Appoints Marshall President of the Red Cross," *New York Times*, September 23, 1949, 1. For a description of those "democratizing" changes, see "Red Cross Revision Favored by Group," *New York Times*, September 21, 1946, 9.

23 Linda Molm, Jessica Collett, and David R. Schaefer, "Building Solidarity through Generalized Exchange: A Theory of Reciprocity," *American Journal of Sociology* 113, no. 1 (2007): 205–42. President Truman echoed this theory of extended benevolent exchange: "In the continuance of our diligent work toward a just and enduring peace, it is very heartening to observe that however peoples may differ on political and economic issues, under the banner of the Red Cross they can unite for the betterment of mankind." "Truman Says Unity Is Red Cross Role," *New York Times*, June 19, 1946, 20.

24 Guglielmo, "Red Cross, Double Cross."

25 "Red Cross Revision Favored by Group," *New York Times*, September 21, 1946, 9.

26 John D. Rockefeller Jr., "Address Introducing the Mayor at the Opening Rally of the Greater New York Fund" (February 24, 1938), Office of the Messrs. Rockefeller III 2Z, B4, F166, Rockefeller Archive Center.

27 "CIO Agency Ends Red Cross Tie-Up," *New York Times*, April 15, 1946, 29. Expressing the hope that the Red Cross would become "a truly people's organization," the letter "recalled that on Nov. 15, 1945, Mrs. Eugene Meyer, wife of the Publisher of The Washington Post, and co-chairman of the women's foundation committee on reorganization of community services, charged that a group of conservatives within the American Red Cross had determined to force Mr. O'Connor out of his position on the ground that he was too friendly to labor." Mrs. Meyer had claimed, "Your very respectable, supposedly honorable but very bitter and very obtuse old fuddy-duddy leaders resent the fact that labor is gaining a foothold in the management of the Red Cross." See "Red Cross Warned against Reaction," *New York Times*, November 16, 1945, 10.

28 William M. Farrell, "Red Cross Decries United Campaigns: Independent Fund Raising Is Fostered in Pamphlet at National Convention," *New York Times*, June 29, 1949, 25. Local chapters faced suspension of their charters for joining such federated drives. The Pittsburgh chapter received such a warning after making a local decision to join the federated drive "was spurred by the preference of a number of Pittsburgh industrial plants for consolidation of philanthropic appeals to their employees." William M. Farrell, "Red Cross Warns Pittsburgh Unit," *New York Times*, June 28, 1949, 31.

29 Tellingly, the champions of the Red Cross portrayed their rivals as nationally centralized despite the considerable evidence that both the Community Chest and United Fund models

centered control in municipal or corporate communities.

30 "Why the American National Red Cross Does Not Permit Participation in Any Joint Fund Raising Campaigns" (issued April 30, 1946; attached to ECS 625), American National Red Cross, RG 200, Box 548, 221.012, National Archives and Records Administration, College Park, Maryland. This policy memo explained that in 1929 ARC Central Committee adopted a policy that required locals to "solicit memberships and funds independent of any other joint fund raising agencies." In 1941, the Community Chests proposed "ONE WARTIME CAMPAIGN," but the Red Cross declined. "In the earlier days, as previously indicated, a storm of protests always broke when a Red Cross chapter proposed severing its Chest connection. In every such community identically the same arguments were advanced against this move, including the prediction that other agencies would follow suit with the result that the very existence of the Chest would be jeopardized. However, no stampede ever took place and interestingly enough most Chest officials, where separations were affected, soon came to the conclusion that they were in a better position by not having the responsibility for raising the large sums required by the Red Cross from year to year. This conviction was strengthened by the interesting discovery that a contributor does not tend to reduce the amount he gives to other agencies because of his Red Cross contribution any more than is the case in his financial support of the church. Therefore, Chests in most instances continued to be supported on much the same level as was the case previous to the separation. On the other hand, by independent campaigns, chapters uniformally [*sic*] experienced no difficulty in securing greatly enlarged sums of money, for both local and national Red Cross purposes, and as a by-product were able to reinstate a consciousness of individual membership in the Red Cross." Foster Rhea Dulles, *American Red Cross* (New York: Harper and Brothers, 1950), 332–33.

31 "WHY THE AMERICAN RED CROSS IS OPPOSED TO PARTICIPATION IN ANY JOINT FUND RAISING CAMPAIGNS," October 1, 1945. National American Red Cross, RG3, Box 548, 221.012 COMMUNITY CHESTS, National Archives and Records Administration.

32 Chester Barnard, president of the USO, captured something of this type of conflict in a letter to John D. Rockefeller Jr. (February 16, 1944): "I am a little reluctant to be too positive in assuming extravagance in the Red Cross because I know there are a number of spots in which the same charge could be made against us by anyone not knowing all the circumstances and the conditions which inhibit prompt curtailment. Nevertheless, I have much difficulty in understanding why the amounts spent by the Chapters should be so large or should have increased so much and there are things brought to my attention which would lead me to scrutinize that part of the budget pretty carefully. However, I am increasing my subscription to the Red Cross 50% notwithstanding."

33 "Joint Fund Drives by Red Cross Hit: O'Connor Assails Approval of Coordinated Campaigns in Industrial Plants," *New York Times*, August 15, 1951, 39. Echoing the late 1920s, the theme of voluntary fund-raising as a prophylactic against expanded taxation regularly appeared in arguments for the Red Cross. Defending the size of the organization's projected budget in 1949, President E. Roland Harriman questioned the demand that the Red Cross return to its prewar scale: "Why should Red Cross be the only organization, Government, welfare or business to return to

any predetermined level? … America still is growing and all of us are doing everything in our power to keep it growing. Red Cross is part and parcel of that growth, particularly with respect to national defense." The failure to support those activities would have undesirable political consequences, he warned: "If the Red Cross and other agencies do not give the people what they need and what they have learned they want and can get, the only road left open may be for the Government to take over. That means taxation instead of voluntary contributions." "Harriman Fights Cut in Red Cross," *New York Times*, January 7, 1949, 26.

34 Gladwin Hill, "Red Cross Declares Itself Tired of Aiding Ingrate Crisis Areas," *New York Times*, March 15, 1954, 1.

35 "First Lady Spurs Red Cross Drives," *New York Times*, March 22, 1953, 2.

36 Marcel Mauss, *The Gift: The Form and Reason for Exchange in Archaic Societies* (1950; New York: W. W. Norton, 1990).

37 William L. Laurence, "Red Cross Leaves Blood Bank Group," *New York Times*, May 21, 1945, 29; Richard M. Titmuss, *The Gift Relationship: From Human Blood to Social Policy* (New York: Pantheon, 1971).

38 Morris, *Limits of Voluntarism*.

39 Mrs. Oswald B. Lord, Board of Trustees, CSS to Mrs. David Rockefeller, mid-winter 1947, in Folder 75 "Community Service Society," Box 7, OMR III 2 P, Rockefeller Archive Center.

40 Rockefeller Archive Center, OMR III 2 P, Box 7, Community Service Society, Folder 75. Draft of Report from Yorkville District Committee (April 24, 1947).

41 Rockefeller Archive Center, OMR III 2 P, Box 7, Community Service Society, Folder 75. Community Service Society, Symposium I—Human Relations in Science and Practice, January 29 and 30, 1948.

42 Frederick Sheffield to Laurance S. Rockefeller (November 15, 1939). Rockefeller Archive Center, OMR III 2 P, Box 7, Community Service Society, Folder 75.

43 Rockefeller Archive Center, OMR III 2 P, Box 7, Community Service Society, Folder 75. A Memorandum to Private Businesses and Executives of Corporations From the Community Service Society, 1948.

44 Advising in response to a request from the Community Service Society, Arthur W. Packard of the Rockefeller Family Office suggested to Mrs. Laurance Rockefeller that "Unless a gift were to be made because of friendship with a solicitor, we would not recommend that any other gifts be made by members of the family." Arthur W. Packard to Mrs. Laurance S. Rockefeller (January 21, 1949). Rockefeller Archive Center, OMR III 2 P, Box 7, Community Service Society, Folder 75.

45 This accommodation was not always made without complaint. At the Rockefeller Family Office, Arthur W. Packard provided a rather grumpy rationale for not replying to a particular solicitation. "This is a form letter with a stamped signature which has been sent to all contributors of the Community Service Society. Since it is not a personalized letter to Mr. Rockefeller and even though he usually answers even form letters from Mr. Gifford, I believe it would be best to ignore this letter. … The only type of reply Mr. Rockefeller could make would be a reply expressing appreciation for Mr. Gifford's letter and pointing out that he personally has not been contributing for some years now and that the pledge of the Davison Fund which he established some years ago has already been made. This of course is a fact of which the officers of the Society are well aware, and I should think it would be better to ignore the letter than for Mr. Rockefeller to make a reply of that character." Arthur Packard to Janet Warfield, October 30, 1941.

Rockefeller Archive Center, OMR III 2 P, Box 7, Community Service Society, Folder 75.

46 Mrs. JDR 3rd to Keith McHugh, March 26, 1957. Rockefeller Archive Center, OMR III 2 P, Box 7, Community Service Society, Folder 75.

47 STATUS REPORT OF THE CSS FAMILY FUND, Rockefeller Archive Center, OMR III 2 P, Box 7, Community Service Society, Folder 75.

48 Mayer Zald and Patricia Denton, "From Evangelism to General Service: The Transformation of the YMCA," *Administrative Science Quarterly* 8, no. 2 (1963): 214–34.

49 Barman, *Contesting Communities.*

■ CHAPTER 2

Class Structure in Major Industrialized Countries

Editor's Introduction

This chapter starts by introducing key arguments of functionalist elite theorists via distinguishing between the ruling class and strategic elites. Hartmann describes emerging studies in meritocratic elites and elite consensus in five leading industrialized nations. He stresses that elites have one thing in common: their upper-middle or upper-class background. He uses functionalist elite theory to describe the ruling class through a set of general habits, customs, and cultural and behavioral patterns, such as strictness of social backgrounds and attendance at prestigious educational institutions. Hartmann also examines the concepts of *pluralist subelites* and the *power elite*, and why he prefers Anthony Giddens's thoughts on the *governing class* to explain the link between economic power and political rule.

READING 2 Elites and Class Structures

Michael Hartmann

Today the discussion on elites is clearly dominated by functionalist approaches which continue to define a large majority of theoretical and—especially—empirical studies. The credo here is: There are no longer any ruling classes or homogeneous elites; what we have today are competing, more or less equally powerful subelites that must be seen as open in social terms because access to them is determined mainly by individual performance, no longer by descent or social background. This, it is argued, is the reason why today the consensus among elites on which parliamentary democracy is predicated can no longer be established on the basis of social homogeneity but has to be sought by way of debate and competition among individual functional elites.

In view of the above-outlined process of elite formation in the major industrialized countries, an approach of this kind raises three central questions:

1. What role does performance really play in the recruitment of elites, and how socially heterogeneous are these elites?
2. Is it a fact that the business elite does not really enjoy a special position which enables it to exert considerably greater influence on the development of society than other groups?
3. What is the nature of the (inter)relationship between elites and classes within society?

Meritocratic Elites and Elite Consensus

The empirical studies published on the career trajectories of top executives and politicians, high-ranking civil servants and judges in Germany, France, Britain, Japan, and the US call for more than a measure of skepticism with respect to the core statement of all functionalist elite theories, namely that access to subelites is based principally on performance. After all, highly selective social recruitment processes can be observed in all five leading industrialized nations; the large majority of elite positions are held by people from the upper middle classes or the upper class. Granted, there are differences between the individual countries—social origin, for example, tends to be somewhat more exclusive in France and Britain than in Germany or the US—as well as between the various sectors, with the business sector generally having the highest percentage of upper middle-class children and the political sector the lowest; but even so, none of these disparities have any pronounced influence impact on the general impression we gain. The important sectors of society (with a few exceptions, such as the German political elite) are clearly dominated by the upper-middle classes, indeed to a large extent by persons from an upper-class background.

Functionalist elite researchers who, on the whole, are aware of these facts, attempt to use two arguments to integrate them into the structures of their theories. First, they point out that the disproportions in social recruitment can be explained primarily by disparate academic achievements and as such are basically not in conflict with the performance principle as the key access criterion. While it is true that they do not deny the connection between social origin and the acquisition of academic titles, they still argue that this is accounted for primarily by disparities in performance and motivation. Second, based on the correlation found between education and professional career, and borrowing on classic modernization theories, they assume a clear-cut tendency toward more meritocracy, i.e., a social opening of elites. Existing links between social background and access to elites, they contend, have been loosened, if not completely broken, as a result of the reform and expansion of higher education.

At first sight, there is something to be said for both arguments; yet they do not bear up to closer scrutiny. If we take a look first at the correlation between academic success and access to elites, we find that there is clearly such a connection. Neither can we simply dismiss the argument that the exclusive academic qualifications generally required for top positions cannot be obtained without extraordinary achievements.

For example, one in three of the approximately 30,000 (of over two million) US high school graduates who achieve 700 or more points on the verbal SAT, go on to one of the top ten universities, while a further 10 percent are accepted at one of the universities ranked among the highest 20 (Greene and Greene 2000). However, even if we disregard the argument that social origins affect strengths and weaknesses in achievement, one fact remains: places at the sought-after elite institutions such as Harvard or Yale are not allocated purely on grounds of achievement. The social background of candidates, defined in terms of the criterion "personality," plays a very direct and central role here. This is true of all exclusive educational institutions, be they the famous private universities in the US, the renowned Grandes écoles, the distinguished public schools in the UK, or the top universities in Japan.

If we at the same time consider the great significance attached to personality-related criteria in the admission procedures of elite educational institutions, we very soon find ourselves face to face with the basic weakness of the functionalist approach. While individual achievement does indeed play a major role here, even if we disregard the social conditions bearing on achievement, we find that there is still a second career factor that is equally, or possibly even more, important, i.e., that of class-specific habitus, the acquisition of which is easily comparable with the factor of inheritance. A social background in thc "better circles" still functions as a door opener to top positions.

This goes for Germany no less than it does for the other major industrialized nations. The only difference lies in the actual mechanisms involved. Whereas social selection in France or the US, for example, operates primarily by means of the admission procedures of the exclusive educational institutions, the German education system only serves as a rough preliminary filter in this process. In Germany much more of the decisive selection process is shifted to the course of a person's professional career. The effect is ultimately the same. Access to the important elites is largely reserved for the offspring of the upper-middle and—to an even greater extent—upper classes.

In certain respects the political sector is an exception to this rule. Here we do in fact find some major differences as regards the social origins of top politicians, because the structure of political parties may differ quite considerably from country to country. The extremes are represented by Germany on the one hand and France and Japan on the other. Whereas in Germany the selection process in the major popular parties has meant that candidates from the broad population have notably better chances of advancement than in other sectors of society, in France and Japan the typical party structures, dominated as they are by dignitaries and clientelism, give clear preference to politicians with a middle-class background. It is not social proximity to the electorate but degrees from elite national educational institutions that determine whether or not aspirants are nominated as candidates for high political offices. What this means in effect is that the social background of the political elite differs relatively little from that of the business or administrative elite.

In view of such social recruitment practices, the question is of course whether functionalist elite theory is wrong—both in terms of its core thesis regarding socially heterogeneous meritocratic elites and in its assumption that consensus and cooperation among subelites is obstructed by the latter's functional specialization and autonomy no less than by heterogeneous social backgrounds. The situation in France and Japan militates, even at first sight, against any such premise. The two languages even have specific expressions for the very close relationships between the business, political, and administrative elites. In France the now common process by which high-ranking officials from government administration move into top positions in major companies is referred to as *pantouflage*, and the people involved are called *catapultés* or *parachutes* (those have been catapulted upward or those who have parachuted down), because they have landed at the top instead of having to climb up the ladder of internal company hierarchies. In Japan there is a very similar term for this process. It is termed "amakudari," that is, "those who have descended from the heavens."

More than half of the 100 largest French companies are headed by such men, 40 of them by former members of the famed Grands Corps. In Japan the same situation is typical for the financial sector, where one-time high-ranking MoF or Bank of Japan officials head one in four of the country's 150 largest banks. Such moves are less frequent in industry, though they are not uncommon. For instance, top figures from MITI later move on, almost without exception, to top positions in business (generally as presidents or vice-presidents of large corporations) (Cutts 1997: 197; Kerbo and McKinstry 1995: 95). The picture in the political sphere is similar. Approximately one in four members of the Japanese parliament and more than one in three prime ministers have previously held a high-ranking position in a ministry. Indeed, nearly two-thirds of French presidents and prime ministers over the last 30 years had previously been members of one of the administrative Grands Corps.

The close links between the personnel in administration, business, and politics are largely the result of the time such people have spent together in the country's exclusive elite educational institutions. Since graduates from these elite institutions are appointed to most top positions in all important spheres of society, moves from one sector to another do not constitute a problem. It ultimately makes no difference whether an Enarque, after a period at the Inspection des Finances, or a Todai graduate, after holding office in the MoF, moves to the top echelon of a major bank previously under his control or is appointed to a cabinet position. Be it here or there, he will be among people very much like himself. Having attended the same elite institutions, these people have known each other for years, irrespective of their fields of activity or political affiliations. This, combined with similar social backgrounds, provides the basis for a large measure of shared attitudes and behaviors. To cite an example, there is little doubt that the discreet discussions conducted directly between the Socialist government and the employers' associations in the second half of the 1990s were greatly facilitated by the fact that Socialist Prime Minister Jospin and the chairman of the French employers' association, at the same time CEO of the Wendel corporation, de Seillière—both ENA graduates—shared an office for three years as members of a Grand Corps in the French foreign ministry. If we further bear in mind the fact that almost all major positions are concentrated in the capital cities of Paris and Tokyo, we cannot fail to see that it is far less difficult than functionalists are fond of maintaining for the elites from different sectors to forge a basic consensus.

The situation in the US is typified far more by close links between business and politics than by career moves by high-ranking administrative officials to the top echelons of other sectors. Over the last 30 years in particular, the number of cabinet members who have previously held top management positions in large corporations has grown to extraordinarily levels. Under President George W. Bush, this goes for nearly half of all the highest-ranking members of government, including Vice-President Cheney, Defense Secretary Rumsfeld, and Secretary of Commerce

Evans. Constant moves from influential political offices to top positions in large corporations, and vice versa, are characteristic here. Compared with Japan in particular, in the US we also find brisk and active exchange processes between politics and academia. A man like the current President of Harvard University, Summers, Treasury Secretary under President Clinton, is no exception here. The present Secretary of the Treasury, Snow, was also once a university professor. Another factor further conducive to mutual understanding is the high percentage of graduates from elite universities active in all sectors.

The Special Role of the Business Elite

One of the most significant differences between the representatives of functionalist elite research on the one hand and critical elite theorists (such as Bourdieu and Mills) on the other lies in their assessment of the influence of the business elite as compared with that of other elites. Bourdieu and Mills repeatedly point to the former's structurally conditioned predominance. In his early studies Bourdieu states quite clearly that economic capital is "at the root of all other types of capital" (Bourdieu 1983 [1986/1997]), and in his more recent publications he still speaks of the markedly strong effects of the business sector. Mills is even more clear on this point. He goes as far as to describe the "chief executives" as "those who, by fact and by proxy, hold the power and the means ..." and against whom "no powers effectively and consistently countervail" (Mills 1959). There can be no doubt that both Mills and Bourdieu see a special role for the business elite.

It is precisely this special role that is disputed by the representatives of functionalist elite research. Suzanne Keller's arguments are the most systematic in this respect. In her book on *Strategic Elites* she uses the example of a conflict between U.S. Steel and US President Kennedy over a planned hike in steel prices to assert that the times are past in which, in pursuing its own interests, the business elite also appeared to be pursuing general national interests. The saying, What's good for U.S. Steel is good for the country, Keller argues, no longer holds true. She then goes deeper into the matter. Regardless of their importance, she argues, today economic goals are only one of a number of desirable goals. Thus the business elite is forced to compete with other elites for available resources. A country's economic performance generally constitutes only *one* measure of its social progress, and this one element must always be weighed up against other factors such as military strength, international prestige, mass education, or scientific success. Indeed, Keller goes a step further, criticizing even the manner, crimped in her eyes, in which Parsons assigns roles to given functions. She even questions the validity of his statement, made in connection with his AGIL paradigm, that one of the four functional imperatives of society, adaptation to the environment, is performed largely by business. For Keller, the military, the diplomatic sphere, and the academic sphere, to name only these, are likewise in charge of discharging key tasks in this connection (Keller 1963). She thus explicitly rejects the notion that the business elite plays any pre-eminent role. Many other representatives of the functionalist approach assign to the political elite (implicitly or explicitly) the particular position of power which they refuse to accept for the business elite.

In countries such as Japan or the US, where the ties between the business world and the world of politics are traditionally much closer than in Germany, more than a shade of doubt is cast on this functionalist view. In addition to the direct and indirect means of gaining influence on political decisions common in Germany, there is another key matter: the role played by financial support of politicians in their election campaigns. In Japan, at the beginning of the 1990s, the average cost of an election campaign was calculated at approximately ¥400 million (over €3 million) per LDP parliamentary seat; the major share of this sum was raised by businesses (Rothacher 1993: 29–30). The classic country for election campaign contributions, however, is the US, where, for example, as long ago as 1976, successful candidates for Senate seats spent an average of $610,000 on their election campaigns. In the following ten years this sum rose dramatically to $3 million, only to more than double again by the year 2000, when the figure reached $7.7 million. While a seat in the House of Representatives is a good deal cheaper, it still costs $840,000, twice the figure it had reached ten years ago. The reason why these sums have increased so enormously is that in 90 percent of cases it is the candidate who spends more money on his election campaign who ultimately wins. The total of the sums raised for Congressional elections increased from $659 million in 1992 to $1.05 billion in 2000, and the figure for presidential elections rose in the same period from $331 million to $529 million. George W. Bush alone, even without any primaries, will have a "war chest" of almost $200 million to fall back on. All of the ten largest contributors to these funds are large banks or investment companies, such as UBS or Merrill Lynch.

This was no different in the last election period in 2000. The financial and real-estate sectors paid out almost $300 million (in addition to over 200 million dollars spent on lobby work) in support for candidates. The money is either paid directly to the target candidates or, and this is more effective in view of the donation ceiling of $2,000, it is channeled via company employees and members of their families. Another increasingly popular approach is to give candidates indirect rather than direct donations, what is known as "soft money." This soft money now accounts for almost 20 percent of donations, considerably more than the official support provided by the state, which amounts to less than 10 percent. If we further bear in mind the fact that about three quarters of donations from individuals comes from people with annual incomes of more than $200,000, i.e., people who belong to the top 2 percent of the population, and that candidates themselves put their own money into their election campaigns on a scale approaching the official state support they receive, we cannot fail to miss the influence exerted by the business elite and the upper class on the filling of important political offices. The situation with respect to high-level judicial posts is similar. Since under the US system these jobs are usually elected posts, donations are coming to play an increasingly important role here as well.

Indeed, the rates of increase over the past ten years have been even higher than in the field of politics. To cite an example, in 1994 a successful candidate for the Michigan Supreme Court spent an average of $287,000 for his election campaign, and six years later this figure had risen to $1.3 million (Phillips 2002: 323–9).

This situation reminds many observers, including the Nobel laureate in economics, Paul Krugman, or Nixon's one-time adviser Kevin Phillips, of practices typical of the late nineteenth and early twentieth centuries. At that time, not only did one in three senators number among the country's approximate 5,000 millionaires, but seats in the Senate were regularly purchased by the major railroad companies. How prevalent this practice was can be seen in the fact that a motion was proposed at that time that aimed at removing all senators in possession of bought seats. The motion was rejected by the Senate with the argument that the body would in that case be without a quorum (ibid: 292–30). The alliance between business and political elite was at that time so close that the period, known as the "Gilded Age" in a term coined by Mark Twain, became a synonym for the almost unrestricted power of large corporations and millionaires as well as for widespread political corruption. How remunerative donations to election campaigns can be for businesses today is demonstrated not only by the awards of contracts after the end of the Iraq war but also by the legislation of the past 20 years aimed at deregulating the American financial markets or providing tax relief for businesses. Even though major legislation can clearly not be explained solely in terms of direct financial benefits to politicians and intensive lobbying by industry and trade associations, and has had far more to do with the structural supremacy of capital, the effectiveness of donations and lobbyists should not be underestimated.

It is, in any case, more expedient to weigh up the influence of the business elite on the "basis of a number of key decisions," as recommended by Beyme (Beyme 1971: 203), rather than to seek to explain the effect on the basis of network analyses, as functionalist-oriented studies tend to do. Any attempt to determine the relative weight of the various sectoral elites by looking into their most important contacts and partners when it comes to solving cross-organizational problems is bound to suffer from a number of weaknesses. Two of them are crucial. First, many functionalist authors deliberately fail—and this is occasionally acknowledged (for instance by Higley et al. 1991: 47)—to analyze specific positions of power on the basis of the practical impacts of decisions or of criteria other than membership in the elite circles under study. It is simply assumed that these circles have a relatively egalitarian structure. Second, the central position of the political elite established by the findings of a given study is frequently predetermined by the way in which the problem under consideration is formulated. Typical of this approach is Hoffmann-Lange's comparatively precise and theoretically grounded evaluation of a Mannheim survey conducted in 1981. She concludes that the "representatives of the political-administrative system," with their share of over 50 percent, play a key role in the central circle of the elite, and she is only being logically consistent when she points to the "central role played by the political sector" (Hoffmann-Lange 1992: 386–7, 403–4). However, if we take a closer look at the central question involved in the survey, we find that this finding is anything but surprising. If we start out by asking an interviewee about the one field in which he has sought most intensely to "influence political decisions or public opinion," following up by asking him to name his most important contacts in this endeavor, then the question itself will necessarily prompt a response in which politicians are named high up on the list. This is not the way to determine where true influence lies.

Here the only possible approach is to look into decisions of central importance. Even if we disregard company-related decisions that may have substantial impacts on whole regions or even countries (for instance, large-scale company mergers), though they are generally made by top management, without consulting with or informing others in advance, we cannot possibly overlook the dominance of the business elite even on immediately political decisions. Tax policy is a good example here in that it provides the financial basis for any state's capacity to act, and as such is the central element behind all political action. In the US, the pioneer of capital-friendly tax policies, the share of corporate taxes in total tax revenues has declined radically over the past few decades, i.e., during a period when the tax burden of the general population has risen sharply. About 30 years ago the level of income and Social Security tax (FICA) revenues was roughly the same as that of corporate tax revenues; recent figures show a relation of 3:1, despite a four- to fivefold increase in corporate profits over the past two decades (Phillips 2002: 149–50). In addition to the multitude of opportunities corporations have to cash in on loopholes in tax law, this development has been influenced primarily by the Reagan administration's tax reforms.

However, tax reform has not only benefited corporations, it has also worked in favor of those in high income-tax brackets and large property owners. While real incomes (after taxes) fell slightly in the US for average wage earners between 1977 and 1999, the incomes of the top percent have more than doubled, reaching a figure of over $500,000 today. In the 1990s alone their share of national income rose from 8.2 to 16.3 percent, with the result that these persons now earn more than the bottom 40 percent of the population. The top 0.1 per mill, that is, about 13,000 families, alone account for 3 percent, while the bottom fifth earns no more than 5 percent. If we look at assets, these inequalities are even more glaring. The top 1 percent now owns over 40 percent of all assets, twice as much as at the end of the 1970s. They own over 60 percent of business assets and bonds and one-half of all share and trust assets, and the top five per mill own almost one third of all shares and almost half of all bonds.

Tax policy has played an important role in this concentration of income and assets. The greatest effect was certainly achieved by the Reagan administration's reduction of the top income-tax rate from 50 percent to just under 30 percent. This, however, was only the extension of a broad trend that had been observed since the 1970s. Whereas in the 1960s the effective tax rate for the top 1 percent of society was six to seven times higher than it was for the average American family, by 1980 this figure had been reduced to a ratio of 3:2, and over the subsequent ten years the ratio was to reach a level of 1:1 (Henwood 1998: 67; Krugman 2002; Phillips 2002: 96, 121–4, 129, 150; Werner 2003: 31). George W. Bush has recently effected a further drastic reduction in the tax burden of rich US citizens and corporations by pushing through tax cuts amounting to $550 billions, and one of the core goals of his program is to halve, and ultimately abolish (by 2007), the tax on stock dividends. In 2001 he also signed a law designed to wholly abolish the inheritance tax, which has already been reduced several times, by the year 2011. This would most benefit the top per mill of the population, who at present account for more than half of the $20 billion in revenues stemming from this particular tax (Beckert 2003: 137–8).

Tax legislation is a good indication of the enormous influence wielded by the business elite on key political decisions. The interests of this elite are largely identical with those of the upper classes in general. Both stand to gain double benefits from these tax reforms. First, their personal income is taxed at a considerably lower rate, and second, thanks to the reduction in their tax burden, corporations are able to pay out more of their profits, and this in turn mainly benefits the upper classes and top executives. In the last 20 years the latter have succeeded in dramatically increasing their incomes, in the US from 50 times to 400 times an average worker's earnings. The record is held by Larry Ellison, head of Oracle, who managed to earn over $700 million in 2001. The gulf in Germany, where top earnings are "only" 100 times those of workers' earnings, is not as wide, but the trend is the same. In the period from 1997 to 2002 alone, the board members of the 30 DAX-listed companies have succeeded in raising their remuneration by about two-thirds. DaimlerChrysler leads the field here. On average its board members are paid €3.7 million in cash, excluding the comprehensive stock options they are offered. As an individual, the board spokesman of the Deutsche Bank, Joseph Ackermann, topped the list with an income in 2003 of about €11 million. He was able to increase his income by almost 60 percent over the previous year. With such incomes, the top executives of Germany's leading corporations are among the top 0.1 per mill of all income earners in Germany.

The comprehensive stock options provided to them in addition to salaries mean that board members themselves are important shareholders. For example, if all DaimlerChrysler board members were to cash in on their options, almost 10 percent of the company would belong to them. The most important executives at the Deutsche Bank, the Group Executive Committee, already own over 7 percent of their company's shares. In no way, then, can we speak of a control by corporate management in the sense meant by Burnham, and there are plainly and simply no conflicts of interest between managers and capital owners.

The Ruling Class and Power Relations in Society

The enormous concentration of productive wealth in the hands of a few per mill of the population, the levels of board-member incomes, and the tax reforms which benefit this circle more than any other illustrate not only the close ties between business elite and upper classes, with their enormous influence, these developments also permit us to draw some general conclusions on the relationship between elites and classes. This includes the connections between individual elites and the links between these elites and the upper classes, not to forget the relationship between class structures in society and the influence of elites on society.

If we start out by looking at the relationships between individual elites, we find that in all major industrialized countries there has been marked growth in the inter-dependencies among the key elites in business, politics, and administration, as well as, to a lesser extent, in the judiciary and the media. In countries like France and, less markedly, in Japan and the US, this process is already relatively far advanced. True, there are still different elite positions, but the fact that a considerable proportion of those in such positions regularly make career moves to other sectors means that the boundaries between the individual elites are blurring to an increasing extent. This is particularly the case in present-day Italy. In the person of Silvio Berlusconi this process of amalgamation has reached a dimension which only 20 years ago would have been decried as a particularly distorted caricature born of leftist propaganda. Presumably, hardly anyone could, at the end of the 1980s, have conceived that the richest man in one of the world's largest industrialized nations could at the same time be head of government and hold control over both the country's privately and publicly owned television networks. Such a concentration of power in the hands of a single person would at that time have been equally as inconceivable in an industrial society as the possibility that a parliament might pass laws which so obviously benefit the economic interests of this one particular person. Even though the spontaneous impression may be somewhat deceptive—this blatant amalgamation of public and private interests is increasingly meeting with resistance, for instance in the refusal of Italian President Ciampi to sign two laws which would have secured Berlusconi a large measure of immunity from criminal prosecution and served to further strengthen his media empire, it clearly indicates the close nature of the ties between the individual subelites on the one hand

and between these elites and the upper classes on the other.

This, however, brings us face to face with the question of whether the concept ruling class is in fact closer to reality than the strict rejection of the term by functionalist elite research and the tentative use of the concept made by Mills and (more recently) Bourdieu would suggest. Keller gives the most precise summary of the arguments of functionalist elite theorists when she distinguishes between the "ruling class" and "strategic elites." In Keller's view what distinguishes a ruling class from an elite is that the former is far broader and more durable, its activities are less specialized, membership is less optional, and that its members share not only their professional and functional positions but also have a set of general habits, customs, and cultural behavior patterns in common. Its members are recruited from families with more or less monopolized access to the most important elites and who are able to pass down their advantages to the next generation. All this, Keller contends, distinguishes ruling classes fundamentally from elites, which are specialized in given sectors and display a tendency toward functional autonomy, since, in her view, no one person would be able to hold elite positions in more than one sector at one time. Elites are, she argues, recruited on the grounds of their individual skills and performance, which are no longer bound to specific social origins. As long as the core group was mainly recruited from a small and exclusive circle, i.e., the upper class, it was difficult if not impossible to distinguish between strategic elites and the class from which most of their members originated. In this age of a modern, functionally differentiated and specialized society, however, even the core group is forced to specialize, a development which has served to make access to individual elites relatively open in social terms. There is no longer one pyramid with one apex but a number of pyramids, each with its own elite at the top (Keller 1963: 57–60, 83).

If we look at the important elites in large industrialized nations from the point of view of these criteria, we find a number of good reasons to speak of the existence of a ruling class. Although Keller's basic distinction between elites and ruling class is analytically correct, in reality the boundaries are becoming increasingly blurred. Even if Berlusconi, bringing together several top offices in his person, is excluded from the analysis as a particularly extreme case, there are still a considerable number of people who hold elite positions in various sectors, many of them nearly at the same time. US Vice-President Cheney, for example, did actually give up his position as CEO of Halliburton for his term of office, but when his term is up he is more than likely to return there. Regular changeovers between various elite positions, known as *pantouflage* in France and *amakudari* in Japan, point in the same direction. There is, in any case, no convincing reason to speak here of a clear distinguishing line between individual elites. Furthermore, a large proportion of key elites have one thing in common: their backgrounds in upper-middle and (more importantly) upper-class milieus. Assuming the form of a class-specific habitus, this background ensures that they will have the same or similar "habits, customs, and cultural behavior patterns." It is not only their "professional and functional positions" that they share. The central role played by an upper middle-class or upper-class habitus in elite recruitment shows plainly that access to elite positions is far less open than Keller and the entire field of functionalist elite research maintain. The benefits of an upper middle-class or upper-class habitus are passed on from generation to generation, roughly in the same way that material benefits are passed down. Even if we ignore differences in background-related school and university achievements and degrees, what counts in gaining access to important elites is not only—indeed often not even primarily—individual performance. After all, the growing complexity of modern industrial society does not automatically entail any functional autonomy of individual elites, nor, in fact, do the "communication problems of the business and political elites" cited by Behme as his principal argument in rejecting Mills' concept of the power elite (Beyme 1971: 206).

The business elite of course seeks to ensure that it is adequately represented in the political elite. As Beyme correctly notes, the influence of the "economically powerful" cannot be measured in terms of the number of people who seek to directly "articulate" such interests "in the state's power apparatus," because this group also has other means of achieving this end; however, the "overrepresentation of certain socially powerful strata and groups" increases their chances of influencing the power apparatus from the outside, because overrepresented groups act as influence "facilitators" (Beyme 1971: 220–1). Even in Germany key political positions are for this reason occupied by members of the business elite, or at the least by members of the upper classes. At present this applies not only for high offices in the cabinets of state governments ruled by the CDU/CSU and FDP but also for the Red-Green governments in power in Berlin and the state of North Rhine-Westphalia), where the interior ministry and the finance ministry are headed by sons of a steel works CEO and a regional court president, respectively.

All in all, today it is quite difficult to distinguish clearly "between the strategic elites and the class from which most of their members are recruited." There are good reasons to proceed neither on the premise of a system of competing pluralist subelites, as the functionalist elite theorists do, nor of a power elite in Mills' sense. Instead it would appear to make more sense (borrowing on a definition provided by Giddens) to proceed on the assumption of a diluted variant of the concept ruling class, namely the "governing class." For Giddens, a governing class of this kind is characterized by relatively closed social recruitment (mainly from the upper class) and a relatively high degree of integration. This class is distinguished from the classic "ruling classes" chiefly by the clear limitations set to its power by the fact that it is controlled (more or less) from below: its holders are forced to pay due regard to the population at large (Giddens 1974: 5–9).

If Giddens' thoughts are taken further, then, the term ruling class can be taken to mean not simply bourgeoisie, upper-middle class, upper class, or classe dominante in Bourdieu's sense. Instead, the ruling class must be seen as made up of—and here we would be well advised to heed Mills' criticism of any assumption of an overly direct link between economic power and political rule—a circle of people recruited mainly from the key elites and the core of the upper-middle to upper classes. This group includes neither all members of the important elites nor all members of the upper classes, because the fact that someone holds a top position or stems from an upper-class family is simply not sufficient to justify membership in it. If one is really to belong to the ruling class, one must be permanently embedded in it, and in this way be in a position to exert significant influence on the development of society.

There are three different ways to achieve this. First, a person may hold a top position for such a long period of time that he or she is successfully integrated into this class, irrespective of social origins. Politicians like Helmut Kohl in Germany belong to this category, whereas ministers of German state or federal governments (in particular SPD members) from ordinary parental backgrounds who serve only, say, one term in office and then return to their former professions or become ordinary members of parliament do not. The second means is to belong to the ruling class by birth. This path, however, is open only to a very small circle of heirs to very large estates (for example, the children of former German industrialist and majority BMW shareholder Herbert Quandt) who belong to the business elite simply by dint of the capital they own. This path normally remains closed to the son of a regional court president or chief physician; he will first have to hold a top position on his own merits, at least for a certain period of time. This, then, is the third variant. A person may find access to the ruling class if he or she holds a top position for a more or less brief period of time and then turns to a lower-level leadership position—provided this person was born into an upper middle-class or (preferably) upper-class family. This is the best short cut on the path to integration.

Generally speaking, and this is the blind spot of most elite theories and studies, the successes and failures of the business elite, as well as of the entire ruling class, depend largely on the power relations in society as a whole. The ongoing radical reforms of tax laws illustrate this point very clearly. On the one hand, reforms on this scale have only been possible because potential opposition forces in parties and—above all—in labor unions, had already been substantially weakened by other developments. There have been two key processes at work here. The internationalization of the economy and the associated—real or supposed—comprehensive new options it has opened up for capital have markedly reduced the influence of both unions and left-wing or classic social-democratic parties and organizations. The effect of this development, which has been underway since the late 1970s, was boosted substantially after 1989 by the collapse of what was known as "real socialism." The dramatic weakening of the unions, including a decline in membership over the last 30 years from—in many cases—50 percent to a level of 10 percent or lower in the US and France—or the rapid demise of the only *real* social alternative to capitalism—were the factors that set the stage for the seemingly unstoppable offensive of neoliberal ideas and concepts in politics.

On the other hand, changes in German tax laws, which constitute a core, if not *the* core element of this allegedly unstoppable development, serve both to cement and further consolidate this shift in power relations in German society. The ongoing discussion in Germany on the need for longer weekly working hours in the public sector illustrates this point very clearly. The reason cited by the German state governments for the need to increase working hours from 38.5 to 42 hours a week is that they lack sufficient tax revenues. This development, however, is largely a result of the tax policies pursued over the past 20 years. Should the authorities actually succeed in pushing through this drastic increase in working hours, private companies will inevitably follow suit in due course. This would again lead to a shift in the balance of power in society to the detriment of the population at large, further increasing the scopes of action open to the ruling class.

All these changes clearly favor the business elite to the detriment of the political elite. As Mills clearly demonstrates in his "Power Elite" with reference to the New Deal, the political elite inevitably has a relatively large amount of influence and leeway when social movements and forces are able to curb the power of capital. But it is precisely the opposite that has occurred over the past few years. Business has been dictating the frameworks for major political decisions, with the consequence that the independent influence of politics is on the wane. The political process is playing an increasingly smaller role in the making of decisions, which are influenced more and more by the ways in which they are "staged" by the media (Sunday evening political talk shows on television instead of congress as the principle arena for political discussion). With counterforces in society having lost a good deal of their influence, and congress being increasingly sidelined on important issues, decision-making processes are coming more and more to be concentrated in small circles. The business elite prefers to make central decisions in intimate circles together with a handful of compliant politicians.

This has triggered a downward spiral that is further and further weakening the political parties. It is commonly argued that if politics lacks the clout it needs to shape the course of events, it will in the end have no choice but to follow, for better or for worse, the laws of the world market—a development that is bound to spell the end of any broad-based political engagement. In the US the turnout for even the most important elections is never higher than 40 percent (for Congressional elections) or nearly 60 percent (for presidential elections). All a candidate now needs to become president of the United Sates is to secure the votes of less than one-quarter of the registered electorate.

This has one further consequence. Since turnout figures vary substantially as a function of income and education levels, the influence of the well-to-do and the rich is also growing accordingly. According to data from the U.S. Census Bureau, the upper quarter of the working population who possess a university degree (bachelor or higher), and thus have incomes between one and a half and three times as high as the average, have a turnout of almost 80 percent, whereas the bottom 20 percent, with a maximum of three years' high school education, turn out to vote at rates of only about 30 percent. What this means in effect is that the top quarter accounts for five times as many actual voters (about 36 percent) as the bottom fifth (just over 7 percent). If we take this one step further, we see that winning the votes of the top 25 percent is close to sufficient to be elected president of the US. It can at any rate be said that it is far more important to cater to the interests of this group than to those of the bottom half of the population, which is hardly ever able to mobilize as many voters as the former group. This social imbalance among the electorate is an additional factor serving to consolidate the influence on politics of the business elite and the upper class.

The overall development in the US, and not at all only in the US, can be accurately characterized in the words of Warren Buffett, the second richest man in the world, who summed up the situation in his 2004 annual shareholders newsletter as follows: "If class warfare is being waged in America, my class is clearly winning." Those who, like Keller and the rest of her mainstream functionalist colleagues, pin their hopes on the insight of elites when it comes to creating better living conditions (Keller 1963: 279), defining the role of the general population, the so-called mass, in this process as a largely passive one, are, it would seem, victims of an illusion. The ruling class will as a rule turn to its account whatever opportunities are offered it by the state of the power relations in society.

Discussion Questions

1. What role does performance play for the recruitment of elites?
2. How socially heterogeneous or homogeneous are the elites?
3. Does the business elite enjoy a special position which enables it to exert considerably greater influence on the development of society than other elites?

4. What is the nature of the relationship between elites and classes within society?
5. Is there a ruling class today?

Bibliography

Becker, I. and Hauser, R. (2003) *Anatomie einer Einkommensverteilung. Ergebnisse der Einkommens-und Verbrauchsstichproben 1969–1998*, Berlin: Sigma.

Beckert, J. (2003) "Demokratische Umverteilung: Erbschaftsbesteuerung und meritokratisches Eigentumsverständnis in den USA," in W. Fluck and W. Werner (eds), *Wie viel Ungleichheit verträgt die Demokratie? Armut und Reichtum in den USA*, Frankfurt a.M.: Campus, pp. 119–43.

Beyme, K. von (1971) *Die politische Elite in der Bundesrepublik Deutschland,* Munich:R. Piper & Co.

Blau, P.M. and Duncan, O.D. (1967) *The American Occupational Structure*, New York: Wiley.

Bourdieu, P. (1974) "Avenir de classe et causalité du probable," in *Revue française de sociologie* 15: 9–42; Ger. "Klassenschicksal, individuelles Handeln und das Gesetz der Wahrscheinlichkeit," in P. Bourdieu, L. Boltanski, M. de Saint Martin and P. Maldidier (1981), *Über die Reproduktion sozialer Macht*, Frankfurt a.M.: EVA, pp. 169–226.

——— (1979) *La distinction, Critique sociale du jugement*, Paris: Éditions de Minuit: Engl. *Distinction. A Social Critique of the Judgement of Taste*, Cambridge, Mass.: Harvard University Press 2004 (original printing 1984/1986).

——— (1980) *Le sens pratique*, Paris: Éditions de Minuit; Engl. *The Logic of Practice*, Stanford: Stanford University Press 1990.

——— (1983) "Ökonomisches Kapital, kulturelles Kapital, soziales Kapital," in R. Kreckel (ed.) *Soziale Ungleichheiten. Soziale Welt*, Sonderband 2. Göttingen: Otto Schwartz & Co.: 183–98; Engl. "The (three) forms of capital," in J.G. Richardson (ed.), *Handbook of Theory and Research in the Sociology of Education*, New York & London: Greenwood Press 1986, pp. 241–58 (Reprint in A.H. Halsey, P. Brown and W.A. Stuart (eds), *Education, Culture, Economy, and Society*, Oxford: Oxford University Press 1997, pp. 46–58).

——— (1984) *Homo academicus*. Paris: Éditions de Minuit; Engl. *Homo academicus*, Cambridge: Polity Press 1988.

——— (1989a) *La noblesse d'Etat. Grandes écoles et esprit de corps*, Paris: Éditions de Minuit: Engl. *The State Nobility. Elite Schools in the Field of Power*, Cambridge: Polity Press 1996.

——— (1989b) *Satz und Gegensatz. Über die Verantwortung der Intellektuellen*, Berlin: Wagenbach Verlag.

——— (1992) "Die feinen Unterschiede," in M. Steinrücke (ed.), *Die verborgenen Mechanismen der Macht*, Hamburg: VSA-Verlag, pp. 31–47.

——— (1993a) *Soziologische Fragen*; Engl. *Sociology in Question*, London: Sage Publications.

——— (1993b) "From ruling class to the field of power," an interview with Pierre Bourdieu on "La Noblesse d'État," *Theory, Culture & Society* 10: 3, 19–44.

——— (1994) *Raisons pratiques. Sur la théorie de l'action*, Paris: Seuil; Engl. *Practical Reason: On The Theory of Action*, Cambridge: Polity Press 1998.

——— and Boltanski, L. (1975) "Le titre et le poste: rapports entre le système de reproduction," *Actes de la recherche en sciences sociales*, 2/3: 95–108; Ger. "Zum Verhältnis von Bildung und Beschäftigung," in P. Bourdieu, L. Boltanski, M. de

——— and Passeron, J.C. (1964) *Les héritiers. Les étudiants et la culture*, Paris: Éditions de Minuit, Engl. *The Inheritors. French Students and their Relation to Culture*, Chicago: University of Chicago Press 1979.

——— and Saint Martin, M. de (1978) "Le patronat," *Actes de la recherche en sciences sociales*, 20/21: 2–82.

——— and Saint Martin, M. de (1982) "La sainte famille. L'épiscopat français dans la champ du pouvoir," *Actes de la recherche en sciences sociales* 44/45: 2–53.

——— and Saint Martin, M. de (1987) "Agrégation et ségrégation. Le champ des grandes écoles et le champ du pouvoir," *Actes de la recherche en sciences sociales* 69: 2–50.

——— and Wacquant, L.J.D. (1992) *Réponses pour une anthropologie réflexive*, Paris: Seuil; Engl. *An Invitation to Reflexive Sociology*, Chicago: University of Chicago Press.

——— Boltanski, L. and Saint Martin, M. de (1973) "Les stratégies de reconversion. Les classes sociales et le système d'enseignement," *Social Science Information* 12: 61–113, Engl. "Changes in social structure and changes in the demand for education," in S. Giner and M. Scotford-Archer (eds), *Contemporary Europe. Social Structures and Cultural Patterns*, London: Routledge and Kegan Paul 1977, pp. 197–227.

Cutts, R.L. (1997) *An Empire of Schools. Japan's Universities and the Molding of a National Elite*, Armonk: M.E. Sharp.

Giddens, A. (1974) "Elites in British class structure," in P. Stanworth and A. Giddens (eds), *Elites and Power in British Society*, Cambridge: Cambridge University Press, pp. 1–21.

Goldthorpe, J.H. (2002) "Globalisation and social class," in *West European Politics* 25: 3, 1–28.

Greene, H.R. and Greene, M. (2000) *Inside the Top Colleges. Realities of Life and Learning in America's Elite Colleges*, New York: Cliff Street Books.

Hartmann, M (1999) "Auf dem Weg zur transnationalen Bourgeoisie? Die Internationalisierung der Wirtschaft und die Internationalität der Spitzenmanager Deutsch lands, Frankreichs, Großbritanniens und der USA," *Leviathan* 27: 113–41.

——— (2002) *Der Mythos von den Leistungseliten. Spitzenkarrieren und soziale Herkunft in Wirtschaft, Politik, Justiz und Wissenschaft*, Frankfurt a.M.: Campus.

Henwood, D. (1998) *Wall Street. How it works and for whom*, London and New York: Verso. Herzog, D.

Higley, J., Hoffmann-Lange, U., Kadushin, C. and Moore, G. (1991) "Elite integration in stable democracies: a reconsideration," *European Sociological Review* 7: 35–53.

Hoffmann-Lange, U. (1992) *Eliten, Macht und Konflikt*, Opladen: Leske + Budrich.

Höpner, M. (2003) *Wer beherrscht die Unternehmen? Shareholder Value, Managerherrschaft und Mitbestimmung in Deutschland*, Frankfurt a.M.: Campus.

Keller, S. (1963) *Beyond the Ruling Class. Strategic Elites in Modern Society*, New York: Random House.

B. Krais and Gebauer, G. (2002) *Habitus*, Bielefeld: transcript Verlag.

Krugman, P. (2002) "For Richer," *New York Times*, October 20.

Marceau, J. (1989a) *A Family Business? The Making of an International Business Elite*, Cambridge: Cambridge University Press.

Mills, C.W (1959) *The Power Elite*, New York: OUP/ Galaxy Books (original printing Oxford: Oxford University Press 1956).

Phillips, K. (2002) *Wealth and Democracy. A Political History of the American Rich,* New York: Broadway Books.

Rothacher, A. (1993) *The Japanese Power Elite*, London: Macmillan Press.

Werner, W. (2003) "Zurück in die Zeit des Great Gatsby? Änderungen in der amerikanischen Einkommensverteilung im späten 20. Jahrhundert," in W. Fluck and W. Werner (eds), *Wieviel Ungleichheit verträgt die Demokratie? Armut und Reichtum in den USA*, Frankfurt a.M.: Campus, pp. 23–46.

■ CHAPTER 3

Mass Media and Agency Design

Editor's Introduction

Chapter 3 describes the significance of media, as the government's watchdog, in political accountability . Ruder examines media and power within the context of shaping voter awareness. In the first section of the chapter, Ruder focuses on presidential control over agencies and the effects of that control on agency responsibility. The second part of Ruder's chapter examines 150,000 news articles to study the variety of coverage from different agencies and their design features between 1987 and 2007. This time frame covers four presidential administrations, from the end of the Reagan to the first seven years of the Bush administration. In doing so, Ruder provides a picture of how an individual's awareness is shaped in relation to how frequently journalists mention the president in relation to their agency. His findings demonstrate that the news has an obligation to include agency design information because without that information, voters cannot make retrospective judgments and may therefore assign responsibility incorrectly. The chapter raises some important questions: How do agency design features lead voters to attribute responsibility of an agency's actions to the president? If information of presidential authority is added, will an agency's responsibility have any substantial change? Why do individuals tend to visualize details of the relationship between political control and the agency before they consider attributing responsibility?

READING 3 Agency Design, the Mass Media, and the Blame for Agency Scandals

Alex I. Ruder

Government agencies are responsible for the regulation and enforcement of laws that affect nearly every aspect of society. Their responsibilities range from the implementation of major health care and financial reform to the criminal enforcement of antitrust laws and the collection of taxes. Yet democratic institutions rarely provide a direct electoral check on bureaucrats. Political accountability of agencies thus requires that voters credit or blame elected officials with formal authority over those agencies.

The process by which voters learn which elected officials are responsible for an agency is complicated by institutional structures that feature multiple political principals, layers of bureaucracy, and complicated decision-making procedures often hidden from public view. A large body of research has thus focused on institutional design features that enhance the clarity of responsibility for agency actions (e.g., Kagan 2001). However, even with this research, we know little about how these features moderate voter attribution of blame. Are responsibility attributions for agency actions influenced by the institutional clarity of responsibility?

Proper allocation of blame and credit is necessary for democratic governance. Voters learn who is responsible for an action, form judgments about their performance in office, and then vote according to those judgments (Fiorina 1981; Key 1966). Concerns about the proper allocation of blame motivates many scholars to advocate for more presidential control over agencies. However, in order for increased presidential formal authority to enhance political accountability, voters must actually know that the president wields that authority.

How do voters learn about the complex institutional details concerning government agencies? As scholars have argued in the context of legislative institutions, voters learn about the institutional context through the mass media (Rudolph 2003). Unlike lawmaking, which has tallied roll-call votes and often a formal signing statement given by the president, most agency policy making occurs in a *black box* (Kagan 2001). Citizens, without media coverage, are unlikely to know which elected officials or bureaucrats are responsible for agency policy making or performance.

The informational role of the media has been shown to enable accountability by increasing voter knowledge of elected officials, which, in turn, creates incentives for those officials to be more responsive to their constituents (Prat and Strömberg 2011; Snyder and Strömberg 2010). In American politics, mass media provides voters with much information about political institutions and officials such as congressional actions (Arnold 2004) and the president's public agenda (Barabas 2008). The media also serves Congress and voters as a crucial watchdog over the actions of government agencies (Rosen 1998).

One challenge facing observational studies seeking to identify the influence of agency institutional context on responsibility attributions is controlling and measuring the information that voters encounter in the news. In this article, I use a survey experiment to identify the effect

Alex I. Ruder, "Agency Design, the Mass Media, and the Blame for Agency Scandals," *Presidential Studies Quarterly*, vol. 45, no. 3, pp. 514-539.

of agency design information on attributions of responsibility for an agency scandal. The survey experiment allows me to manipulate the information that respondents receive about agency design, while holding constant other potentially confounding details about the agency.

In the experiment, respondents read a real newspaper article about an agency scandal. Scandals provide an opportunity to study one of mass media's most important functions—revealing government malfeasance to citizens. Officials themselves are unlikely to provide information to the public about misdoings in government. Absent these disclosures of wrongdoing, the mass media is the public's only source of information concerning officials who are not representing their interests (Snyder and Puglisi 2011). Thus, out of all types of media coverage, coverage of agency scandals is arguably the most important place to convey information about political control of the bureaucracy. In addition, using news coverage allows me to manipulate an information source that is readily available to the public and is a primary source to voters about agency actions and institutional context.

In one experimental condition, I include agency-design information—the institutional context—that explains how the agency is structured to allow greater presidential influence over its operations. I provide respondents with agency-design details widely promoted by scholars as enhancing presidential control: presidential appointments and removal of agency leadership, the agency's location in the president's cabinet, and centralized regulatory review by the White House Office of Management and Budget (OMB). The second experimental condition presents the same newspaper article but with no information on agency design.

I find that informing respondents about agency-design features that enhance presidential control significantly increases attributions of responsibility to the president. This result is consistent with presidential control theorists who argue that increasing presidential formal authority over agencies enhances clarity of responsibility for voters.

Coverage of scandals, however, is only one part of the media's role informing voters about public affairs. Simple media attention to the day-to-day activities of regulatory agencies enhances accountability by providing voters with crucial information about the numerous ways that agency activity influences them and society. To assess mass media attention to federal agencies, I investigate how much opportunity voters have to learn about agencies through the news. I collect over 150,000 newspaper articles about a large sample of U.S. federal agencies and examine how coverage varies by agency, agency-design features, and regulatory activity. I match news coverage to data about agency-design characteristics from Lewis's work (2003, 2008) and regulatory review activity from the OMB. The analysis presents a mixed assessment of how well the news enables accountability of federal agencies. I demonstrate a high degree of heterogeneity across agencies in both the attention they receive in the news and the frequency with which journalists mention the president along with the agency. Some agencies with vast regulatory powers—such as the Food and Drug Administration (FDA)—receive relatively little coverage that mentions the president, despite the president's significant powers over that agency.

The article is organized into the following sections. The first section reviews the institutional context of government agencies, paying particular attention to design features that increase the president's formal authority over agencies. The second section describes the theoretical motivation and hypothesis. The third section presents the experimental design and results. The fourth section places the experimental results in a broader context of press coverage of government agencies. The fifth section concludes.

The Institutional Context: Agency Design

When creating agencies, elected officials balance political control with agency performance (Bawn 1995; Huber and McCarty 2004). The fundamental trade-off is that more political influence and control—through appointees rather than experts—reduce the autonomy of agencies to pursue what expert bureaucrats consider good public policy.

A second consideration is how much authority the president wields over an agency relative to Congress and the agency bureaucrats (Moe and Wilson 1994; Volden 2002). Theorists suggest that Congress resists presidential control of agencies when the president is ideologically opposed to Congress. Other works suggest that congressional control obscures responsibility for agency actions (e.g., Lowi 1979) and that greater presidential control enhances clarity of responsibility and greater political accountability (Kagan 2001).

Battles over agency structure can lead to a variety of complex agency structures, but scholars simplify the empirical analysis of agency design by focusing on four broad categories of institutional design. Each category is defined by a set of institutional features that enhances or limits presidential control over the agency.[1] In Table 3.1, I list the principal agency types identified by Lewis (2003, 2008), along with their design characteristics and examples of agencies.

These broad categories, of course, mask significant within-type heterogeneity. However, given their prominence in the literature, they provide a useful starting point to analyze differences in coverage. Political battles over agency

TABLE 3.1 Insulation Characteristics of Different Agency Types

Design	Description	Example
Executive Office of the President	Located within the White House, under the direct control of the president's Chief of Staff	Council on Environmental Quality, Office of Management and Budget.
Cabinet/Subcabinet	Officials serve at president's will; agencies within cabinet face additional budgetary pressure from presidentially appointed secretaries.	Homeland Security, Food and Drug Administration
Executive Agency	Located outside the cabinet structure. Budget line independent of cabinet departments. President still can remove officials at will.	Environmental Protection Agency
Regulatory Commission	Led by multimember, bipartisan commission with staggered terms. For-cause removal of officials only.	Securities and Exchange Commission

Note: Types are listed in increasing order of insulation, with regulatory commissions being the most insulated from presidential control. Classification of agency types adapted from Lewis (2003).

design often focus on these broad categories. For example, congressional Republicans have continued to challenge the powerful Consumer Financial Protection Bureau and call for a change in leadership structure from a single agency director to a bipartisan regulatory commission (McCoy 2013). Another example involves the Federal Emergency Management Agency (FEMA), where critics, angered by perceived politicization of the agency, called for FEMA to be removed from the president's cabinet and made into an independent agency (Cilluffo et al. 2009). Agencies located within the Executive Office of the President and the president's cabinet feature the highest levels of presidential control. For cabinet departments such as Justice and Homeland Security, the president has significant control over budgets, personnel, and policy through regulatory review. Power over cabinet departments extends to agencies that belong within the cabinet departments. This subcabinet level includes agencies such as the FDA and FEMA.

The president also has these powers over executive agencies such as the Environmental Protection Agency (EPA). In terms of political insulation, executive agencies are not substantially different than cabinet-level agencies. The design feature that distinguishes these agencies is that their budget line in the federal budget is independent of any particular cabinet department budget.

Regulatory commissions are the agencies most insulated from presidential control through several mechanisms (Barkow 2010). First, commission members are removable only for cause and not simply at the president's will. Second, a commission is not required to submit significant regulations to the OMB for cost–benefit analysis. Third, a commission cannot be composed of commissioners from a single party; moreover, members serve staggered, fixed-length terms. All these factors reduce the president's ex ante and ex post ability to control a commission's policy and enforcement agenda.

Theoretical Expectations

Arguments for greater political control often focus on the president and features of the executive branch that increase the clarity of responsibility for voters (Kagan 2001; Lessig and Sunstein 1994). Even the judicial branch, especially since the Supreme Court's *Chevron* decision, justifies judicial deference to executive agencies due to their being under the direction of an electorally accountable executive (*Chevron U.S.A., Inc.* v. *Natural Resources Defense Council* 1984). However, more presidential authority would have little effect on electoral accountability if voters were unaware of this power.

The implicit assumption in this literature is that voter knowledge of agency design moderates attributions of blame. In other words, voters adjust their attributions of blame to be consistent with the formal degree of control a president holds over an agency. This behavior is consistent with arguments that voters are sophisticated in allocating blame, meaning voters consider factual details in order to form their opinions regarding responsibility.

The literature of blame attribution suggests several reasons why institutional context moderates blame attribution. One prominent theme in this literature focuses on the clarity of responsibility provided by features of political systems. Responsible party government focuses on the ease with which voters can hold a single party responsible for government actions (Schattschneider 1942). Economic voting studies find that features of political institutions, such as a greater share of control by governing parties, periods of unified government, budgetary power, or proposal power, increase clarity of responsibility for economic outcomes (Alt and Lowry 1994; Duch and Stevenson 2008, 2013; Powell and Whitten 1993; Rudolph 2003). In comparative politics, the debate over presidential and parliamentary constitutions includes discussions of the clarity of responsibility provided by presidential systems, which feature a single elected official responsible for governmental outcomes (Cheibub 2007; Mainwaring and Shugart 1997).

As Anderson (2000) shows, formal features of a political system moderate the strength of the relationship between economic conditions and blame or reward. This explanation of institutional complexity underlies more recent studies of blame attribution in the wake of disaster, where scholars have focused on the complexity of responsibility attributions in a federalist system (Arceneaux and Stein 2006; Gomez and Wilson 2008; Maestas et al. 2008; Malhotra and Kuo 2008).

Many features of agency design are directly intended to increase or decrease the president's responsibility over a given agency. Ruder (2014), for example, shows how bipartisan commission structures insulate the president from attributions of responsibility. An open question, however, is how features that enhance presidential control provide greater clarity of responsibility to voters seeking to allocate blame in the wake of an agency scandal. Based on the discussions of agency design in the first section and institutional moderators of blame attribution in this section, I state the following hypothesis:

> **Centralized Control Hypothesis:** Voters are more likely to blame the president when news includes information about formal institutional structures that give the president more control over an agency, compared to when news does not include information about formal institutional structures that give the president more control over an agency.

The first section suggests several features of agency design suitable to test the hypothesis. Commissions, for example, feature a bipartisan structure and for-cause removal of officials, both of which reduce presidential control. An alternative approach is to focus on agency-design features that increase presidential control. The advantage of this approach is that it addresses a key argument in favor of increasing presidential control over agencies: the enhanced accountability derived through clarity of responsibility.[2]

Executive and cabinet agencies both feature several agency-design features that increase presidential control. In the analysis below, I focus on two features in particular: the appointment power and centralized control of presidential power through regulatory review. The appointment power is an Article II power granted to the president and remains one of the most important ways that the president manages the executive branch (Lewis 2008).

White House review of agency rulemaking is a feature of institutional design that has received considerable attention from presidential and public-law research (Acs and Cameron 2013; Croley 2003; West 2006). The OMB, serving the president, has been called a gatekeeper for agency regulations and annually reviews hundreds of significant agency regulations (Government Accountability Office 2003). The review of agency regulations allows the White House, through the OMB, to ensure that agency regulations "reflect Presidential priorities and … ensure that economic and other impacts are assessed as part of regulatory decision-making" (OMB 2013).

Experimental Design and Results

To test the hypothesis regarding agency design and blame attribution, I conduct a survey experiment about the Minerals Management Service (MMS) oversight of the oil and gas industry, leading to the Deepwater Horizon explosion and oil spill in the Gulf of Mexico in April 2010. I choose this particular agency scandal for several reasons. Most importantly, the scandal represents a regulatory failure, with congressional hearings, independent investigative reports, and media citing the agency's lax regulatory approach and regulatory capture by the oil and gas industry. Scandals over regulatory failures address a core agency function with costly consequences for public health and safety. Furthermore, agency-design features, such as regulatory review, are specifically structured to provide the president with more or less power over regulation, allowing for a more plausible examination of how these features moderate blame attribution.

The second reason I choose this incident concerns the widespread news coverage and public attention to the disaster. Less than a month after the Deepwater Horizon exploded, nearly 85% of U.S. adults knew *a lot* or *some* about the oil spill (*60 Minutes/Vanity Fair* 2010). Americans were watching the news to learn about the oil spill. News coverage of the spill's aftermath also frequently included President Barack Obama. In other words, the spill scandal is a situation in which the public was widely exposed to the scandal, the agency, and the president. This allows me to assess whether agency-design information can make any difference in attributions, given a media environment saturated with coverage of the president, agency officials, and state and local leaders trading blame for the disaster.[3]

The salience of the disaster also presents a potential weakness of this approach. Considering that so many individuals have knowledge of the disaster, preformed opinions regarding blame attribution may not respond to new information about agency design. Another potential weakness concerns the elapsed time since the disaster and its aftermath. Blame attribution may be most important to study as a scandal unfolds, not years after the event has occurred.

Even so, agency scandals and their aftermath can unfold over long periods of time. As this process unfolds, voters can attribute responsibility immediately after the disaster or retrospectively as more information about the disaster and the government's response becomes available. As recently as March 2014, articles are still being published about health consequences and regulatory decisions linked to the 2010 oil spill (Hays 2014). Congressional investigations can drag on for months, and criminal investigations can take years to complete. Sources or newly discovered information can reveal previously unknown details that lead to new inquires into a scandal. These factors contribute to keeping agency scandals in the news long after such large disasters occur, suggesting that press coverage has the potential to continue to influence blame attributions.

Experimental Design

An observational study would require the unrealistic ability to measure exposure of individuals to news coverage with agency-design information and, controlling for other factors, estimate its effect on blame attributions. A more internally valid method is experimental manipulation of news articles, which has a long tradition in media research on framing effects.

I conduct the experiment using Amazon's Mechanical Turk (MTurk) to recruit 305 respondents in April 2014.[4] I take several standard precautions with regard to subject recruitment from MTurk. I warn subjects that they will not be paid for taking the survey more than once; I check respondent Internet protocol (IP) addresses to reduce the chance that anyone took the survey twice. I also warn respondents that they will not be compensated if they too quickly read the prompts and answer questions, which suggests guessing and not taking the experiment seriously. I also limit the survey to respondents with over a 97.5% task approval rate, which is an indicator of the reliability and quality of the MTurk respondent. The average survey completion time was five minutes and twenty-eight seconds. After respondents completed the survey, they received 60 cents compensation.

To gauge attribution of responsibility, I first ask respondents to read a real news article about the resignation of MMS Director Elizabeth Birnbaum amid criticism of the agency's lax industry oversight.[5] After reading the article, I ask respondents to "Please indicate how much responsibility you think each of the following has for the U.S. Minerals Management Service's role in the Deepwater Horizon disaster." I present respondents with a list of four entities: the Obama administration, the Bush administration, Congress, and the agency leadership. Respondents select *A Lot*, *Some*, *A Little*, or *None*.

I include both the Bush and Obama administrations because the disaster happened only 16 months into the Obama administration; reasonably, individuals could conclude that Bush administration policies led to the disaster. In fact, polling conducted at the time suggests that individuals felt Bush administration policies were a more likely contributor to the regulatory failure. Among U.S. adults, 18% blame the policies of the Bush administration for the conditions that led to the spill, compared to only 3% for the Obama administration (CBS News/*New York Times* Poll 2010). This difference between George W. Bush and Barack Obama is particularly large among Democrats and independents, but even Republicans were more likely to blame the Bush administration.

I randomly assign respondents to one of three experimental conditions. In the first condition, respondents view no news article and simply attribute responsibility for the disaster. This condition provides baseline estimates of attributions of responsibility in the absence of news coverage. In the second condition, which I call the *No Presidential Control* condition, respondents read an article that makes no mention of elected officials or agency-design information. It simply discusses the resignation and the agency's poor enforcement record. In the third condition, the *Presidential Control* condition, I add the following sentences near the beginning of the article:

> MMS is under the direction of Secretary of the Interior Ken Salazar, who has led the cabinet-level department as part of the Obama administration. According to the U.S Office of Management and Budget, since 2009 alone the Obama administration has reviewed and approved several MMS regulations related to deepwater oil exploration.

In addition, the article includes the following text: "Elizabeth Birnbaum, who was appointed director of the Minerals Management Service in June 2009, submitted her resignation to Interior Secretary Ken Salazar." In the third condition, I add "by President Obama" after "… was appointed director of the Minerals Management Service."

The third condition includes three factors related to the hypothesis stated in the second section: the president appointed the leader, MMS is a cabinet-level agency under the direction of a cabinet secretary, and the OMB reviews and approves the agency's regulations related to offshore drilling. The theoretical expectation is that this added information increases attributions of responsibility by clarifying the degree of the president's responsibility over the agency.

The articles and survey instrument are available in Appendix S1 and Appendix S2, respectively.

Results

The ordinal nature of the data in the experiment suggests two alternative strategies for statistical analysis. I use a simple nonparametric test for ordinal variables, the one-sided Mann-Whitney *U* test, which tests the null hypothesis of equality of two groups of responses against the alternative hypothesis that one group is greater than the other. The second approach would be to use ordinal logistic regression, but I choose the nonparametric alternative because I include no pretreatment covariates. The hypothesis in the second is strictly about agency-design information; it is not focused on heterogeneous treatment effects across groups, which I leave for future research. The results presented below are robust to different empirical strategies, such as a chi-square test or transforming the data into dichotomous *high* and *low* attribution groups and performing an equality of proportions test. These additional results are available in Appendix S1.

The results presented in Table 3.2 show the percent of respondents in each response category across the two experimental conditions. In Panel A, I show results from respondent attributions to the Bush administration. The one-sided Mann-Whitney *U* test cannot reject the null hypothesis that attribution levels are the same in both experimental conditions. The information about agency design had no effect on increasing the attributions to the Bush administration. Attributions appear slightly higher in the *No Presidential Control* condition, though the alternative one-sided and two-sided Mann-Whitney tests cannot reject the null hypothesis of equal response distributions.

The results for the Obama administration provide a stark contrast to the results for the Bush administration. The difference in responses across *Presidential Control* and *No Presidential Control* conditions is large and statistically significant. In the *No Presidential Control* condition, 17% of respondents said the Obama administration had *None* as a degree of responsibility. In the *Presidential Control* condition, only 5% of

TABLE 3.2 Results from Experiment Testing the Centralized Control Hypothesis: Percent Respondents in Each Cell by Experimental Condition

A. Bush Administration					
Condition	**A Lot**	**Some**	**A Little**	**None**	**Mean Attribution**
No Presidential Control	17%	48%	29%	7%	0.58
Presidential Control	18%	37%	28%	18%	0.51
Mann-Whitney Test Statistic: $U = 4{,}550$, $p = 0.92$					
B. Obama Administration					
Condition	**A Lot**	**Some**	**A Little**	**None**	**Mean Attribution**
No Presidential Control	11%	40%	33%	17%	0.48
Presidential Control	23%	48%	25%	5%	0.62
Mann-Whitney Test Statistic: $U = 6{,}437$, $p < 0.01$					

Note: Panel A shows results from the Bush administration response. Panel B shows results from the Obama administration response. One-sided Mann-Whitney test statistics and *p*-values shown. $n = 202$, with 101 respondents assigned randomly to each experimental condition.

respondents chose *None*. Moreover, only 11% of respondents chose *A Lot* in the *No Presidential Control* condition, while 23% chose *A Lot* in the *Presidential Control* condition.

One way to simplify the presentation of these results is to recode the four attribution levels into a single continuous measure that ranges from 0 (no attribution) to 1 (the highest degree of attribution). I recode *none* to 0.00, *a little* to 0.33, *some* to 0.66, and *a lot* to 1.00. The implied assumption of this recoding is that the response values are equidistant from each other. Once recoded, I calculate the average value of this variable and call it *mean attribution*. The measure is presented in the final column of Table 3.2. For the Bush administration, the difference in mean attribution between the two experimental conditions is −0.07 (0.51–0.58). In contrast, the difference in mean attribution for the Obama administration is 0.14 (0.62–0.48).

Blame of Other Officials

The survey also asked respondents to attribute responsibility to other officials with formal responsibility over the agency. These other officials are Congress and the agency leadership. These results provide an assessment of how respondents change blame attributions to other officials when provided with information about presidential control. For example, learning about presidential control over the agency may reduce the respondents' propensity to blame Congress or the agency leadership. Alternatively, if respondents do not treat responsibility for agency failures as zero-sum, then respondents may not change their attributions to Congress and the agency leadership when presented with information about presidential control.

The results for Congress and the agency leadership are in Table 3.3. For simplicity, I present only the mean attribution scores. The mean attribution scores are considerably higher for the agency leadership (column 2) than for Congress (column 3), or for the Bush and Obama administrations, as presented in Table 3.2. The *Presidential Control* treatment has a small negative effect reducing attributions of responsibility to these two actors, though these results are only significant at the 0.10 level. This result suggests that respondents allocate blame away from these officials and toward the administration.

Treatment Comparison to Baseline Attributions

The results presented in the sections above compare the effect of information about presidential control relative to a baseline in which respondents read a newspaper without information on presidential control. This experimental design tests the hypothesis as described in the second section. An alternative strategy is to examine how information on presidential control changes attributions of responsibility relative to a baseline group who receives no experimental intervention. While not a test of the centralized

TABLE 3.3 Allocation of Blame to Other Officials

Condition	Agency Leadership	Congress
No Presidential Control	0.86	0.63
Presidential Control	0.82	0.56
p-value	0.054	0.058

Note: Results show mean attribution scores to both agency leadership and Congress, by experimental condition. *p*-values are for one-sided Mann-Whitney test of the alternative hypothesis that attribution in the *Presidential Control* condition is less than attribution in the *No Presidential Control* condition.

TABLE 3.4 Results from Experiment Examining Treatments Compared to *No Media Baseline* Condition

A. No Presidential Control Comparison

Condition	Agency Leadership	Congress	Bush Administration	Obama Administration
No Media Baseline	0.69	0.61	0.52	0.54
No Presidential Control	0.86	0.63	0.58	0.48
p-value	<0.01	0.74	0.24	0.19

B. Presidential Control Comparison

Condition	Agency Leadership	Congress	Bush Administration	Obama Administration
No Media Baseline	0.69	0.61	0.52	0.54
Presidential Control	0.82	0.56	0.51	0.62
p-value	<0.01	0.18	0.80	0.04

Note: All cells contain mean attribution to the president. One-sided Mann-Whitney test statistics and *p*-values shown. 103 respondents assigned to *No Media Baseline* condition.

control hypothesis, this strategy illuminates how respondents allocate responsibility absent media coverage and how different types of media coverage change those allocations of responsibility.

In Table 3.4, I present results of both the *No Presidential Control* and *Presidential Control* conditions, when compared to a baseline condition where I simply ask respondents to attribute responsibility to the four officials. Panel A shows the mean attribution scores for the *No Presidential Control* condition and the baseline *No Media Baseline* condition. When asked to attribute responsibility for each official, respondents in the *No Media Baseline* condition are more likely to blame the agency leadership than Congress or the presidential administrations.

Respondents allocate similar degrees of attribution to the Bush and Obama administrations (0.52 and 0.54, respectively), which differs from results of polls conducted after the disaster. The results presented here are not strictly comparable as there was extensive media coverage of the disaster and its response in 2010 and several years have passed since the event. The relatively equal levels of attribution could reflect uncertainty over the details of the disaster, the federal agency in charge, or the exact dates involved in the scandal.

Presenting respondents with a news article without presidential control information has the largest change on attributions of responsibility to the agency leadership (0.69 to 0.86). This large change is most likely driven by the content in the news article, which focuses on the resignation of agency leadership. The *No Presidential Control* condition shows no statistically significant differences in attribution of responsibility for the remaining officials. Respondents were slightly more likely to blame the Bush administration and slightly less likely to blame the Obama administration when compared to the *No Media Baseline* condition. This pattern is more consistent with the national polling results from 2010, in which the Bush administration received more blame than the Obama administration.

Panel B in Table 3.4 shows results for the *Presidential Control* condition and the *No Media Baseline* condition. As with the results in Panel A, significantly more respondents allocate responsibility to the agency leadership after reading the news article when compared to respondents in the *No Media Baseline* condition (from 0.69 to 0.82). The results for the presidential administrations are substantively comparable to the results presented in Table 3.2: the *Presidential Control* treatment causes a statistically significant increase in attributions of responsibility toward the Obama administration. There is no significant difference in attributions to the Bush administration.

Summary of Experimental Results

The results in Table 3.2 provide support for the centralized control hypothesis: information in the news about the president's centralized control over the agency increases attributions of blame to the president, relative to news that omits that information. The results support the hypothesis only with regard to the Obama administration.

What explains the absence of an effect with regard to the Bush administration? One likely explanation involves the sophisticated allocation of blame for the conditions that led to the disaster. Without a clear understanding of presidential formal authority over the agency, respondents are more likely to blame eight years of Bush administration regulatory policy and the failures that occurred under that administration (which are mentioned in the experiment's news article). However, once informed about the influence the Obama administration wields over the agency—through appointment of the agency leadership, removal of the agency leadership, and regulatory review—respondents were more likely to allocate blame to the Obama administration. Respondents, however, may also be acting myopically (Bartels 2008) by irrationally allocating more blame to the current administration than it actually deserves.

The change does not mean that respondents place no blame on the Bush administration, but that respondents shift toward more blame on the Obama administration. More information about presidential control clarifies for respondents how much responsibility the Obama administration had for the agency; before respondents were exposed to the agency-design information, they possibly had a vague or inaccurate notion of presidential responsibility for the agency. Knowledge of the institutional context, in other words, enhanced clarity of responsibility.

The News and Federal Agency Accountability

Results in the preceding section show that news coverage that emphasizes the agency institutional context increases attributions of responsibility to the president during a major agency scandal. Providing details about the institutional context is not the only way that journalists enable the political accountability about agencies. Journalists, for example, can use different frames to describe policy (Bolson, Druckman, and Cook 2014; Ruder 2014), slant coverage toward a particular ideology (Gentzkow and Shapiro 2010; Groseclose and Milyo 2005), or emphasize some issues while ignoring others (Larcinese, Puglisi, and Snyder 2011; Puglisi 2011). Scandals, too, are not the only events that attract journalists to agencies. Agencies issue and enforce major regulations across the public policy domain. It is important to assess whether the public gets information about these day-to-day agency activities and does not learn about agencies only when the press covers relatively infrequent agency scandals.

A minimal requirement for accountability is simply covering agencies so that the voting public receives information about agency policy making. In the congressional context, Arnold (2004) shows that media coverage affects voter awareness of representatives and challengers in elections. Similarly, Snyder and Strömberg (2010) show that voters who live in areas with less press coverage about their

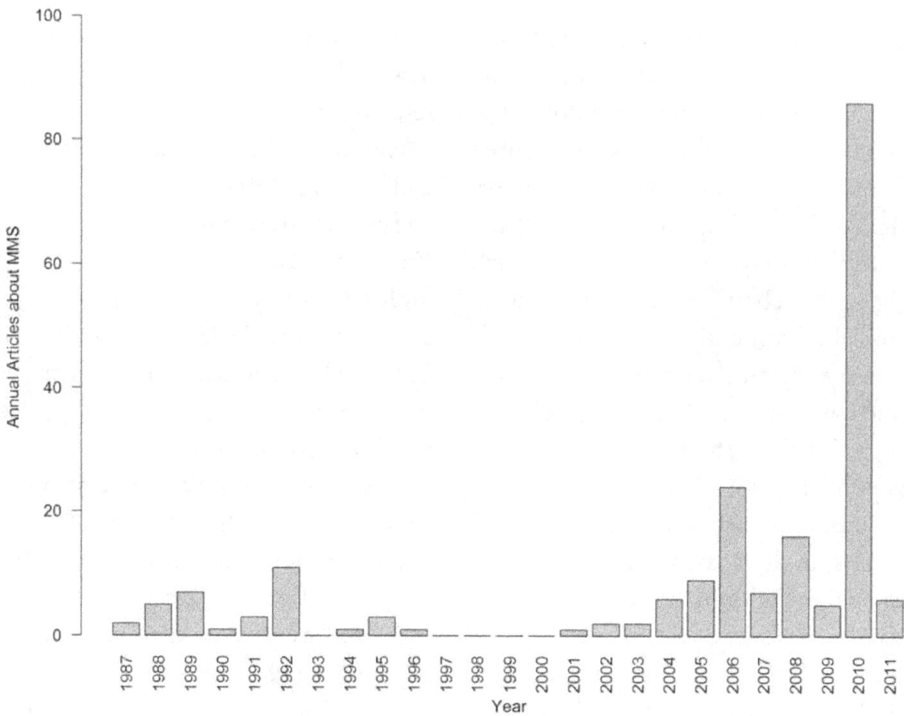

FIGURE 3.1 Annual Articles about the Minerals Management Service.

Sources: New York Times Annotated Corpus and ProQuest Newspapers.

congressional representative are less likely to recall their representative's name or evaluate their performance in office. According to their findings, coverage impacts more than voter knowledge; it affects the responsiveness of elected officials to their constituencies (Snyder and Strömberg 2010).

To understand the information available to voters about federal agencies, it is first important to know which agencies receive extensive coverage in the press and which agencies do not. Some agencies, such as the MMS, make significant policy-making decisions yet infrequently make the news. Other major agencies, such as the FDA, are featured far more frequently in the press. This variation in coverage has implications for whom the public holds accountable for federal agencies, what the public knows about federal agencies, how the public approves or disapproves of an agency's performance, and how agency officials conduct policy.

Gallup, for example, regularly polls the American public to ask their approval of select federal agencies (Gallup 2013). An important question is how the public obtains the information necessary to make these evaluations. The public has direct experience with some of the agencies Gallup uses in the survey, such as the Internal Revenue Service, allowing the public to use that direct experience in their evaluations. The public is far less likely to have direct interaction with many other federal agencies in the survey, such as the Central Intelligence Agency. This makes press coverage of these agencies an important provider of information about agency performance and official oversight.

For example, between 1987 and 2011, MMS approved over 21,000 applications to drill in the Gulf of Mexico. Between 1987 and 2007, the agency proposed 114 rules to the OMB; three of those rules were economically significant. The public had limited opportunity to learn of this activity through the news. The dark bars in Figure 3.1 show the number of news articles published annually about the MMS. Overall, the agency receives fairly little coverage. The median number of articles published annually is only three. The maximum number of articles published (86) is in 2010, the year of the oil spill.[6] The second highest annual total of articles, in 2006, was largely driven by another scandal, which concerned nonpayment of oil royalties.

I now present patterns of newspaper coverage of U.S. federal agencies. I show that considerable heterogeneity exists in the extent to which journalists cover agencies and in the frequency that journalists mention the president along with the agency—a minimum requirement to connect the agency's policies to the president. I then focus on regulators whose regulations are subject to presidential oversight through OMB regulatory review. I find that even the nation's largest regulators rarely receive coverage that features the president. The goal of this analysis is not to explain the variation in coverage but to provide descriptive patterns of media coverage of federal agencies. The knowledge of these patterns itself is an important step toward understanding accountability of these agencies and formulating questions for future research.

Aggregate Newspaper Coverage of the Bureaucracy

Newspapers are a major source of news for the public. Approximately 25% of U.S. adults use national newspapers for news, while 69% use local newspapers (Harris Interactive 2010). Editors and journalists at these local newspapers rely on influential papers such as the *New York Times* to set the agenda (Gans 1979; Wilhoit and Weaver 1991).

The data source for this analysis is the *New York Times Annotated Corpus* (*Times*), which includes nearly all articles published by the *Times* between 1987 through 2007 (Sandhaus 2008). Unfortunately, the corpus is limited to these years, but its coverage spans four presidential administrations, including the complete Clinton administration and seven years of the Bush administration. This coverage limits the potential for finding results that are idiosyncratic to a single president or biased by period-specific events such as a presidential election.

The *Times*, given its influence and focus on politics and regulation, is ideally suited to study agencies. Scholars have frequently used the *Times* to study presidential politics (see Gilens, Vavreck, and Cohen 2007). For decades, the *Times* has maintained its position as the country's leading paper. Presidents and national politics receive extensive coverage in the *Times* (Cohen 2008). I also find that the *Times* is not unique in its extensive coverage of regulatory agencies. Other major papers, such as the *Wall Street Journal* and the *Washington Post*, devote similar amounts of coverage to federal agencies.

I create a list of nearly every agency in the U.S. federal government using three sources: the *U.S. Government Manual*, the official Web site of the White House, and Lewis's agency-design data sets.[7] To identify subcabinet agencies, I use two sources. First, I use the OMB's database on rulemaking activity. This list identifies every subcabinet agency or office that has issued a rule or regulation. I supplement this list with Lewis's data set. While this list misses some obscure subcabinet agencies or offices, it still includes over 150 entities. All agencies used in the analysis are listed in Appendix S1.

After creating the list of agencies, I search the *Times* corpus for news articles that mention any of these agencies. I then organize the articles into five separate document corpora corresponding to institutional design of the agency.[8] I organize by the broad categories of agency design, rather than substantive policy area, to highlight how coverage varies across different institutional contexts. The number of articles and agencies collected is listed in Table 3.5.

Table 3.5 shows that agencies, at this aggregate level, receive extensive coverage in the newspaper. Three categories—cabinet departments, subcabinet agencies, and regulatory commissions—each contain nearly 50,000 articles published. The table also shows considerable variation in coverage across agency type. The last column reports the first, second, and third quartile of the annual number of articles published about agencies within each agency type. For example, the median article count for cabinet departments is 110. That high value is a stark contrast to the subcabinet, where 50% of annual agency observations have a value of zero. Many of these subcabinet agencies and offices are small (measured by staff and budget) and have a minimal regulatory impact on society (measured by regulations issued), which is one explanation for the limited news coverage. In addition, coverage of the subcabinet agencies often refers only to the parent cabinet department, although the action was taken by a subcabinet agency. Thus, there are fewer opportunities for these agencies to receive press coverage.

Newspaper Coverage of U.S. Regulatory Agencies

Table 3.5 counts articles from a wide variety of agencies. Some of these agencies have neither regulatory nor enforcement authority, leading the aggregate numbers in Table 3.5 to mask how coverage varies by an agency's regulatory impact on society. An alternative approach is to focus on regulatory agencies only, that is, focus on agencies that promote social and economic regulations on American businesses and individuals (see Coglianese and Howard 1998 for analysis of EPA regulatory coverage). Accountability of regulatory agencies is particularly important given the significant benefits and costs associated with agency regulations. In 2013, the president's regulatory budget eclipsed $58 billion; those funds pay salaries of over 290,000 agency personnel (Dudley and Warren 2012). Also in 2013, the

TABLE 3.5 Number of Articles That Mention Department, Agency, or Office by Agency Type

Institution Type	Agencies	Articles	Quartiles of Annual Articles per Agency
Executive Office of the President	7	7,298	3, 15, 79
Cabinet Department	15	55,456	61, 110, 195
Subcabinet Agency or Office	154	56,574	0, 0, 3
Executive Agency	16	20,471	2, 17, 53
Regulatory Commission	27	48,673	0, 12, 60

Note: The number of department, agency, or office within each type is also listed. Last column reports the first, second, and third quartile of the number of articles published annually for all entities within type.

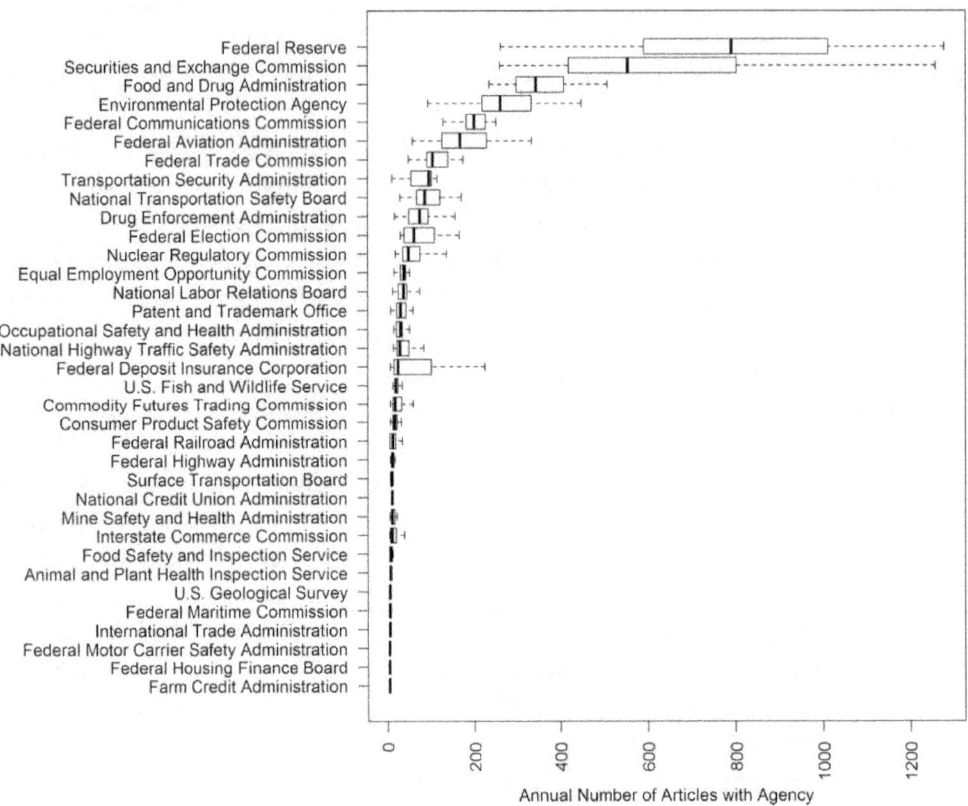

FIGURE 3.2 Number of Annual Articles by Regulatory Agency.

Note: Agencies sorted by median annual number of articles. Difference in group means significant at the .01 level according to analysis of variance test: $F = 65.7$.

OMB reviewed 418 proposed agency regulations; 104 of those regulations OMB deemed economically significant.[9] Since 1987, the OMB has received over 28,000 agency regulations.[10]

Figure 3.2 shows boxplots of annual newspaper coverage of a large sample of U.S. regulatory agencies.[11] The figure shows high variation in press coverage across and within agencies. The Federal Reserve, the Securities and Exchange Commission, and the FDA receive the most coverage. Other agencies, such as the Consumer Product Safety Commission, the Interstate Commerce Commission (abolished in 1995), and the Transportation Security Administration receive relatively little attention in the news.

When journalists cover agencies, they enable the public to learn about agency actions. An additional step toward political accountability involves journalists connecting agencies' actions to the elected officials who oversee those agencies. Given the large size of the data set, and the research focus on general media attention to the president and the agency, I limit the analysis to a simple measure: the share of articles about an agency that mentions the president and the agency together. This measure captures media attention to the broad range of issues that involve the president and federal agencies: appointments, political controversy, and public discussions of agency policy. The advantages to this approach are ease of replication and low cost in terms of

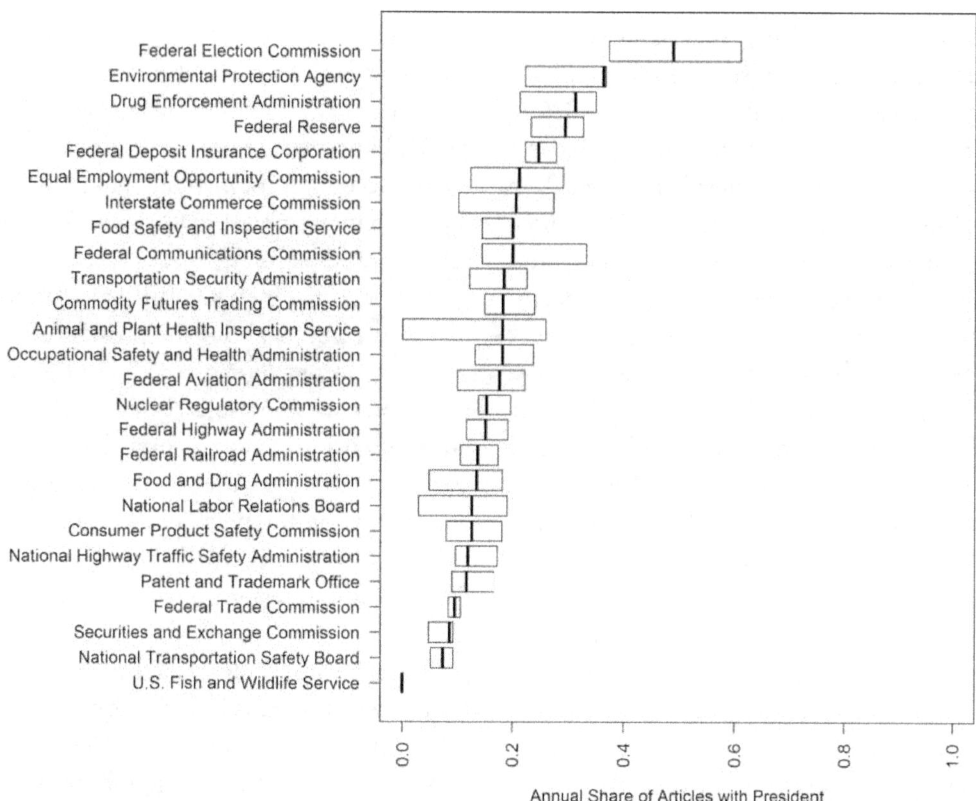

FIGURE 3.3 Annual Share of Published Articles That Mention the President, by Regulatory Agency.

Note: Agencies sorted by median share of articles that mention the president. Observations weighted by annual number of articles that mention the agency. Weighted analysis of variance test rejects equality of group means at the .01 level: $F = 30.9$.

human coding. The principal disadvantages are a lack of context and a risk of counting incidental mentions of the president's name that make no connection between the president and the agency.

In Figure 3.3, I show first, second, and third quartiles of the annual share of articles about each regulatory agency that mentions the president's name.[12] Observations are weighted by the annual number of articles that feature the agency. Agencies that receive the most coverage do not necessarily receive the most coverage that mentions the president. The agencies with the greatest share of articles that mention the president are the Federal Election Commission and the EPA. The EPA is prominent in both the total coverage it receives and the share of coverage that mentions the president. In contrast, the Securities and Exchange Commission and the National Transportation Safety Board receive relatively little coverage that features the president.

Political accountability requires accurate attributions of responsibility. Figure 3.3 reveals one possible way that the accurate assignment of blame can be undermined by news coverage of agencies. Specifically, even some agencies that are relatively insulated from presidential control receive a large share of articles that mention the president. The Federal Reserve, for example, is arguably the most politically insulated regulatory commission, but news coverage of the Federal Reserve still mentions the president in over 20% of articles per year. Approximately 11% of these articles that mention the Federal Reserve and the president suggest presidential influence to readers by mentioning appointments.[13]

Coverage of the Federal Reserve can take many forms, each with different implications for voter attribution of responsibility. Many of these articles are about general economic policy; the president and the Federal Reserve wield significant influence in economic policy and are likely to appear in articles together due to each actor wielding significant influence over economic affairs. However, in some of these articles, by discussing the political issues surrounding Federal Reserve policy, journalists can be using a political frame to discuss the Federal Reserve. Political frames, when compared to more policy-focused frames, can reduce support for policy and influence attributions of responsibility (Bolson, Druckman, and Cook 2014; Ruder 2014). In each case, if journalists exclude agency-design information from articles about these independent agencies, then they may fail to increase the institutional clarity of responsibility for some readers. Readers may then misjudge the president's authority over the agency and, ultimately, improperly allocate blame for the agency's action.

Newspaper Coverage of Agencies Subject to OMB Regulatory Review

Figure 3.3 includes agencies whose regulations are not subject to formal OMB review. One of the main justifications for OMB review is that voters, when seeking to assign blame, will know that the president has set an agency's regulatory agenda. The White House itself seems to accept this view, stating, as quoted in the second section, that OMB review is intended to ensure that regulations *reflect presidential priorities*. However, for OMB regulatory review to enable accountability, voters must know which regulations are subject to OMB review and thus reflect presidential priorities.

How can the news fulfill this function of informing voters about the president's control over regulatory agencies? One possibility is that every news article about a rule or regulation mentions that the president has review authority. At the other extreme, news could never mention the president's centralized control powers and instead focus on the policy details and interest group activity surrounding the rule.

The experiment described in the third section reveals how this information can influence attributions of responsibility. Recall that the MMS is a cabinet-level agency whose leaders are appointed and removed at will by the president. The treatment mentions the president's review of agency regulations, which is one component of the agency-design information that increases attributions of responsibility to the president.

To assess the actual coverage patterns, I use OMB regulatory reports to calculate the 10 agencies with the most economically significant regulations reviewed between 1981 and 2007.[14] I focus on the top 10 regulation producers in order to simplify the presentation of results and focus on the agencies with the largest regulatory impact on society. In addition, to more accurately represent coverage that focuses on regulations, I limit the news collection to articles that mention *rule*, *regulation*, or *rulemaking*. I list these agencies and the share of articles that mention the president's name in Figure 3.4.

Once again, the figure reveals considerable heterogeneity in coverage across agencies.

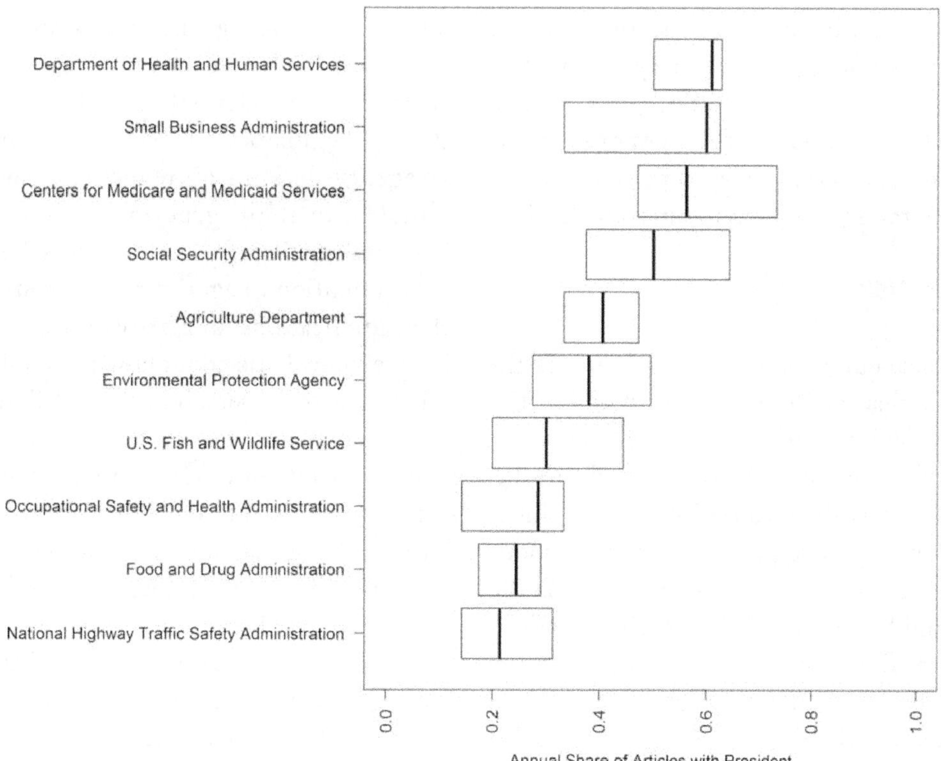

FIGURE 3.4 Average Annual Share of Published Articles That Mention the President, by Regulatory Agency.

Note: Only 10 agencies with the most economically significant rules proposed are shown. Agencies sorted by median share of articles that mention the president. Observations weighted by annual number of articles that mention the agency. Weighted analysis of variance test rejects equality of group means at the .01 level: $F = 7.73$.

Coverage patterns match neither of the extreme conditions stated above. For seven of these agencies, less than 50% of news coverage mentions the president. Only three regulators—the Department of Health and Human Services, the Small Business Administration, and the Centers for Medicare and Medicaid Services—receive coverage that mentions the president more than 50% of the time. Meanwhile, coverage of the powerful FDA mentions the president approximately 25% of the time. Voters are thus often reading about many prominent regulators as though they operate independently from the president and his influence.

It is notable that agencies, such as the FDA, receive such a low frequency of coverage that mentions the president. FDA regulations and decisions on drug approvals have significant consequences for industry and personal health and well-being. The White House maintains authority over the FDA, including the power to overrule approvals of drugs and medical devices. Despite these controls, the media infrequently associate this agency with the president and, as Carpenter (2011) noted in a *New York Times* op-ed, presidents infrequently interfere with it. Only once in FDA history has a presidential administration overruled an FDA decision.

Therefore, the infrequent appearance of the president in FDA agency news may reflect a hesitancy to politicize technocratic agency decision making (see Bawn 1995). That power to overrule the agency, however, is always present and can influence the agency's actions on some level.

Discussion

This article builds on work that examines the influence that institutional context and clarity of responsibility have on retrospective evaluations of elected officials. Many works in this literature study the relationship between institutional clarity of responsibility and economic voting (Alt and Lowry 1994; Anderson 2000; Duch and Stevenson 2008; Powell and Whitten 1993; Rudolph 2003); others focus more broadly on blame allocation given the institutional complexity of a multilayered federalist government (Arceneaux and Stein 2006; Gomez and Wilson 2008; Maestas et al. 2008; Malhotra and Kuo 2008).

There is a lack of empirical work that focuses on the comparative analysis of agency-design features that influence how voters perceive the relative influence of various elected officials. This absence is puzzling for several reasons. First, unitary executive theorists in public law argue that agency-design features that enhance presidential control over agencies also increase clarity of responsibility (Calabresi 1995; Kagan 2001). Second, political battles over agency design often center on how much power over an agency the president wields relative to Congress (Lewis 2003; Moe and Wilson 1994). Third, a long tradition in bureaucratic politics posits that legislators delegate authority to agencies, whose complex structures obscure responsibility, in order to mask their own involvement and avoid blame (Fiorina 1982; Lowi 1979). Fourth, one of the most significant developments in the expansion of executive power—increased centralized presidential control over agencies through regulatory review—is fundamentally an agency-design feature meant to enable the president to align agency policy with administration priorities.[15] In summary, scholars pay great attention to agency-design features and their implications for clarity of responsibility, but we know little about how the public actually learns of or perceives these differences.

In this article, I show that agency-design features that enhance formal presidential authority can also lead voters to increase attributions of responsibility for an agency's actions to the president. The findings suggest that these agency-design features lead to greater institutional clarity of responsibility. Informing voters of the institutional context, or the formal structures that enhance or insulate the agency from the president, allows voters to form more accurate retrospective judgments and assign responsibility correctly.

Forming retrospective evaluations for agency scandals, and agency actions more generally, is particularly challenging. Presidents who are no longer in office still exert control over agency policy through appointments of officials such as commission members. For agency actions, voters must determine how much responsibility the current administration bears relative to the previous administration. In this article, respondents in the survey experiment are more likely to blame the Obama administration for the conditions that led to the Deepwater Horizon disaster. It is not clear that this is the strictly rational reaction; the Bush administration implemented years of regulatory actions that formed the U.S. energy policy in the Gulf of Mexico. With respect to this agency scandal, respondents may be myopic (Bartels 2008), believing a new administration bears more responsibility than it deserves. At the same time, respondents may be acting rationally, because President Obama appointed the agency leader who was in charge during the disaster and had approved many regulations related to offshore oil drilling.

These results highlight the need for scholars in executive and bureaucratic politics to consider an important point when discussing the increasing trend of centralized presidential control: voters lack perfect information about the president's formal authority. Thus, White House approval or disapproval of an agency regulation can lead to greater accountability only if voters know that the agency's regulations are subject to review. The news, as a key source of political information for voters, is but one way voters can learn about the institutional context when forming retrospective judgments.

The results add an additional consideration to discussions of blame attribution in the wake of a scandal. Certainly a complex federal system, a multilayered bureaucracy, and elites shifting blame all obscure responsibility. However, the institutional context of agencies themselves can enhance the clarity of responsibility during an agency scandal. Formal authority resolves some of the ambiguity regarding responsibility.

One line of future research should consider how the president's internal staff manages agency crises in the wake of a scandal. Previous work that studies presidential involvement in scandals and their lasting impact on the president (e.g., Hacker, Giles, and Guerrero 2003; Rottinghaus and Berenznikova 2006) can be expanded to consider how presidents manage blame when agencies are insulated from their influence.

An additional line of future research should focus on how partisan identifications moderate attributions of responsibility in the context of bureaucratic politics. As discussed above, scholars studying legislative institutions have found that partisan rationalizations moderate the effect of the legislative institutional context on attributions of responsibility for economic outcomes.

There is at least one reason to expect that the moderating effects of partisanship may differ in the context of bureaucratic politics. For example, agencies possess their own policy preferences, which have been scaled onto the liberal/conservative ideological spectrum (Bertelli and Grose 2011). Voters may consider the ideological distance of an agency from the president when deciding whether to attribute responsibility to the president if they believe there is a systematic relationship between the degree of political control and the ideological distance between an agency and the president.

Notes

1 I exclude government corporations because they are technically not regulatory or enforcement agencies, but rather independent corporations subsidized by the government.

2 In related work, I show that commission features reduce attributions of responsibility in the context of antitrust cases (Ruder 2014).

3 A different approach is to study attribution in the context of less salient events where the public has little prior knowledge of the agency's actions. Ruder (2014) takes this approach by focusing on routine agency actions and not scandals.

4 Berinsky, Huber, and Lenz (2012) discuss the benefits and drawbacks of the MTurk subject pool. They show that the MTurk subject pool is comparable to other student and adult convenience samples and is often more representative of the U.S. adult population. However, the samples tend to be younger, more educated, and more liberal than U.S. population averages.

5 Article used based on Kauffman (2010).

6 Additional years for the *Times* acquired from ProQuest Online Newspapers. See Appendix S3 and Appendix S5 for search terms and results and search parameters for statistics on oil leasing. Oil leasing data from online database of Bureau of Ocean Energy Management. Review data from OMB.

7 I use two data sets from Lewis's work. The *Politicization Over Time* data includes all agencies included in the Office of Personnel Management Central Personnel Data File, which includes nearly all agencies in existence. See Lewis's data set codebook for the few exceptions, available on Professor Lewis's Web site, https://my.vanderbilt.edu/davidlewis/data/ (accessed May 3, 2015). For additional coverage, I also use Lewis's *Administrative Agency Insulation* data, which include all agencies created during 1946–97, as listed in the *U.S. Government Manual*, http:// ww.gpo.gov (accessed May 3, 2015). I exclude the military branches, primarily because the Constitution places these agencies under presidential control, which reduces the ambiguity of control and the public's reliance on media for knowledge of who is in charge.

8 The corpora are not mutually exclusive.

9 According to Executive Order 12866, any rule that meets the following criteria is economically significant: (1) has an annual economic impact of over $100 million, (2) creates a serious inconsistency with other agency policy, (3) alters the budgetary impact of entitlements, and (4) raises novel legal or policy issues.

10 Figures from http://www.reginfo.gov.

11 I include all regulatory agencies used in Lewis (2008). Lewis obtained the list, which I independently verified, from the Washington University at St. Louis' Weidenbaum Center on the Economy, Government, and Public Policy at http://wc.wustl.edu/regulatory_reports.

12 To be able to calculate the share of articles, I remove agencies with less than five observations, eliminating zeros and agencies with very few observations.

13 See Appendix S4 for searches to obtain these numbers.

14 The first year available in OMB's .xml reports at time of access is 1981. I collapse two subcabinet agencies within the Agriculture Department to just the Agriculture Department. While the Centers for Medicare and Medicaid Services (established 2001) and the FDA are part of the Department of Health and Human Services, I list them separately because OMB lists those subcabinet agencies issuing the regulations, and they receive prominent press coverage, independent of the parent cabinet department.

15 West (2005, 78), for example, calls regulatory review "arguably the most significant constitutional extension of executive power in decades."

References

60 Minutes/Vanity Fair. 2010. "Gulf Oil Spill/Technology." Poll conducted by CBS News, May 6–9. http://www.ropercenter.uconn.edu/ipoll-database/ (accessed May 3, 2015).

Acs, Alex, and Charles M. Cameron. 2013. "Does White House Regulatory Review Produce a Chilling Effect and 'OIRA Avoidance' in the Agencies?" *Presidential Studies Quarterly* 43 (3): 443–67.

Alt, James E., and Robert C. Lowry. 1994. "Divided Government, Fiscal Institutions, and Budget Deficits: Evidence from the States." *American Political Science Review* 88 (4): 811–28.

Anderson, Christopher. 2000. "Economic Voting in a Comparative Perspective." *Electoral Studies* 19 (2): 151–70.

Arceneaux, Kevin, and Robert Stein. 2006. "Who Is Held Responsible When Disaster Strikes? The

Attribution of Responsibility for a Natural Disaster in an Urban Election." *Journal of Urban Affairs* 28 (1): 43–53.

Arnold, R. Douglas. 2004. *Congress, the Press, and Political Accountability*. Princeton, NJ: Princeton University Press.

Barabas, Jason. 2008. "Presidential Policy Initiatives: How the Public Learns about State of the Union Proposals from the Mass Media." *Presidential Studies Quarterly* 38 (2): 195–222.

Barkow, Rachel E. 2010. "Insulating Agencies: Avoiding Capture through Institutional Design." *Texas Law Review* 89 (15): 16–78.

Bartels, Larry M. 2008. *Unequal Democracy: The Political Economy of the New Gilded Age*. Princeton, NJ: Princeton University Press.

Bawn, Kathleen. 1995. "Political Control Versus Expertise: Congressional Choices about Administrative Procedures." *American Political Science Review* 89 (1): 62–73.

Berinsky, Adam J., Gregory A. Huber, and Gabriel S. Lenz. 2012. "Evaluating Online Labor Markets for Experimental Research: Amazon.com's Mechanical Turk." *Political Analysis* 20 (3): 351–68.

Bertelli, Anthony M., and Christian R. Grose. 2011. "The Lengthened Shadow of Another Institution? Ideal Point Estimates for the Executive Branch and Congress." *American Journal of Political Science* 55 (4): 767–81.

Bolson, Toby, James N. Druckman, and Fay Lomax Cook. 2014. "How Frames Can Undermine Support for Scientific Adaptations: Politicization and the Status-Quo Bias." *Public Opinion Quarterly* 78 (1): 1–26.

Calabresi, Steven G. 1995. "Some Normative Arguments for the Unitary Executive." *Arkansas Law Review* 48 (1): 23–104.

Carpenter, Daniel. 2011. "Free the F.D.A." *New York Times*, December 13.

CBS News/*New York Times* Poll. 2010. "Gulf Oil Spill." June 16, 2010. Sample: U.S. national adult with oversample of gulf state residents. http://www.ropercenter.uconn.edu/ipoll-database/ (accessed May 3, 2015).

Cheibub, Jose Antonio. 2007. *Presidentialism, Parliamentarism, and Democracy*. New York: Cambridge University Press.

Chevron U.S.A., Inc. v. Natural Resources Defense Council. 477 U.S. 837 (1984).

Cilluffo, Frank J., Daniel J. Kaniewski, Jan P. Lane, Gregg C. Lord, and Laura P. Keith. 2009. *Serving America's Disaster Victims: FEMA, Where Does It Fit?* Issue Brief. Washington, DC: Homeland Security Policy Institute, George Washington University. http://cchs.gwu.edu/sites/cchs.gwu.edu/files/downloads/IssueBrief_3_HSPI.pdf (accessed April 17, 2015).

Coglianese, Cary, and Margaret Howard. 1998. "Getting the Message Out: Regulatory Policy and the Press." *Harvard International Journal of Press Politics* 3 (3): 39–50.

Cohen, Jeffery E. 2008. *The Presidency in an Era of Twenty-Four Hour News*. Princeton, NJ: Princeton University Press.

Croley, Steven. 2003. "White House Review of Agency Rulemaking: An Empirical Investigation." *University of Chicago Law Review* 70 (3): 821–85.

Duch, Raymond M., and Randolph T. Stevenson. 2008. *The Economic Vote*. New York: Cambridge University Press.

———. 2013. "Voter Perceptions of Agenda Power and Attribution of Responsibility for Economic Performance." *Electoral Studies* 32 (3): 512–16.

Dudley, Susan, and Melinda Warren. 2012. *Growth in the Regulators' Budget Slowed by Fiscal Stalemate: An Analysis of the U.S. Budget for Fiscal Years 2012 and 2013*. St. Louis, MO: Washington University in St. Louis, Weidenbaum Center on the Economy, Government, and Public Policy.

Fiorina, Morris P. 1981. *Retrospective Voting in American National Elections*. New Haven, CT: Yale University Press.

———. 1982. "Legislative Choice of Regulatory Forms: Legal Process or Administrative Process?" *Public Choice* 39 (1): 233–67.

Gallup. 2013. "Government Agency Ratings and Government Power." May 20–21. http://www.gallup.com/poll/162764/americans-views-irs-sharply-negative-2009.aspx (accessed May 3, 2015).

Gans, Herbert J. 1979. *Deciding What's News*. New York: Pantheon.

Gentzkow, Matthew, and Jesse M. Shapiro. 2010. "What Drives Media Slant? Evidence from the U.S. Daily Newspapers." *Econometica* 78 (1): 35–71.

Gilens, Martin, Lynn Vavreck, and Martin Cohen. 2007. "The Mass Media and the Public's Assessment of Presidential Candidates, 1952–2000." *The Journal of Politics* 69 (4): 1160–75.

Gomez, Brad T., and J. Matthew Wilson. 2008. "Political Sophistication and Attributions of Blame in the Wake of Hurricane Katrina." *Publius: The Journal of Federalism* 38 (4): 633–50.

Government Accountability Office. 2003. *Rulemaking: OMB's Role in Reviews of Agencies' Draft Rules and the Transparency of Those Reviews*. GAO Report GAO-03-929. http://www.gao.gov/new.items/d03929.pdf (accessed April 17, 2015).

Groseclose, Tim, and Jeffrey Milyo. 2005. "A Measure of Media Bias." *Quarterly Journal of Economics* 120 (4): 1191–237.

Hacker, Kenneth L., Maury Giles, and Aja Guerrero. 2003. "The Political Image Management Dynamics of President Bill Clinton." In *Images, Scandal, and Communication Strategies of the Clinton Presidency*, eds. Robert E. Denton Jr. and Rachel L.Holloway. Westport, CT: Praeger, 1–38.

Harris Interactive. 2010. "Troubles for Traditional Media—Both Print and Television." October 28. http://www.harrisinteractive.com/NewsRoom/HarrisPolls/tabid/447/mid/1508/articleId/604/ctl/ReadCustom%20Default/Default.aspx (accessed April 17, 2015).

Hays, Kristin. 2014. "BP Bids in Gulf of Mexico Lease Sale after U.S. Lifts Ban." *Associated Press*, March 19.

Huber, John D., and Nolan McCarty. 2004. "Bureaucratic Capacity, Delegation, and Political Reform." *American Political Science Review* 98 (3): 481–94.

Kagan, Elena. 2001. "Presidential Administration." *Harvard Law Review* 114 (8): 2245–385.

Kauffman, Tim. 2010. "Minerals Management Service Chief Resigns." *Federal Times*, May 27.

Key, V. O. 1966. *The Responsible Electorate*. Cambridge, MA: Harvard University Press.

Larcinese, Valentino, Riccardo Puglisi, and James M. Snyder. 2011. "Partisan Bias in Economic News: Evidence on the Agenda Setting Behavior of Newspapers." *Journal of Public Economics* 95 (9–10): 1178–89.

Lessig, Lawrence, and Cass R Sunstein. 1994. "The President and the Administration." *Columbia Law Review* 94 (1): 1–123.

Lewis, David. E. 2003. *Presidents and the Politics of Agency Design*. Stanford, CA: Stanford University Press.

———. 2008. *The Politics of Presidential Appointments: Political Control and Bureaucractic Performance*. Princeton, NJ: Princeton University Press.

Lowi, Theodore J. 1979. *The End of Liberalism*. 2nd ed. New York: W. W. Norton.

Maestas, Cherie D., Lonna Rai Atkeson, Thomas Croom, and Lisa A. Bryant. 2008. "Shifting the Blame: Federalism, Media, and Public Assignment of Blame Following Hurricane Katrina." *Publius: The Journal of Federalism* 38 (4): 609–32.

Mainwaring, Scott, and Matthew S. Shugart. 1997. "Juan Linz, Presidentialism, and Democracy: A Critical Appraisal." *Comparative Politics* 29 (4): 449–71.

Malhotra, Neil, and Alexander G. Kuo. 2008. "Attributing Blame: The Public's Response to Hurricane Katrina." *The Journal of Politics* 70 (1): 120–35.

McCoy, Kevin. 2013. "Consumer Protection Bureau is Under Attack, but Working." *USA Today.* June 6.

Moe, Terry M., and Scott A. Wilson. 1994. "Presidents and the Politics of Structure." *Law and Contemproary Problems* 57 (Spring): 1–44.

Office of Management and Budget. 2013. "The Mission and Structure of the Office of Management and Budget, Office of Management and Budget, the White House." www.whitehouse.gov/omb/organization_mission (accessed December 3, 2013).

Powell, G. Bingham Jr., and Guy D. Whitten. 1993. "A Cross-National Analysis of Economic Voting: Taking Account of the Political Context." *American Journal of Political Science* 37 (2): 391–414.

Prat, Andrea, and David Strömberg. 2011. "The Political Economy of Mass Media." Working Paper. http://www.columbia.edu/~ap3116/papers/mediasurvey11.pdf (accessed April 17, 2015).

Puglisi, Riccardo. 2011. "Being the New York Times: The Political Behavior of a Newspaper." *The B.E. Journal of Economic Analysis and Policy* 11 (1): art. 20.

Rosen, Bernard. 1998. *Holding Government Bureaucracies Accountable.* 3rd ed. Westport, CT: Praeger.

Rottinghaus, Brandon, and Zlata Berenznikova. 2006. "Exorcising Scandal in the White House: Presidential Polling in Times of Crisis." *Presidential Studies Quarterly* 36 (3): 493–505.

Ruder, Alex I. 2014. "Institutional Design and the Attribution of Presidential Control." *Quarterly Journal of Political Science* 9 (3): 301–35.

Rudolph, Thomas J. 2003. "Institutional Context and the Assignment of Political Responsibility." *The Journal of Politics* 65 (1): 190–215.

Sandhaus, Evan. 2008. *The New York Times Annotated Corpus.* Philadelphia: Linguistic Data Consortium.

Schattschneider, Elmer Eric. 1942. *Party Government.* New York: Rinehart.

Snyder, James M., and David Strömberg. 2010. "Press Coverage and Political Accountability." *Journal of Political Economy* 118 (2): 355–408.

Snyder, James M., and Riccardo Puglisi. 2011. "Newspaper Coverage of Political Scandals." *The Journal of Politics* 73 (3): 931–50.

Volden, Craig. 2002. "A Formal Model of the Politics of Delegation in a Separation of Powers System." *American Journal of Political Science* 46 (1): 111–33.

West, William F. 2005. "The Institutionalization of Regulatory Review: Organizational Stability and Responsive Competence at OIRA." *Presidential Studies Quarterly* 35 (1): 76–93.

———. 2006. "Presidential Leadership and Administrative Coordination: Examining the Theory of a Unified Executive." *Presidential Studies Quarterly* 36 (3): 433–56.

Wilhoit, G. Cleveland, and David H. Weaver. 1991. *The American Journalist: A Portrait of U.S. News People and Their Work.* Bloomington: Indiana University Press.

■ CHAPTER 4

Women and Democracy

Editor's Introduction

Chapter 4 explains how government affects feminist movements. Fallon and Viterna highlight the differences among Eastern European, Western, and developing nations concerning feminist issues. The authors expand on the feminist view by considering its relationship with democracy and development. Men's dominance in government is essential to the first section of this chapter. The authors explain how gender roles have historically limited women's ability to influence government. Western nations, in particular, tend to be classified as male-dominated countries with laws that keep women reliant on men. However, successful women's movements have created incremental improvement for women's political and social environments in these nations. Fallon and Viterna stress that the dominance of men (and thereby the exclusion of women) in the formation of modern democracies has strongly influenced where we are today. According to Fallon and Viterna, colonization is the primary factor as to why men maintained power structures and why women were relegated to domestic roles. A discussion of democracy in developing countries concludes the chapter. Fallon and Viterna posit that female involvement in developing states has positive regulatory outcomes for society.

READING 4 Women, Democracy, and the State

Kathleen M. Fallon and Jocelyn Viterna

What role do states and democracies play in development? Although many scholars have addressed this question, fewer have done so with respect to women. In this chapter, we argue that renewed attention to the relationship between states and women would powerfully improve existing sociological analyses of development. We begin by defining how states are fundamentally gendered institutions, and how states both create and reproduce gender relations in the societies they govern. We then turn to the question of whether states are valid sites of contestation for empowering and emancipating women. We examine this question across three different categories of states: Western nations, East European nations, and developing nations. We conclude that a feminist perspective of the state would powerfully extend existing theories about whether and how states influence "development." This is especially true for a new generation of state-centered development research that examines how individuals, through social mobilization and participatory democracy, can influence state development practices (see, e.g., Baiocchi, Heller, and Silva 2011; Evans 2010; Lee 2007; Wolford 2010. See also Paul Almeida's chapter in this volume).

Our chapter is premised on the understanding that gender[1] is always implicated in sociological analyses of development, regardless of how development is formally defined. Our arguments below prioritize a capabilities approach to development, where the importance of gender is relatively straightforward. In this approach, an "ideally" developed society requires that every individual's rights, resources, and "capabilities" exist wholly independently of his or her gender or sexuality (Nussbaum 2000). Yet we note that the more traditional, market-based approaches to development are also fundamentally gendered (see Valentine Moghadam's and Rae Lesser Blumberg's chapters in this volume). The way a society defines "men" and "women" in turn structures the organization of its families, its labor markets, its wealth transfers, its use of technology, and its knowledge production, among other factors commonly analyzed in development studies. Gender, we argue, mediates states' influence on these development processes.

Gender and the State

To best understand the relationship between states and gender, feminist scholars advocate studying both the *gender of governance* and the *governance of gender* (Brush 2003). In the former, gender systems structure states. In most West European countries, democracies began with men in rule and with women excluded from political participation (Yuval-Davis 1997). During that time period, women were viewed as nurturing and were expected to remain in the home, attend to domestic affairs, or work within feminine-related occupations, such as education or tailoring. The West European society shaped the political realm, and these societal and political constructions were later exported through the process of colonization (Mamdani 1999; Oyěwùmí 1997). Although pre-colonial countries did not necessarily structure their governance according to male leadership, colonizers exerted their force and implemented

Kathleen M. Fallon and Jocelyn Viterna, "Women, Democracy, and the State," *The Sociology of Development Handbook*, ed. Gregory Hooks, pp. 414-429.

male-dominated government institutions (Fallon 2008; Parpart and Staudt 1990). Because of men's historical dominance in society, leading to the initial creation of male-only national governments, men continue overwhelmingly to occupy the most powerful positions within government today. For example, in 2014, men held approximately 78.2 percent of all parliamentary positions around the world, whereas women made up only 21.8 percent (Inter-Parliamentary Union 2014). Based on the historical development of state institutions, the assumptions of male dominance continue to influence the structuring of state agencies, laws, and programs in countless ways.[2]

The gender of governance leads, in turn, to the governance of gender; scholars agree that all states "govern" gender because their institutions, policies, and practices help create, maintain, and reproduce the categories of men and women in both direct and indirect ways (Phillips 2012). Directly, states use the categories of "men" and "women" to dictate, among other things, who can vote, who can go to school, who can marry whom, who has the right to control their own sexual and reproductive behavior, and who can be drafted into military service. Indirectly, states shape gender in countless additional ways: for example, social welfare programs formally define what can constitute a "family"; taxations systems place differential values on paid and unpaid labor; the presence, absence, or form of parental leave programs shape expectations and opportunities for mothers and fathers; the availability of affordable child care mitigates mothers' access to paid labor and economic independence; and public health-care systems determine who can control their own sexual health and reproduction through the drugs and procedures they provide (Brady 2009; Misra, Moller, and Budig 2007; Orloff 2009).

Whether using the frame of the gender of governance or the governance of gender, feminist scholars overwhelmingly agree that states are gendered institutions. However, they frequently disagree about whether states are valid sites of contestation and change for citizens seeking gender equity (Borchorst 1999; Brush 2003; Phillips 2006). In the more pessimistic camp, scholars argue that fighting for women's rights within a masculine state has ultimately been self-defeating because it reifies the category "woman" (Squires 2001, 2008), changes women's dependence from private patriarchy to public patriarchy (Eisenstein 1981; Holter 1984), or simply augments state power and control over citizens in ways that reinforce the existing "condition and construction of women" (Brown 1995, 173). Others see "the state" as too ambiguous and unwieldy to be a useful category for analysis or a useful target for activists (Allen 1990; Kantola 2007). The most radical in this camp argue that the state is simply irredeemable: it is too sexist and too masculine to serve as a vehicle for change (Gould 2014; Davis 2001; MacKinnon 1989; Smart 1989). Therefore, pessimists often suggest that feminist activism is more profitably targeted at other social relations, such as gendered interactions in day-to-day relationships, rather than at "state transformation."

By contrast, scholars in the more optimistic camp argue that states are "where the power is" (Brush 2003, 3; see also Dahlerup 1994). These scholars agree that state structures, policies, and ideologies generally work to reinforce masculine privilege. They maintain, however, that state institutions still provide important sites of contestation and negotiation for women (Chapman 1993; O'Connor, Orloff, and Shaver 1999; Orloff 1996; True and Mintrom 2001; Watson 1990). Indeed, scholars have documented how women's activism has fundamentally altered states' genders in terms of extending voting rights to women (McCammon 2001; McCammon et al. 2001), expanding welfare benefits to reduce women's dependence on men (Brady 2009; Bolzehndahl and Brooks 2007; Gordon 1994; Koven and Michel 1993; Skocpol 1992), and increasing legal protections against gender discrimination in the workplace, in the legal system, in the home, and surrounding the body (Bauer 2008; Chaudhuri 2010; Cooke 2007; Gelb and Hart 1999; Gould 2014; Rhode 1989). Working within a masculine state structure certainly limits, and sometimes undermines, women's victories, they argue, but the state is simply too powerful an arena for leveraging power for feminists to disassociate from it completely (Brush 2003).

In the next section, we review existing arguments about whether states can be sites for gendered change in Western nations, in Eastern Europe, and in developing countries.

Western Welfare States

Most early theorizing about states and gender in mainstream sociology focused on wealthy nations.[3] In the 1980s, Catherine MacKinnon (1989), Carole Pateman (1988), and others opened the conversation by arguing that (Western) states are inherently male institutions, created by men, in male-dominated societies, to maintain a social order that privileges hegemonic masculinity. Feminist scholars supported these contentions by demonstrating, for example, how welfare systems encouraged women's continued reliance on men (Gordon 1990, 1994), how legal systems were more concerned with regulating—rather than prohibiting—rape (MacKinnon 1989), or how variations in states' support and organization of child care directly affected women's power in labor markets and politics (Ruggie 1984; Siim 1990).

As the field developed, feminist scholars became increasingly interested in gendered variations across welfare states. They sought to document whether some states were more "women friendly" than others (Borchorst 1994; Brady and Burroway 2012; Orloff 1996; O'Connor, Orloff, and Shaver 1999; Sainsbury 1996; Wernet 2008) and what historical processes (especially women's mobilizations) might account for these variations (Abramovitz 1988; Muncy 1991; Skocpol 1992; Sklar 1993; Gordon 1994; Goodwin 1997; Pini, Panelli, and Sawer 2008).[4] They concluded that women's movements' successes in creating more women-friendly states depended on a number of factors: how they framed their issues (Ferree and Gamson 2003; Hobson 2003; Stetson 2001); the organizational structure of the movement (Clemens 1993; Staggenborg 1988); the strategies they utilized (McCammon et al. 2001; Taylor and Van Dyke 2004); the cohesiveness of the movements (Lovenduski 2005); and whether they had allies within the government (Mazur 2001; Stetson 2001). They also found that historically specific characteristics of the state influenced the outcomes of women's mobilizations, attributing cross-national variations to, for example, "strong" versus "weak" states (Koven and Michel 1993), a history of fascism (Bock and Thane 1991), the balance of power among workers, employers, and the state (Pederson 1993), or the demands placed on feminists by the small realm of available allies (Gordon 1994).

These theories demonstrate that states are complex systems of institutions, strategies, and ideologies and tend to reinforce hegemonic masculine privilege in their respective societies, but that states are also vulnerable to change according to historical developments and the influence of (generally women's) mobilizations. Feminist scholars of Western states have given us important tools for theorizing from what types of mobilizations, and under what social and political conditions, gendered change might be possible. However, given their focus on rich, relatively stable nations, these studies often conceptualize states' genders as something that crystallized in the past with the formation of states' welfare systems. They frequently see states as valid sites for contesting gender inequalities, but the changes they study are often incremental, such as modifications of state policies or personnel—the kind of changes expected from social movements operating under the protections, and limitations, of long-standing democratic systems. Thus, feminist theories of Western states provide an important framework from which to start our analysis, but their ability to answer questions about how women's movements might target less-democratic states, or how radical state transformations might lead to more justly gendered political systems, is limited.

Eastern Europe

The political, social, and economic transformation of Eastern Europe in the 1990s encouraged scholars to ask how states' genders might change in moments of radical transformation. Feminist scholars were initially highly optimistic about the possibility of women's empowerment in the transitioning nations of Eastern Europe. Since women were already active within the government and the public sphere under the former communist regimes, scholars anticipated that this historical female presence in political positions would help create a more feminist-oriented state with democratization (Einhorn 1993). Yet, contrary to this expectation, the transition did not create more women-friendly states, and many writers would argue it reinforced the masculinity of the state apparatus (Einhorn 1993; Watson 1993). With democratization, women's participation in the state dropped precipitously, and men came to dominate the national government and its agenda. To illustrate, in the first post-transition elections, women's representation dropped from 29.5 to 6 percent in the Czech and Slovak Federal Republic, from 20.9 to 8.5 percent in Bulgaria, from approximately 50 to 9.5 percent in Poland, and from 33 to 3.5 percent in Romania (Watson 1993). Moreover, maternity leave policies were curtailed, women's legislative quotas were dismantled, funding for child care centers decreased significantly, and there were attempts to end women's rights to abortion (Einhorn 1993; Gal and Kligman 2000; Haney 1994; Pascall and Manning 2000; Watson 1993). After democratization, many of the East European states began to resemble the highly masculine makeup of their West European neighbors.

How did this "democratic" transformation generate more highly masculine government structures? In hindsight, scholars concluded that the original communist states' "women-friendliness" was perhaps only an appearance. Women's representation within the legislative bodies was high because of quotas, but these legislatures were mere window dressings for the Central Committees of the ruling Communist Parties, where the policies and agenda of East European states were determined. Women's representation in the Central Committee for the Communist Party in the Soviet Union was less than 5 percent, and thus women's actual political power in the state was weak. The Communist Party also exalted women as both laborers and reproducers of the nation; thus, they were expected to have children, care for the family, and work regular shift hours (Einhorn 1993; Watson 1993; Haney 1994; Gal and Kligman 2000; Pascall and Manning 2000). Because of these multiple demands, women attempted to subvert the state by using the home as a refuge from the communist state's agenda (Einhorn 1993; Gal and Kligman 2000; Gerber and Perelli-Harris 2012; Haney 1994; Watson 1993).

In addition to overestimating the women-friendliness of the pre-transition states, scholars argued that the former Communist

Party's iron-handed control over political organizing, and the sense that women had in some ways already achieved equality, meant that women were poorly mobilized *as women* before the transition so were not able to act on behalf of women during and after the transition (Einhorn 1993). Although women's organizations existed, they were generally not unified and tended to focus on educational and economic concerns (Berthusen Gottlick 1999; Silova and Magno 2004). Women's organizations in pre-transition Eastern Europe had remained relatively localized, further limiting their connections to the international women's movement (Fallon, Swiss, and Viterna 2012). Moreover, because the former Communist Party expounded a commitment to gender equality, albeit more in ideology than in practice, women as well as men conflated gender equality and feminism with communism in the post-transition period, and they distanced themselves from these terms and representations (Haney 1994; Gal and Kligman 2000).

As the years have progressed post-transition, women's political access to and participation within the state appears to be improving. From the initial drop post-transition to 2014, women's representation increased from 6 percent in the Czech and Slovak Federal Republic to 19.5 percent in the Czech Republic and to 18.7 percent in Slovakia, from 8.5 to 20 percent in Bulgaria, from 9.5 to 24.3 percent in Poland, and from 3.5 to 13.5 percent in Romania (Inter-Parliamentary Union 2014). This increase in representation has occurred despite the fact that Eastern Europe continues to lag behind other regions of the world in the adoption of quotas guaranteeing minimal levels of women's representation (Fallon, Swiss, and Viterna 2012). The initial democratic transition led women to withdraw from, while men usurped, political power. Often, men who held pre-transition political power were the first elected to new political offices with democratization. However, as women became increasingly savvy about how to effectively engage the new democratic systems, post-transition limits on political office eventually helped force old-guard male politicians out of power, creating space for new players. The lessening of state coercion, combined with women's growing familiarization with and trust of the new democratic system, increased women's willingness to engage the state on behalf of their gendered rights (Fallon, Swiss, and Viterna 2012). East European women gradually reentered politics. Moving forward, current research is now beginning to examine how women's increasing physical presence in political structures may promote gender-equitable states (Forest 2006; Fuszara 2010; Millard 2014).

In sum, although democratization in Eastern Europe initially created more highly masculine states rather than more gender equitable states, scholars have not pessimistically dismissed the state as irredeemable. Rather, the East European case has provided additional evidence that states' genders are strongly influenced by path-dependent historical processes and by the presence or absence of feminist movements and allies.

Developing Countries

Feminist scholars of developing nations lament that much theorizing about gender and the state has been developed in Western contexts (Waylen 1996). Such theories do not easily translate to non-Western nations, where men's and women's patterns of political engagement with the state are strikingly different. Often these gendered political patterns in developing nations are rooted in European colonial histories. In many cases, colonizers usurped and restructured existing political institutions to best meet their own needs, often by encouraging women to remain in the domestic realm while encouraging men to become educated or active laborers (Bujra 1986; Fallon 2008; Stamp 1986). For example, among the Igbo in Nigeria, the *obi,* who traditionally represented the needs of the men within the community, were appointed to local government positions by the British. However, the *omu,* who represented the needs of the women within the community, were disregarded by colonial institutions. Similarly, among the Kikuyu in Kenya, male elders, who had held positions within their lineage prior to colonization, were appointed as chiefs, sub-chiefs, and judges under new colonial systems. Yet women, who also traditionally held positions of power within their lineages, were not appointed to new colonial positions.

When European colonies gained independence, their new post-colonial governments often initially proved weak and unstable. Newly independent states seldom had the resources necessary to run governments, and the state institutions they inherited had been created to serve their colonizers' needs rather than the needs of their own populations (Rodney 1972). Often, the withdrawal of colonial authorities left a power vacuum, and, with no institutional process in place for choosing new leaders, many nations experienced political instability. The outcomes of those instabilities varied across nations, with some countries developing formal democratic systems, others coming under control of authoritarian regimes, and still others experiencing years of civil strife.

As a result, most developing nations tend to be weak in their administrative capacities and typically have little funding for social welfare or policy enforcement, which influences how states can interact with women.[5] States most often figure in non-Western women's lives when they transgress some social boundary and are returned to order by brute state force (Rai 1996, 36). Moreover, women in developing nations often have lower levels of literacy and employment and higher levels of income inequality than their West or East European counterparts and are more likely to engage the state outside of conventional politics. Not surprisingly, then, much research on gender and the state in developing nations has called for a broader definition of the political and has focused on the rich tradition of women's mobilizations and participation in civil society as key components of state challenges.

Unfortunately, the result of this focus on women's mobilizations has been the conversion of the state into a secondary character, which is often treated monolithically as "good" or "bad" in its reactions to women's organizing. Yet state structures are important because, as state structures vary, so do their responses to women's mobilizations. One particular variation in state structures, the presence of women, is critical not only in determining responses to women's mobilization but also in determining legislative action. For example, in relation to women's political presence, local councils in South Africa that have more women are more likely to focus on the urgent issue of HIV/AIDS (Lieberman 2012), and, in India, village councils with more than one-third women are more likely to address the needs of women, such as access to drinking water—minimizing women's time spent collecting water from afar (Chattopadhyay and Duflo 2004). At the national level, women legislators in Malaysia worked to address child care, child education, and child safety concerns (Zakuan 2010); in Tanzania, they focused debates on issues ranging from education to health, poverty, water, and energy and managed to pass legislation addressing concerns ranging from sexual offenses to access to land and girls' education (Yoon 2011); in Timor-Leste, women legislators passed a resolution on gender-responsive budgeting (Costa, Sawer, and Sharp 2013). Cross-nationally, as women's legislative representation increases, children's health also improves (Swiss, Fallon, and Burgos 2012). These findings suggest that understanding the gendered state becomes essential to the process of development. Moreover, the role of the gendered state in tandem with women's mobilization is particularly important across developing countries, where political instability and variation of government rule (or lack thereof) exists.

Women's Mobilizations, the Democratizing State, and Pessimism

Over the past several decades, transitions to democracy across Africa, Asia, and Latin America have provided women's mobilizations with unprecedented opportunities to fundamentally transform existing state structures and promote new "women friendly" political institutions (Fallon, Swiss, and Viterna 2012; Hassim 2006; Huiscamp 2000; Viterna and Fallon 2008). Buttressed by international conventions like CEDAW and the international women's movement, local women's movements have routinely taken advantage of the unprecedented political opening of transition to push newly democratizing states to adopt national quotas[6] and to create national political institutions specifically tasked with supporting and maintaining gender equity in state policies and practices (Chen 2010; Krook 2006).

Unlike Eastern Europe, these developing states had little pretext of being "women friendly" prior to their transitions.[7] Whether transitioning from dictatorships or civil strife, undemocratic regimes were highly masculine (Manuh 1993; Tsikata 1989). Unlike men, women could not gain political positions through coups, bribes, or appointments by other men (Tripp 1994). Women who did gain political positions often did so through family members, or they held positions with little influence on government policy (Geisler 1995).

Women's absence from formal political structures in authoritarian states contrasted sharply with women's central role in the civil society mobilizations that forced these authoritarian states into democratic transitions. Feminist research documents extensive and powerful mobilizations of women's organizations against authoritarian states (and especially against their human rights abuses) at precisely the moment when more typically masculine forms of doing politics (political parties, labor unions) were effectively silenced by state repression (Alvarez 1990; Fisher 1990; Noonan 1995). Women also constituted an estimated 30 percent of the guerrilla armies that quite literally fought to dismantle authoritarian regimes in nations like Nicaragua and El Salvador (Viterna 2006, 2013). Given scholars' previous findings that feminist changes in state structures occur most readily when women are mobilized, it is perhaps not surprising that scholars anticipated similar feminist outcomes in transitioning states. Women had proven themselves fearless fighters for political transformation under repressive authoritarian regimes; how could they not continue the political fight for gender equity under new democratic institutions?

Despite the initial optimism about organized women's potential to transform states' gender with democratization, early studies often reported disappointing outcomes.[8] Numerous case studies found that, with democratization, women's gains during pretransition mobilizations were overturned (Cagan 2000; Chinchilla 1994), there was a widespread reassertion of traditional gender expectations (Jaquette 1994; Rai 1996), women's pre-transition mobilizations waned in the post-transition period (Craske 1998), and, in some nations, women's electoral representation in parliament actually declined (Fisher 1993; Jaquette and Wolchik 1998; Jelin 1990). Democratic transitions may have eliminated authoritarian barriers to women's political participation, but studies consistently found that women's political power increased little, if any, with initial democratization (Bystydzienski and Sekhon 1999; Geisler 1995; Friedman 2000; Jaquette and Wolchik 1998; Kelly et al. 2001; Walby 1992), and some argued that women were likely worse off after democratization—politically, socially, and economically—than they were under previous regimes (Hawkesworth 2001).[9]

As in Eastern Europe, scholars of developing countries generated a number of explanations for women's disappointing gains with democratization. First, several scholars argued that the countries' historical and political contexts shaped the *manner* in which women mobilized under authoritarian regimes, and this choice of strategies limited women's ability to gain political power after democratization. By closing down political options typically considered "masculine" (such as political parties and labor unions), repressive authoritarian regimes inadvertently promoted women's "feminine" mobilizations through community-based, family-oriented protests. Women protestors shrewdly incorporated the authoritarian regimes' own gendered discourse of women as pious, self-sacrificing mothers into the framing of their claims against the state. Authoritarian regimes thus found themselves in the uncomfortable position of trying to justify the repression of women who had mobilized around feminine themes that the regime itself had earlier exalted (Alvarez 1990; Chuchryk 1989; Friedman 2000; Okeke-Ihejirika and Franceschet 2002; Ray and Korteweg 1999; Sternbach et al. 1992).[10] With democratization, however, new political players on both the left and the right utilized women's own discourse of motherhood, and of innate gender differences, to encourage women's return to the household (Chinchilla 1994; Fisher 1993; Friedman 1998; Schild 1994).[11]

Second, many argue that democratization marginalizes women because, under democratization, political parties—not social movements—control access to the state (O'Donnell and Schmitter 1986). Given that political parties are typically patriarchal and resistant to women's participation, women have historically found their strongest political voice within social movements. Paradoxically, then, authoritarian states may have opened space for women's mobilizations that was in turn closed by democratization and the institutionalization of conventional political channels (Friedman 2000; Jelin 1990; Nelson and Chowdhury 1994).

A third proposed explanation is that pre-transition women's mobilizations were co-opted or institutionalized by the state and by political parties after democratization (Alvarez 1999; Okeke-Ihejirika and Franceschet 2002; Richards 2004; Vargas 2002). For example, women associated with political parties prior to the transition often found their gender-specific goals subsumed to the party's "mainstream" goals (Luciak 2001). Likewise, states sometimes instituted a new women's office within the state machinery after democratization, but they constrained the effectiveness of these new institutions with laws, bureaucracy, and funding shortages. Leaders of women's movements were often the first to transition to the leadership positions within new women's offices of the state or women's branches of parties, or even new gender-specific NGOs, thus crippling women's social movements by removing many movement leaders at the precise moment of democratic opening (Hassim 2006; Viterna and Fallon 2008). Moreover, women who find themselves in paid positions often tend to be of a higher class, and better educated, than women who remain in community-based social movements, leading to a problem of cohesion and collaboration within the movements themselves (Waylen 1994). This concern about co-optation has led many women's movements in developing nations to declare autonomy from states and political parties, thus giving them freedom to pursue their own agendas and collaborate with a wide range of political interests, even though it may limit their access to the state and their funding options (Alvarez 1999; Beckwith 2000; Jaquette 1994; Tripp 2000; Waylen 1994).[12]

The final argument explaining democracy's disappointing outcomes for women is the one most familiar to development scholars: the neoliberal economic policy changes that typically accompany democratization diminished women's ability to participate in politics by increasing women's already unfair workload (Cagan 2000; Jelin 1998). Privatization and structural adjustment made basic necessities like food, healthcare, and education increasingly difficult to access, thus increasing women's time spent in care-giving roles, while liberalization of the economy reduced wages and opportunities for organizing on the job, especially in export-oriented production work often dominated by women's labor (Blumberg and Salazar-Palacios 2011; Darkwah 2010; Gideon 1999). Because of neoliberal policies accompanying democratization, then, women's free time was restricted, and their associations with individuals and organizations outside the home were limited, resulting in women having little time, resources, or networks to facilitate any sort of political involvement (Yoo 2011).[13]

Women's Mobilizations, the Democratizing State, and Optimism

Amid the many pessimistic prognostications for women's gains with democratization is a small, optimistic literature focusing on gender and revolution. In an initial theoretical investigation of gender and revolution, Valentine Moghadam (1997) argues that some revolutions, like those in Nicaragua, Afghanistan, and South Yemen, are modernizing, egalitarian, and focus on women's emancipation, whereas others, like revolutions in Iran and Poland, stress family and gender differences and reinforce patriarchy. In Latin America, Karen Kampwirth (2004) uses case studies to argue that revolutionary movements inadvertently engendered feminist movements by providing women with new ideologies of equality, new political skills, and new networks with other women activists, both locally and internationally. Both conclude that revolutions may not have transformed the gender of the state, but they did transform the lives of the women activists within the revolution, such that these women have launched strong, vibrant, autonomous feminist movements that are qualitatively different from feminist movements in the West.

More recent studies provide additional reasons to believe that, with time, democratic transitions may improve women's legislative representation, potentially transforming the gender of governance. Similar to Eastern Europe, democratization had a curvilinear effect on women's national political representation in developing states (Fallon, Swiss, and Viterna 2012; Bjarnegård 2013). With the initial transition to democracy, nations often experienced a precipitous drop in representation. However, with each additional year, women's representation improved. Countries that had longer histories with nominally competitive (albeit undemocratic) elections prior to their transitions saw relatively faster increases in women's legislative representation after their transitions, suggesting that women's representation improved as their familiarity with the electoral system increased (Fallon, Swiss, and Viterna 2012). Although all countries gained from democratization, those that transitioned from civil strife appear to have gained the most (Hughes 2009), in part because they were the most likely to initiate working electoral quotas with their transitions (Fallon, Swiss, and Viterna 2012). In short, the implementation of quotas plus women's increasing trust of, and adaptation to, the new political systems seem to account for these gradual improvements in women's political representation (Bjarnegård and Melander 2011; Fallon, Swiss, and Viterna 2012; Tripp and Kang 2008).

Although it remains to be seen how women's increasing legislative presence may affect gender-equitable development, we point to four additional reasons for optimism in state-gender relations among developing nations. First, women's movements in developing nations often connected to the international women's movement prior to democratization, and these transnational resources proved useful for successfully pressuring democratizing states to implement gender-equitable laws and institutions during the transition (Bush 2011; Krook 2009; Viterna and Fallon 2008). These transnational connections seem to have given many women's movements in the Global South an ally that East European women's organizations were slower to expropriate, and we anticipate that transnational allies will continue to be influential.

Second, the new global trend of implementing gender quotas has spread even to nations with low levels of democracy and less powerful women's movements (Bauer 2012; Fallon, Swiss, and Viterna 2012; Paxton, Hughes, and Painter 2010; Stockemer 2014; Tripp and Kang 2008). Given quotas' proven potential for powerfully increasing women's formal political representation, we suggest that quotas may help build women's political power from the top down, even in contexts where bottom-up mobilizations may struggle.

Third, as women gain increased access to state resources and representation, and as they continue to be connected to international mobilization, they also successfully work to implement laws to protect women. Laurel Weldon and Mala Htun (2012), for example, demonstrate that domestic violence laws and resources to support survivors of domestic violence are more successful in countries where women's local and international movements are active.

Fourth and finally, many developing states are experimenting with their own novel practices for equalizing political power, such as the implementation of participatory direct democracy in nations like Brazil and India (Baiocchi, Heller, and Silva 2011). These new options for political participation have already increased women's participation at the local level in at least some instances (Agarwal 2010; Gibson 2012). Given findings that women's formal representation increases as their familiarity with electoral politics improves, we anticipate that the long-term impacts of such local-level participation on state structures may ultimately be very positive.

In sum, although scholars initially reached a largely pessimistic consensus about democracy's ability to create more justly gendered states and societies in developing nations, later studies demonstrate that, as democracy progresses, it does provide new space for women to increase their political power and participation. Women have become more involved with national politics through democratic political structures, and they have lobbied for changes in policies affecting women. Of note, despite the striking differences in national contexts, studies engaging gender and the state within developing countries concur with scholars of Western states that women's activism in social movements—albeit constrained by the path-dependent governance structures and historical political cultures already in place—are the primary vehicles for achieving more gender-equitable states.

Conclusion

Existing studies sometimes suggest that developing state governments, by virtue of their relative institutional weakness, instability, and lack of resources, are not well positioned to shape development outcomes. Yet this review demonstrates how developing nations' relative institutional instability can also open new opportunities for state-led improvements in human capabilities. Women's movements in stable democracies may often benefit from institutionalized state protection and broader social acceptance of feminist ideals, but they seldom achieve more than incremental gender changes when targeting state institutions—institutions that have been stable centers of political power across centuries. In contrast, women's movements in newly emerging democracies have often successfully capitalized on moments of instability and transition to demand that women's rights and needs be integrated into new state offices, policies, and procedures. Indeed, by some measures—particularly the measure of women's political representation in national legislatures—many poor nations have surpassed their rich counterparts in promoting gender equity in state governance. We certainly do not aim to downplay the difficulties that women in developing nations suffer when their national governments provide inadequate and gender-biased legal, judicial, educational, or welfare systems. Rather, we draw attention to how, despite the gutting of state power with neoliberal policies, *all* states' policies and practices continue to shape the different opportunities and identities available to men and women, making states valid sites for studying and supporting a gender-sensitive, capabilities-driven development.

There is still much research needed on the relationship between gender, states, and development. First, scholars still struggle to identify what factors or outcomes would constitute a "woman friendly" or "gender equitable" state. For example, Western nations that adopt more "family friendly" policies successfully increase rates of women's labor force participation, but these same family policies may simultaneously make it harder for women to achieve positions of power in the work place, effectively lowering and hardening the proverbial glass ceiling (Mandel and Semyonov 2005). In Cuba, authoritarian state crack down on some political and social freedoms—like the freedom to organize—but the same authoritarian state guarantees broad access to reproductive health services for women. Rwanda has progressive gender-sensitive laws, more girls than boys in primary school, and the world's highest percentage of women in parliament. Yet most Rwandan women continue to have difficulty accessing their new rights given entrenched social norms about the necessity of marriage (Berry 2015). Given that advances in one arena may come with—or even generate—setbacks in another, and given the masculine bias of all national governments despite level of economic development, what might a gender-equitable state look like?

Second, we need to improve our understandings of how states influence and are influenced by civil society, both at the national and the transnational levels. World-polity theorists argue that transnational networks of international nongovernmental organizations (INGOs) and intergovernmental organizations (IGOs) are creating a new "global culture" that celebrates gender equality (Berkovitch 1999; Meyer et al. 1997)—a process underlying our above discussion of the diffusion of gender quotas and laws against gendered violence. Yet the theories and methods used by world-polity scholars often ignore other powerful agents of global governance—like transnational religious institutions—that are much more likely to retrench, rather than support, women's political, economic, and social rights. The intensifying criminalization of abortion in Latin America (Viterna 2012, 2014a, 2014b) and same-sex relations in Africa (Currier 2012; Kaoma 2012) demonstrates how states may powerfully institutionalize gender discrimination just as easily as they might legislate gender equality in the present transnational world.

Finally, although the presentation of the current literature on gendered theory of the state is presented according to geographical locations, this is not meant to indicate a homogenization of a region or a state. There are, of course, striking variations across countries within all of our categorizations. For example, Romania's access to abortion differs greatly from most other East European nations (Benson, Anderson, and Samandari 2011). States' genders are shaped by their path-dependent histories. Researchers may find it useful to group states by certain shared historical events, like colonialism, but more research investigating why even similarly situated states sometimes have different gender outcomes is needed.

Furthermore, variation is found not just across states but also within states. The way in which state policies influence gender differs across individuals, often according to intersecting characteristics such as age, race, minority status, sexuality, religion, ability, and socioeconomic status. Although some states may appear more women friendly, benefits may accrue primarily to privileged women (Currier 2012; Hughes 2011).[14] Individuals who fall outside the gender binary may face some of the greatest restrictions to state resources. Some scholars have begun to explore these variations (Cabral and Viturro 2006; Canaday 2009; Connell 2012; Smith 2008; Solymár and Takács 2007); however, more research is needed.

Over the past decade, development practitioners have reached an overwhelming consensus that "empowering women" is a—and perhaps *the*—fundamental condition necessary for achieving any form of development.[15] Meanwhile, politicians are increasingly and emphatically using gender—and states' policing of gender roles—to demarcate battle lines in the global "war on terror" (Charrad 2011). Yet despite this clear real-world relevance, scholars of development have paid too little attention to the relationship between states and gender, especially as compared to the vast and varied theories of gendered states that have been developed by political scientists and political sociologists. As development scholars rethink the parameters of a "new" sociology of development—one that takes states seriously, that investigates issues of development in Western nations as well as indeveloping nations, and that is relevant to policy decisions (see Samuel Cohn and Gregory Hooks's introduction to this volume)—they would be wise to investigate how gendered states affect development outcomes in the societies they study as well as how citizen mobilizations can sometimes powerfully shape those development outcomes by promoting gendered transformations in state policies, practices, and institutions.

Notes

1 Although we recognize that gender is not limited to a binary and that it incorporates a multitude of variations, for the purpose of this chapter, gender is used primarily in reference to cisgender women and cisgender men.

2 El Salvador provides a relatively straightforward illustration that the gender of governance continues today. Like most of the world's nations, El Salvador signed onto the U.N. Convention on the Elimination of All Forms of Discrimination Against Women, or CEDAW, in 1981.

To fulfill the expectations of CEDAW, and in response to pressure from local women's movements after democratization, the Salvadoran state created a national-level "women's office" in 1996 (Viterna and Fallon 2008), giving it a mandate to police all other state agencies for gender discriminatory practices. Nevertheless, since its founding, each Salvadoran president has appointed his wife, the First Lady, to head the women's institute. This creates a highly visible gendered division of political power in El Salvador: men are presidents, and their wives run the "women's institute," regardless of whether they have any qualification for that position. The idea that a woman might ever be president, or that a male president could ever have a male spouse, is thus negated by the organizational structure of the very institution that was designed to promote gender equity in state governance. (The projects prioritized by the institute have, not surprisingly, varied in accordance with the political ideologies of the party in power. Nevertheless, the institutionalization of "president" as "heterosexual male" remains the same across any First Lady's gender ideology.)

3 There was, however, a notable literature on women and state-building in developing nations that emerged in the latter part of the 1980s, especially in the Middle East and South Asia. See Valentine Moghadam's chapter in this volume for details.

4 Excellent overviews of feminist state theory, focusing on the Western welfare state, include Brush 2003, Haney 2000, Borchorst 1999, and Orloff 1996. Lynne Haney (1996) further encourages scholars to conceptualize the state as a network of institutions and to study gender variation across those institutions within a single state.

5 Strong states in the Middle East and North Africa are notable exceptions. See Moghadam 2013.

6 Generally speaking, gender quotas are political policies that mandate a certain percentage of seats to be reserved for women in elected or appointed political positions. Many nations have implemented some sort of national or party-level gender quotas, but cross-national variations in quota type, reach, implementation, and effectiveness remain extensive. See Krook 2006 and Fallon, Swiss, and Viterna 2012 for overviews.

7 Some exceptions include communist countries (e.g., Vietnam, Cuba, and China), and authoritarian governments in the Middle East, like Tunisia (which instituted women-friendly laws under a staunchly secular regime) and Algeria (which prioritized some political guarantees of gender equity as an outgrowth of its revolutionary movement, even while maintaining an Islamic state). See Moghadam 2013.

8 Some scholarship did highlight positive outcomes. For example, in South Africa, the Women's National Coalition worked to improve women's representation within the constitution and formal political structures. Yet even in these more positive cases, scholars expressed strong concerns about the durability of feminist advances. Continuing with the South Africa example, the Women's National Coalition was dismantled after the transition to democracy was completed. Similarly, scholars have noted a disconnect between relatively "feminist" laws passed with democratization in the more positive cases and the continuing patriarchal practices within those states' legislative, executive, and judicial systems. Scholars also expressed concern about whether women who gained political power with democratization would continue to work with and for women's on-the-ground organizing. See, e.g., Britton 2002; Hassim 2006; Meer 2005; Seidman 2003.

9 lthough the majority of this literature examines cases in Latin America (Friedman 2000), Jane

Jaquette and Sharon Wolchik (1998) extend the comparison to Eastern Europe, Kathleen Sheldon (1994) and Catherine Scott (1994) find similar trends in Africa, and Valentine Moghadam (2013) explores the complexity of politics and women's rights in the Middle East. Quantitative cross-sectional studies similarly found that levels of democracy had no statistical impact, or a significant but negative impact, on women's legislative representation (Kenworthy and Malami 1999; Paxton 1997; Paxton and Kunovich 2003; Reynolds 1999).

10 Examples of activism that promoted traditional feminine images include motherhood-based human rights groups, where women marched to condemn authoritarian governments for kidnapping and killing their family members (Fisher 1990; Stephen 1997), and movements for social welfare, where women organized as housewives to protest rising prices, shrinking social services, and their increasing difficulty in feeding and caring for their families (Jelin 1990; Neuhouser 1998). Opposition groups also used traditional narratives of "mother" to justify their increasing use of political violence (Viterna 2013). Though certainly strategic, the "mother" identity was also heartfelt (Bayard de Volo 2001); women strongly believed that their status as women made them particularly qualified to talk about suffering and human rights.

11 Although these movements did little to challenge the traditional patriarchal society, some scholars argue that "feminine" movements can and do overlap and develop into "feminist" ideologies (Molyneux 1985; Stephen 1997), but little is written about which movements evolve, which languish, and whether this broadening of movement goals results in gendered changes within the state apparatus.

12 Susan Franceschet (2003) provides an excellent overview of this literature and counters that Chile's state agency for women, the Servicio Nacional de la Mujer, has actually strengthened women's mobilizing.

13 Others have shown how neoliberalism may have generated women's mobilization as well (e.g., Almeida and Delgado 2008; DiMarco 2011; Moghadam 2009).

14 Feminist literature on citizenship delves into these differences. See Dietz 2003 for an overview.

15 To illustrate: the U.N. Development Programme focuses "on gender equality and women's empowerment not only as human rights, but also because they are a pathway to achieving the Millennium Development Goals and sustainable development" (http://www.undp.org/content/undp/en/home/ourwork/womenempowerment/overview.html). CARE, a large international nongovernmental organization, places a "special focus on working alongside poor women because, equipped with the proper resources, women have the power to help whole families and entire communities escape poverty" (http://www.care.org/about/index.asp). Oxfam International simply states, "Human development is driven by empowered women" (http://www.oxfam.org/en/about/how-oxfam-fights-poverty).

References

Abramovitz, Mimi. 1988. *Regulating the Lives of Women: Social Welfare Policy from Colonial Times to the Present.* Boston: South End Press.

Agarwal, Bina. 2010. *Gender and Green Governance: The Political Economy of Women's Presence within and beyond Community Forestry.* New York: Oxford University Press.

Allen, Judith. 1990. "Does Feminism Need a Theory of 'the State'?" In *Playing the State: Australian Feminist Interventions,* edited by Sophie Watson, 21–35. London: Verso.

Almeida, Paul, and Roxana Delgado. 2008. "Gendered Networks and Health Care Privatization." *Advances in Medical Sociology* 10: 273–99.

Alvarez, Sonia E. 1990. *Engendering Democracy in Brazil.* Princeton, N.J.: Princeton University Press.

———. 1999. "Advocating Feminism: The Latin American Feminist NGO 'Boom.'" *International Feminist Journal of Politics* 1, no. 2: 181–209.

Baiocchi, Gianpaolo, Patrick Heller, and Marcelo K. Silva. 2011. *Bootstrapping Democracy: Transforming Local Governance and Civil Society in Brazil.* Stanford, Calif.: Stanford University Press.

Bauer, Gretchen. 2008. "Fifty/Fifty by 2020." *International Feminist Journal of Politics* 10, no. 3: 348–68.

———. 2012. "'Let There Be a Balance': Women in African Parliaments." *Political Studies Review* 10: 370–84.

Bayard de Volo, Lorraine. 2001. *Mothers of Heroes and Martyrs: Gender Identity Politics in Nicaragua, 1979–1999.* Baltimore, Md.: Johns Hopkins University Press.

Beckwith, Karen. 2000. "Beyond Compare? Women's Movements in Comparative Perspective." *European Journal of Political Research* 37: 431–68.

Benson, Janie, Kathryn Anderson, and Ghazzaleh Samandari. 2011. "Reductions in Abortion-Related Mortality Following Policy Reform: Evidence from Romania, South Africa and Bangladesh." *Reproductive Health* 8: 1–12.

Berkovitch, Nitza. 1999. *From Motherhood to Citizenship: Women's Rights and International Organizations.* Baltimore, Md.: Johns Hopkins University Press.

Berry, Marie E. 2015. "When 'Bright Futures' Fade: Paradoxes of Women's Empowerment in Rwanda." *Signs: Journal of Women in Culture and Society* 41, no. 1: 1–27.

Berthusen Gottlick, Jane. 1999. "From the Ground Up: Women's Organizations and Democratization in Russia." In *Democratization and Women's Grassroots Movements,* edited by Jill M. Bystydzienski and Joti Sekhon, 241–61. Bloomington: Indiana University Press.

Bjarnegård, Elin. 2013. *Gender, Informal Institutions and Political Recruitment: Explaining Male Dominance in Parliamentary Representation.* Basingstoke, U.K.: Palgrave Macmillan.

Bjarnegård, Elin, and Erik Melander. 2011. "Disentangling Democratization, Gender, and Peace: The Negative Effects of Militarized Masculinity." *Journal of Gender Studies* 20, no. 2: 139–54.

Blumberg, Rae Lesser, and Andrés Wilfrido Salazar-Palacios. 2011. "Can a Focus on Survival and Health as Social/Economic Rights Help Some of the World's Most Imperiled Women in a Globalized World?" In *Making Globalization Work for Women,* edited by Valentine M. Moghadam, Suzanne Franzway, and Mary Margaret Fonow, 123–56. Albany: SUNY Press.

Bock, Gisela, and Pat Thane, eds. 1991. *Maternity and Gender Policies: Women and the Rise of the European Welfare States, 1880s–1950s.* New York: Routledge Press.

Bolzehndahl, Catherine, and Clem Brooks. 2007. "Women's Political Representation and Welfare State Spending in 12 Capitalist Democracies." *Social Forces* 85, no. 4: 1509–34.

Borchorst, Anette. 1994. "The Scandinavian Welfare States—Patriarchal, Gender Neutral or Woman Friendly?" *International Journal of Contemporary Sociology* 31: 1–23.

———. 1999. "Feminist Rethinking about the Welfare State." In *Revisioning Gender,* edited by Myra Marx Ferree, Judith Lorber, and Beth B. Hess, 99–127. London: Sage Publications.

Brady, David. 2009. *Rich Democracies, Poor People: How Politics Explain Poverty.* New York: Oxford University Press.

Brady, David, and Rebekah Burroway. 2012. "Targeting, Universalism, and Single-Mother Poverty: A Multilevel Analysis across 18 Affluent Democracies." *Demography* 49, no. 2: 719–46.

Britton, Hannah. 2002. "The Incomplete Revolution." *International Feminist Journal of Politics* 4, no. 1: 43–71.

Brown, Wendy. 1995. *States of Injury: Power and Freedom in Late Modernity.* Princeton, N.J.: Princeton University Press.

Brush, Lisa D. 2003. *Gender and Governance.* Walnut Creek, Calif.: Altamira Press.

Bujra, Janet M. 1986. "'Urging Women to Redouble Their Efforts ...': Class, Gender and Capitalist Transformation in Africa." In *Women and Class in Africa,* edited by Claire Robertson and Iris Berger, 117–40. New York: Africana Publishing Company.

Bush, Sarah. 2011. "International Politics and the Spread of Quotas for Women in Legislatures." *International Organization* 65, no. 1: 103–37.

Bystydzienski, Jill M., and Joti Sekhon. 1999. "Introduction." In *Democratization and Women's Grassroots Movements,* edited by Jill M. Bystydzienski and Joti Sekhon, 1–21. Bloomington: Indiana University Press.

Cabral, Mauro (A. I. Grinspan), and Paula Viturro. 2006. "(Trans)Sexual Citizenship in Contemporary Argentina." In *Transgender Rights,* edited by Paisley Currah, Richard M. Juang, and Shannon Price Minter, 262–73. Minneapolis: University of Minnesota Press.

Cagan, Elizabeth. 2000. "Women and Democratization: Lessons from Latin America." In *Advances in Gender Research,* Vol. 4, edited by Vasilikie Demos and Marcia Texler Segal, 91–121. Greenwich, Conn.: JAI Press.

Canaday, Margot. 2009. *The Straight State: Sexuality and Citizenship in Twentieth-Century America.* Princeton, N.J.: Princeton University Press.

Chapman, Jenny. 1993. *Politics, Feminism, and the Reformation of Gender.* New York: Routledge Press.

Charrad, Mounira M. 2011. "Gender in the Middle East: Islam, State, Agency." *Annual Review of Sociology* 37: 417–37.

Chattopadhyay, Raghabendra, and Esther Duflo. 2004. "Women as Policymakers: Evidence from a Randomized Policy Experiment in India." *Econometrica* 72, no. 5: 1409–43.

Chaudhuri, Soma. 2010. "The Fight for Property Rights: How Changes in Movement Actors and History Brought about the Changes in Frames in a Single Movement." *Comparative Studies of South Asia, Africa and the Middle East* 30, no. 3: 633–43.

Chen, Li-Ju. 20010. "Do Gender Quotas Influence Women's Representation and Policies?" *European Journal of Comparative Economics* 7: 13–60.

Chinchilla, Norma Stoltz. 1994. "Women's Movements and Democracy in Latin America: Some Unresolved Tensions." In *Women and the Transition to Democracy: The Impact of Political and Economic Reform in Latin America,* edited by Jane S. Jaquette, 1–19. Washing-ton, D.C.: Woodrow Wilson International Center for Scholars.

Chuchryk, Patricia M. 1989. "Feminist Anti-Authoritarian Politics: The Role of Women's Organizations and the Transition from Dictatorship to Democracy in Peru." In *The Women's Movement in Latin America,* edited by Jane S. Jaquette, 149–84. Boston: Unwin Hyman.

Clemens, Elisabeth S. 1993. "Organizational Repertoires and Institutional Change: Women's Groups and the Transformation of U.S. Politics, 1890–1920." *American Journal of Sociology* 98: 755–98.

Connell, Raewyn. 2012. "Transsexual Women and Feminist Thought: Toward New Understanding and New Politics." *Signs: Journal of Women in Culture and Society* 37, no. 4: 857–81.

Cooke, Lynn Prince. 2007. "Policy Pathways to Gender Power: State-Level Effects on the US Division of Housework." *Journal of Social Policy* 36, no. 2: 239–60.

Costa, Monica, Marian Sawer, and Rhonda Sharp. 2013. "Women Acting for Women." *International Feminist Journal of Politics* 15, no. 3: 333–52.

Craske, Nikki. 1998. "Remasculization and the Neoliberal State in Latin America." In *Gender, Politics and the State,* edited by Vicky Randall and Georgina Waylen, 100–120. London: Routledge Press.

Currier, Ashley. 2012. *Out in Africa: LGBT Organizing in Namibia and South Africa.* Minneapolis: University of Minnesota Press.

Dahlerup, Drude. 1994. "Learning to Live with the State. State, Market, and Civil Society: Women's Needs for State Intervention in East and West." *Women's Studies International Forum* 17, nos. 2–3: 117–27.

Darkwah, Akosua K. 2010. "Education: Pathway to Empowerment for Ghanaian Women?" *IDS Bulletin* 41, no. 2: 28–36.

Davis, Angela. 2001. "The Color of Violence against Women." *Sojourner* (Oct.): 12–13.

Dietz, Mary G. 2003. "Current Controversies in Feminist Theory." *Annual Review of Political Science* 6: 399–431.

DiMarco, Graciela. 2011. "Gendered Economic Rights and Trade Unionism: The Case of Argentina." In *Making Globalization Work for Women: The Role of Social Rights and Trade Union Leadership,* edited by Valentine M. Moghadam, Suzanne Franzway, and Margaret Fonow, 93–122. Albany: SUNY Press.

Einhorn, Barbara. 1993. *Cinderella Goes to Market: Citizenship, Gender and Women's Movements in East Central Europe.* London: Verso.

Eisenstein, Zillah. 1981. *The Radical Future of Liberal Feminism.* New York: Longman.

Evans, Peter B. 2010. Constructing the 21st Century Developmental State: Potentialities and Pitfalls." In *Constructing a Democratic Developmental State in South Africa,* edited by Omano Edigheji, 37–58. Cape Town, South Africa: HSRC Press.

Fallon, Kathleen M. 2008. *Democracy and the Rise of Women's Movements in Sub-Saharan Africa.* Baltimore, Md.: Johns Hopkins University Press.

Fallon, Kathleen, Liam Swiss, and Jocelyn Viterna. 2012. "Resolving the Democracy Paradox: Democratization and Women's Legislative Representation in Developing Nations, 1975–2009." *American Sociological Review* 77, no. 3: 380–408.

Ferree, Myra Marx, and William A. Gamson. 2003. "The Gendering of Governance and the Governance of Gender: Abortion Politics in Germany and the USA." In *Recognition Struggles and Social Movements: Contested Identities, Agency and Power,* edited by B. Hobson, 35–63. Cambridge, Engl.: Cambridge University Press.

Fisher, Jo. 1990. *Mothers of the Disappeared.* Cambridge, Mass.: South End Press.

———. 1993. "Women and Democracy: For Home and Country." *NACLA Report on the Americas* 27, no. 1: 30–36.

Forest, Maxime. 2006. "Emerging Gender Interest Groups within the New States: The Case of the Czech Republic." *Perspectives on European Politics and Society* 7, no. 2: 170–84.

Franceschet, Susan. 2003. "State Feminism and Women's Movements: The Impact of Chile's Servico Nacional de la Mujer on Women's Activism." *Latin American Research Review* 38, no. 1: 9–40.

Friedman, Elisabeth J. 1998. "Paradoxes of Gendered Political Opportunity in the Venezuelan Transition to Democracy." *Latin American Research Review* 33, no. 3: 87–135.

———. 2000. *Unfinished Transitions: Women and the Gendered Development of Democracy in Venezuela, 1936–1996.* University Park: Pennsylvania State University Press.

Fuszara, Malgorzata. 2010. "Citizenship, Representation, and Gender." *Polish Sociological Review* 4, no. 172: 367–89.

Gal, Susan, and Gail Kligman, eds. 2000. *Reproducing Gender.* Princeton, N.J.: Princeton University Press.

Geisler, Gisela. 1995. "Troubled Sisterhood: Women and Politics in Southern Africa." *African Affairs* 94: 545–78.

Gelb, Joyce, and Vivien Hart. 1999. "Feminist Politics in a Hostile Environment: Obstacles and

Opportunities." In *How Social Movements Matter,* edited by Marco Giugni, Doug McAdam, and Charles Tilly, 149–81. Minneapolis: University of Minnesota Press.

Gerber, Theodore P., and Brienna Perelli-Harris. 2012. "Maternity Leave in Turbulent Times: Effects on Labor Market Transitions and Fertility in Russia, 1985–2000." *Social Forces* 90, no. 4: 1297–1322.

Gibson, Christopher. 2012. "Making Redistributive Direct Democracy Matter: Development and Women's Participation in the Gram Sabhas of Kerala, India." *American Sociological Review* 77, no. 3: 409–34.

Gideon, Jasmine. 1999. "Looking at Economies as Gendered Structures: An Application to Central America." *Feminist Economics* 5, no. 1: 1–28.

Goodwin, Joanne L. 1997. *Gender and the Politics of Welfare Reform.* Chicago: University of Chicago Press.

Gordon, Linda. 1990. "The New Feminist Scholarship on the Welfare State." In *Women, the State, and Welfare,* edited by Linda Gordon, 9–35. Madison: University of Wisconsin Press.

———. 1994. *Pitied but Not Entitled: Single Mothers and the History of Welfare.* Cambridge, Mass.: Harvard University Press.

Gould, Laurie A. 2014. "Exploring Gender-Based Disparities in Legal Protection, Education, Health, Political Empowerment, and Employment in Failing and Fragile States." *Women and Criminal Justice* 24, no. 4: 279–305.

Haney, Lynne A. 1994. "From Proud Worker to Good Mother: Women, the State, and Regime Change in Hungary." *Frontiers Editorial Collective* 14, no. 3: 113–50.

———. 1996. "Homeboys, Babies, Men in Suits: The State and the Reproduction of Male Dominance." *American Sociological Review* 61, no. 5: 759–78.

———. 2000. "Feminist State Theory: Applications to Jurisprudence, Criminology, and the Welfare State." *Annual Review of Sociology* 26: 641–66.

Hassim, Shireen. 2006. *Women's Organizations and Democracy in South Africa.* Madison: University of Wisconsin Press.

Hawkesworth, Mary E. 2001. "Democratization: Reflections on Gendered Dislocations in the Public Sphere." In *Gender, Globalization and Democratization,* edited by Rita Mae Kelly, Jane H. Bayes, Mary E. Hawkesworth, and Brigitte Young, 223–36. New York: Rowman and Littlefield.

Hobson, Barbara, ed. 2003. *Recognition Struggles and Social Movements: Contested Identities, Agency and Power.* Cambridge, Engl.: Cambridge University Press.

Holter, Harriet. 1984. "Women's Research and Social Theory." In *Patriarchy in a Welfare Society,* edited by Harriet Holter, 9–25. Oslo: Universitetsforlaget.

Hughes, Melanie. 2009. "Armed Conflict, International Linkages, and Women's Parliamentary Representation in Developing Nations." *Social Problems* 56, no. 1: 174–204.

———. 2011. "Intersectionality, Quotas, and Minority Women's Political Representation Worldwide." *American Political Science Review* 105, no. 3: 604–20.

Huiscamp, Gerard. 2000. "Identity Politics and Democratic Transitions in Latin America: (Re)organizing Women's Strategic Interests through Community Activism." *Theory and Society* 29, no. 3: 385–415.

Inter-Parliamentary Union. 2014. "Women in Parliaments: World Classification." Accessed Dec. 10, 2014. http://ipu.org/wmn-e/classif.htm.

Jaquette, Jane S. 1994. "Conclusion: Women's Political Participation and the Prospects for Democracy." In *The Women's Movement in Latin America: Participation and Democracy,* 2d ed., edited by Jane S. Jaquette, 223–38. Boulder, Colo.: Westview Press.

Jaquette, Jane S., and Sharon L. Wolchik, eds. 1998. *Women and Democracy: Latin America and Central and Eastern Europe.* Baltimore, Md.: Johns Hopkins University Press.

Jelin, Elizabeth J., ed. 1990. *Women and Social Change in Latin America*. London: Zed Books.

———. 1998. "Women, Gender and Human Rights." In *Constructing Democracy: Human Rights, Citizenship, and Society in Latin America*, edited by Elizabeth Jelin and Eric Hershberg, 177–96. Boulder, Colo.: Westview Press.

Kampwirth, Karen. 2004. *Feminism and the Legacy of Revolution: Nicaragua, El Salvador, Chiapas*. Athens: Ohio University Press.

Kantola, Johanna. 2007. "The Gendered Reproduction of the State in International Relations." *British Journal of Politics and International Relations* 9, no. 2: 270–83.

Kaoma, Kapya. 2012. "Exporting the Anti-Gay Movement." *The American Prospect* 23, no. 4: 44.

Kelly, Rita Mae, Jane H. Bayes, Mary Hawkesworth, and Brigitte Young, eds. 2001. *Gender, Globalization and Democratization*. New York: Rowman and Littlefield.

Kenworthy, Lane, and Melissa Malami. 1999. "Gender Inequality in Political Representation: A Worldwide Comparative Analysis." *Social Forces* 78: 235–69.

Koven, Seth, and Sonya Michel, eds. 1993. *Mothers of the New World: Maternalist Politics and the Origins of the Welfare States*. New York: Routledge Press.

Krook, Mona Lena. 2006. "Reforming Representation: The Diffusion of Candidate Gender Quotas Worldwide." *Politics and Gender* 2, no. 3: 303–27.

———. 2009. *Quotas for Women in Politics: Gender and Candidate Selection Reform Worldwide*. New York: Oxford University Press.

Lee, Cheol Sung. 2007. "Labor Unions and Good Governance: A Cross-national Comparative Analysis." *American Sociological Review* 72, no. 4: 585–609.

Lieberman, Evan S. 2012. "Descriptive Representation and AIDS Policy in South Africa." *Contemporary Politics* 18, no. 2: 156–73.

Lovenduski, Joni. 2005. *Feminizing Politics*. Cambridge, Engl.: Polity.

Luciak, Ilja A. 2001. *After the Revolution: Gender and Democracy in El Salvador, Nicaragua, and Guatemala*. Baltimore, Md.: Johns Hopkins University Press.

MacKinnon, Catherine. 1989. *Toward a Feminist Theory of the State*. Cambridge, Mass.: Harvard University Press.

Mamdani, Mahmood. 1999. "The Historicizing Power and Responses to Power: Indirect Rule and Its Reform." *Social Research* 66, no. 3: 859–86.

Mandel, Hadas, and Moshe Semyonov. 2005. "Family Policies, Wage Structures, and Gender Gaps: Sources of Earnings Inequality in 20 Countries." *American Sociological Review* 70: 949–67.

Manuh, Takyiwaa. 1993. "Women, State and Society under the PNDC." In *Ghana under PNDC Rule*, edited by Emmanuel Gyimah-Boadi, 176–95. Dakar, Senegal: Council for the Development of Social Science Research in Africa.

Mazur, Amy G. 2001. *State Feminism, Women's Movements, and Job Training: Making Democracies Work in the Global Economy*. New York: Routledge Press.

McCammon, Holly J. 2001. "Stirring up Suffrage Sentiment: The Formation of the State Woman Suffrage Organizations, 1866–1914." *Social Forces* 80, no. 2: 449–80.

McCammon, Holly J., Karen E. Campbell, Ellen M. Granberg, and Christine Mowery. 2001. "How Movements Win: Gendered Opportunity Structures and U.S. Women's Suffrage Movements, 1866–1919." *American Sociological Review* 66: 49–70.

Meer, Shamim. 2005. "Freedom for Women: Mainstreaming Gender in the South African Liberation Struggle and Beyond." *Gender and Development* 13: 36–45.

Meyer, John W., John Boli, George M. Thomas, and Francisco O. Ramirez. 1997. "World Society and the Nation-State." *American Journal of Sociology* 103: 144–81.

Millard, Frances. 2014. "Not Much Happened: The Impact of Gender Quotas in Poland." *Communist and Post-Communist Studies* 47, no. 1: 1–11.

Misra, Joya, Stephanie Moller, and Michelle Budig. 2007. "Work Family Policies and Poverty for Partnered and Single Women in Europe and North America." *Gender and Society* 21, no. 6: 804–27.

Moghadam, Valentine M. 1997. "Gender and Revolutions." In *Theorizing Revolutions*, edited by John Foran, 137–67. New York: Routledge Press.

———. 2009. *Globalization and Social Movements: Islamism, Feminism, and the Global Justice Movement*. Lanham, Md.: Rowman and Littlefield.

———. 2013. *Modernizing Women: Gender and Social Change in the Middle East*. 3d ed. Boulder, Colo.: Lynne Rienner Publishers.

Molyneux, Maxine. 1985. "Mobilization without Emancipation? Women's Interests, State and Revolution in Nicaragua." *Feminist Studies* 11, no. 2: 227–53.

Muncy, Robyn. 1991. *Creating a Female Dominion in American Reform, 1890–1935*. New York: Oxford University Press.

Nelson, Barbara J., and Najma Chowdhury, eds. 1994. *Women and Politics Worldwide*. New Haven, Conn.: Yale University Press.

Neuhouser, Kevin. 1998. "'If I Had Abandoned My Children': Community Mobilization and Commitment to the Identity of Mother in Northeast Brazil." *Social Forces* 77, no. 1: 331–58.

Noonan, Rita K. 1995. "Women against the State: Political Opportunities and Collective Action Frames in Chile's Transition to Democracy." *Sociological Forum* 10, no. 1: 81–111.

Nussbaum, Martha C. 2000. *Women and Human Development: The Capabilities Approach*. New York: Cambridge University Press.

O'Connor, Julia S., Ann S. Orloff, and Sheila Shaver. 1999. *States, Markets, Families*. New York: Cambridge University Press.

O'Donnell, Guillermo, and Philippe C. Schmitter. 1986. *Transitions from Authoritarian Rule: Tentative Conclusions about Uncertain Democracies*. Vol. 4. Baltimore, Md.: Johns Hopkins University Press.

Okeke-Ihejirika, Philomina, and Susan Franceschet. 2002. "Democratization and State Feminism: Gender Politics in Africa and Latin America." *Development and Change* 33, no. 3: 439–66.

Orloff, Ann. 1996. "Gender and the Welfare State." *Annual Review of Sociology* 22: 51–78.

———. 2009. "Gendering the Comparative Analysis of Welfare States: An Unfinished Agenda." *Sociological Theory* 27, no. 3: 317–43.

Oyěwùmí, Oyèrónké. 1997. *The Invention of Women: Making an African Sense of Western Gender Discourses*. Minneapolis: University of Minnesota Press.

Parpart, Jane, and Kathleen Staudt, eds. 1990. *Gender and the State in Africa*. Boulder, Colo.: Lynne Rienner Press.

Pascall, Gillian, and Nick Manning. 2000. "Gender and Social Policy: Comparing Welfare States in Central and Eastern Europe and the Former Soviet Union." *Journal of European Social Policy* 10, no. 3: 240–66.

Pateman, Carole. 1988. *The Sexual Contract*. Stanford, Calif.: Stanford University Press.

Paxton, Pamela. 1997. "Women in National Legislatures: A Cross-National Analysis." *Social Science Research* 26: 442–64.

Paxton, Pamela, Melanie Hughes, and Michael Painter. 2010. "Growth in Women's Political Representation: A Longitudinal Exploration of Democracy, Electoral System and Gender Quotas." *European Journal of Political Research* 49, no. 1: 25–52.

Paxton, Pamela, and Sheri Kunovich. 2003. "Women's Political Representation: The Importance of Ideology." *Social Forces* 82, no. 1: 87–114.

Pederson, Susan. 1993. *Family, Dependence, and the Origins of the Welfare State: Britain and France, 1914–1945*. New York: Cambridge University Press.

Phillips, Anne. 2006. "'Really' Equal: Opportunities and Autonomy." *Journal of Political Philosophy* 14, no. 1: 18–32.

———. 2012. "Representation and Inclusion." *Politics and Gender* 8, no. 4: 512–18.

Pini, Barbara, Ruth Panelli, and Marian Sawer. 2008. "Managing the Woman Issue." *International Feminist Journal of Politics* 10, no. 2: 173–97.

Rai, Shirin. 1996. "Women and the State in the Third World." In *Women and Politics in the Third World,* edited by Haleh Afshar, 25–39. New York: Routledge Press.

Ray, Raka, and Anne C. Korteweg. 1999. "Women's Movements in the Third World: Identity, Mobilization, and Autonomy." *Annual Review of Sociology* 25: 47–71.

Reynolds, Andrew. 1999. "Women in the Legislatures and Executives of the World Knocking at the Highest Glass Ceiling." *World Politics* 51: 547–72.

Rhode, Deborah L. 1989. *Justice and Gender: Sex Discrimination and the Law.* Cambridge, Mass.: Harvard University Press.

Richards, Patricia. 2004. *Pobladoras, Indigenas, and the State: Conflicts over Women's Rights in Chile.* Newark, N.J.: Rutgers University Press.

Rodney, Walter. 1972. "How Europe Underdeveloped Africa." In *Beyond Borders: Thinking Critically about Global Issues,* edited by Paula S. Rothenberg, 107–25. New York: Worth Publishers.

Ruggie, Mary. 1984. *The State and Working Women: A Comparative Study of Britain and Sweden.* Princeton, N.J.: Princeton University Press.

Sainsbury, Diane. 1996. *Gender, Equality and Welfare States.* New York: Cambridge University Press.

Schild, Verónica. 1994. "Recasting 'Popular' Movements: Gender and Learning in Neighborhood Organizations in Chile." *Latin American Perspectives* 21, no. 2: 59–80.

Scott, Catherine. 1994. "'Men in Our Country Behave like Chiefs': Women and the Angolan Revolution." In *Women and Revolution in Africa, Asia, and the New World,* edited by Mary Ann Tetreault, 89–110. Columbia: University of South Carolina Press.

Seidman, Gay W. 2003. "Institutional Dilemmas: Representation versus Mobilization in the South African Gender Commission." *Feminist Studies* 29, no. 3: 541–63.

Sheldon, Kathleen. 1994. "Women and Revolution in Mozambique: A Luta Continua." In *Women and Revolution in African, Asia, and the New World,* edited by Mary Ann Tetreault, 33–61. Columbia: University of South Carolina Press.

Siim, Birte. 1990. "Women and the Welfare State: Between Public and Private Dependence." In *Gender and Caring: Work and Welfare in Britain and Scandinavia*, edited by Clare Ungerson, 80–109. London: Harvester/Wheatsheaf.

Silova, Iveta, and Cathryn Magno. 2004. "Gender Equity Unmasked: Democracy, Gender, and Education in Central/Southeastern Europe and the Former Soviet Union." *Comparative Education Review* (Special Issue on Global Trends in Comparative Research on Gender and Education, guest editors N'Dri Assié-Lumumba and Margaret Sutton) 48, no. 4: 417–42.

Sklar, Kathryn K. 1993. "The Historical Foundations of Women's Power in the Creation of the American Welfare State, 1830–1930." In *Mothers of a New World: Maternalist Politics and the Origins of Welfare States,* edited by Seth Koven and Sonya Michel, 43–93. New York: Routledge Press.

Skocpol, Theda. 1992. *Protecting Soldiers and Mothers.* Cambridge, Mass.: Harvard University Press.

Smart, Carol. 1989. *Feminism and the Power of Law.* New York: Routledge Press.

Smith, Miriam. 2008. *Political Institutions and Lesbian and Gay Rights in the United States and Canada.* New York: Routledge.

Solymár, Bruce, and Judit Takács. 2007. "Wrong Bodies and Real Selves: Transexual People in the Hungarian School and Healthcare System." In *Beyond the Pink Curtain: Everyday Life of LGBT*

People in Eastern Europe, edited by Roman Kuhar and Judit Takács, 141–98. Ljubljana: Peace Institute.

Squires, Judith. 2001. "Feminism and Democracy." In *The Blackwell Companion to Political Sociology,* edited by Kate Nash and Alan Scott, 366–74. Malden, Mass.: Blackwell Publishing.

———. 2008. "Deliberation, Domination and Decision-Making." *Theoria: A Journal of Social and Political Theory* 55, no. 117: 104–33.

Staggenborg, Suzanne. 1988. "The Consequences of Professionalization and Formalization in the Pro-Choice Movement." *American Sociological Review* 53: 585–605.

Stamp, Patricia. 1986. "Kikuyu Women's Self-Help Groups." In *Women and Class in Africa,* edited by Claire Robertson and Iris Berger, 27–46. New York: Africana Publishing Company.

Stephen, Lynn. 1997. *Women and Social Movements in Latin America: Power from Below.* Austin: University of Texas Press.

Sternbach, N. A., M. Navarro-Aranguren, Patricia Chuchryk, and Sonia E. Alvarez. 1992. "Feminisms in Latin America: From Bogota to San Bernardo." *Signs: Journal of Women in Culture and Society* 17, no. 2: 393–434.

Stetson, Dorothy McBride, ed. 2001. *Abortion Politics, Women's Movements, and the Democratic State: A Comparative Study of State Feminism.* New York: Oxford University Press.

Stockemer, Daniel. 2014. "Women's Descriptive Representation in Developed and Developing Countries." *International Political Science Review* (first published online Apr. 24). Accessed Mar. 5, 2015. http://ips.sagepub.com/content/early/2014/04/24/0192512113513966.full.pdf+html.

Swiss, Liam, Kathleen Fallon, and Giovani Burgos. 2012. "Reaching a Critical Mass: Women's Political Representation and Child Health in Developing Countries." *Social Forces* 91, no. 2: 531–58.

Taylor, Verta, and Nella Van Dyke. 2004. "'Get up, Stand up': Tactical Repertoires of Social Movements." In *The Blackwell Companion to Social Movements,* edited by David A. Snow, Sarah A. Soule, and Hanspeter Kriesi, 262–93. Malden, Mass.: Blackwell Publishers.

Tripp, Aili Mari. 1994. "Gender, Political Participation and the Transformation of Association Life in Uganda and Tanzania." *African Studies Review* 37: 107–31.

———. 2000. "Rethinking Difference: Comparative Perspectives from Africa." *Signs: Journal of Women in Culture and Society* 25: 649–75.

Tripp, Aili Mari, and Alice Kang. 2008. "The Global Impact of Quotas: On the Fast Track to Increased Female Legislative Representation." *Comparative Political Studies* 41: 338–61.

True, Jacqui, and Michael Mintrom. 2001. "Transnational Networks and Policy Diffusion: The Case of Gender Mainstreaming." *International Studies Quarterly* 45, no. 1: 27–57.

Tsikata, Edzodzinam. 1989. "Women's Political Organisations 1951–1987." In *The State Development and Politics in Ghana,* edited by Emmanuel Hansen and Kwame A. Ninsin, 73–93. London: Council for the Development of Social Science Research in Africa.

Vargas, Virginia. 2002. "The Struggle by Latin American Feminisms for Rights and Autonomy." In *Gender and the Politics of Rights and Democracy in Latin America,* edited by Nikki Craske and Maxine Molyneux, 199–221. Basingstoke, U.K.: Palgrave.

Viterna, Jocelyn. 2006. "Pulled, Pushed and Persuaded: Explaining Women's Mobilization into the Salvadoran Guerrilla Army." *American Journal of Sociology* 112, no. 1: 1–45.

———. 2012. "The Left and 'Life': The Politics of Abortion in El Salvador." *Politics and Gender* 8, no. 2: 248–54.

———. 2013. *Women in War: The Micro-processes of Mobilization in El Salvador.* New York: Oxford University Press.

———. 2014a. "Conceiving while Poor; Imprisoned for Murder." *NACLA Report on the Americas* 47, no. 3: 34–37.

———. 2014b. "Radical or Righteous? Using Gender to Shape Public Perceptions of Political Violence." In *Dynamics of Political Violence: A Process-Oriented Perspective on Radicalization and the Escalation of Political Conflict,* edited by Lorenzo Bosi, Chares Demetriou, and Stefan Malthaner, 189–216. Surrey, U.K.: Ashgate Publishing.

Viterna, Jocelyn, and Kathleen Fallon. 2008. "Democratization, Women's Movements, and Gender-Equitable States: A Framework for Comparison." *American Sociological Review* 73, no. 4: 668–89.

Walby, Sylvia. 1992. "Women and Nation." *International Journal of Comparative Sociology* 32, nos. 1–2: 81–100.

Watson, Peggy. 1993. "The Rise of Masculinism in Eastern Europe." *New Left Review* 198: 71–82.

Watson, Sophie. 1990. *Playing the State: Australian Feminist Interventions.* London: Verso.

Waylen, Georgina. 1994. "Women and Democratization: Conceptualizing Gender Relations in Transition Politics." *World Politics* 46, no. 3: 327–55.

———. 1996. *Gender in Third World Politics.* Boulder, Colo.: Lynne Rienner Publishers.

Weldon, Laurel, and Mala Htun. 2012. "The Civic Origins of Progressive Policy Change: Combating Violence against Women in Global Perspective, 1975–2005." *American Political Science Review* 106, no. 3: 548–69.

Wernet, Christine A. 2008. "An Index of Pro-Woman Nation-States: A Comparative Analysis of 39 Countries." *International Journal of Comparative Sociology* 45, no. 1: 60–80.

Wolford, Wendy. 2010. "Participatory Democracy by Default: Land Reform, Social Movements, and the State in Brazil." *Journal of Peasant Studies* 37, no. 1: 91–109.

Yoo, Eunhye. 2011. "International Human Rights Regime, Neoliberalism, and Women's Social Rights, 1984–2004." *International Journal of Comparative Sociology* 52, no. 6: 503–28.

Yoon, Mi Yung. 2011. "More Women in the Tanzanian Legislature: Do Numbers Matter?" *Journal of Contemporary African Studies* 29, no. 1: 83–98.

Yuval-Davis, Nira. 1997. *Gender and Nation.* London: Sage Publications.

Zakuan, Ummu Atiyah Ahmad. 2010. "Women in the Malaysian Parliament: Do They Matter?" *Intellectual Discourse* 18, no. 2: 283–322.

■ CHAPTER 5

The Power of Hope: A Theory of Hope for Racial Justice

Editor's Introduction

This chapter contends that political entities commonly discriminate, providing unfair treatment, partiality, or favoritism for the benefit of dominant groups. Lawrence and Lawless's initial goal for this study was to construct a documentary based on the steps taken to rebuild the small rural community of Pinhook, Missouri, following a Mississippi River flood. Lawrence and Lawless's research took an unexpected turn when they discovered the stories from this community. Their findings describe incidents of governmental racism and how these actions were perceived in the small agricultural community. For many years, the town struggled to receive compensation for the flood devastation. This was largely due to how they were perceived by authorities in, for example, their high levels of unemployment. In this vein, the chapter raises an important question: Is the value of unemployed people invisible in the eyes of the government? In this case, the Pinhook community residents were stereotyped as "nobodies." In contrast, Lawrence and Lawless suggest that race, ethnicity, or social class should not serve as a barrier for receiving benefits from governmental emergency agencies. To that end, the authors present a theory of hope for racial justice and that a sense of collective identity is important for communities to flourish in the face of adversity. In this chapter, the reader will identify why social change is necessary and how change generates opportunities for growth in society.

READING 5 Conclusion: The Power of Hope Through Community

David Todd Lawrence and Elaine J. Lawless

> Our struggle for racial justice, a struggle we must continue even if—as I contend here—racism is an integral, permanent, and indestructible component of this society. The challenge has been to tell what I view as the truth about racism without causing disabling despair.
>
> —**DERRICK BELL**, *Faces from the Bottom of the Well*

Frustrations Abound

When we first embarked on this endeavor in Missouri's Bootheel region, our intention was to write a book about the Mississippi River flood of 2011 and the thoughtless destruction of the African American town of Pinhook, located in the Birds Point–New Madrid Floodway. We wanted to document what had happened and why. We presumed also that our work would follow the displaced Pinhook residents as they applied for funding and began the slow, but hopeful, process of rebuilding their town. We pledged to stand with them in their claim that the government had, in fact, destroyed their town, and that it should make good on the promise of funding for relocation and rebuilding Pinhook. Similarly, when we began the filming that would become our documentary film, *Taking Pinhook*, we hoped the final scenes would be filled with images of people with hammers building houses. In 2012, these outcomes seemed to be a possibility, although we all had our doubts about what might actually happen. Since those first few months of fieldwork in southern Missouri, we have come to understand much more about the racial politics in Missouri's Bootheel region and have recognized how race may have factored into the decision to flood the spillway and why destroying the town of Pinhook was not seen as problematic for government officials who made that call.

Missouri's Bootheel region, particularly the counties that were flooded (Mississippi, Pemiscot, Dunklin, New Madrid, Stoddard, and parts of other contiguous counties), has a reputation for being an underserved and under-resourced region with high levels of poverty and unemployment. Yet, we were taken aback by what Judge Stephen N. Limbaugh said to us when we asked him whether or not the existence of a town called Pinhook had been discussed during the deliberations on whether the Corps could breach the levee. Self-possessed and utterly confident, he flipped through the hundreds of pages of court documentation, while assuring us, "Yes, yes, there was a little bit of testimony about that area—yeah, they had a couple of landowners testify. … Yeah, Yeah, I'm sure it was. Yeah." Yet, just minutes before, he had made statements that seemed to dismiss the Bootheel as insignificant. He told us that the Bootheel was still "a feudal society." For emphasis, he reiterated, "That's how it is. It's a fact."

The Bootheel is largely a poor, rural region with little or no industry beyond agriculture and no towns larger than Sikeston, which boasted a population of 16,494 in 2013. Mississippi County, where Pinhook was located, has one of the largest populations of African Americans in

David Todd Lawrence and Elaine J. Lawless, "Conclusion: The Power of Hope Through Community," *When They Blew the Levee: Race, Politics, and Community in Pinhook, Missouri*, pp. 163-172, 180-181, 183-188.

the state and is also one of the poorest. Given the definition of a "feudal society," we wondered just what the judge meant with his remark. Certainly, at one time, his reference might have suggested a hierarchical social strata with (white) landowners as the "lords" and the (African American) farmworkers as "vassals" or "serfs." In 2013, when we interviewed him, his remark suggested, instead, a commonly-held negative stereotype about the Bootheel and the people who live there. For some who disparage the region as backward and of little value, there may be a generalized opinion that the rural poor in this region fit what historian Marc Lamont Hill has recently characterized as "nobodies," those who are systematically disadvantaged, particularly black and brown people who are regarded in this country as persons who can easily be ignored if they are seen as not worthy of attention or regard (Hill).

Most certainly, the judge's remark suggests that he did not know anything about the black farmers of Pinhook who owned and operated their own land in the Bootheel and had done so for over seventy years. Even though Pinhook has been clearly marked on Missouri state maps for more than fifty years, we may assume the judge had no knowledge of the actual community of Pinhook, a town complete with well-groomed yards and houses, a stately church and community center, streets marked with standard street signs, and carefully tended, productive fields. Perhaps the Army Corps of Engineers did not know anything about this town either, or they might not have been so quick to destroy what the Pinhook farmers had developed in the Bootheel. On the other hand, perhaps they would not have cared to know the facts about Pinhook and might have proceeded with the breach and the intentional flooding regardless. The result was basically the same: ignore the town and the residents who lived there; flood it, and it disappears. The implication being: those people down there are, after all, "nobodies."

A wide variety of factors related to race and class were put into play even before the 1940s, continued to affect the Pinhook community up until the breach in 2011, and persist to this day. We have attempted to articulate some of the reasons the folks residing in this rural town were virtually invisible to those making decisions about the raging Mississippi River in 2011. Ignorance and incorrect assumptions about those living in the spillway worked in tandem to make it possible for the Army Corps and the legal and regional emergency agencies involved to ignore Pinhook residents and to refuse to include them in the discussions prior to the breach, to assist them in their evacuation and temporary housing, and, then, to provide the appropriate assistance for funding and restitution following the breach. Exactly what did happen to the Pinhook community immediately after the flooding, and for years following, has become a way of life for the displaced people—a life of one crushing disappointment after another.

* * *

Only days after the flood, the assessment of the damage done was acknowledged as severe and worthy of federal funding for restitution. Kay Phillips, FEMA Individual Assistance Specialist, speaking after the flood, assured those who had been displaced that help was available to them.

> I think the devastation here was terrible. I find that the extent of the damage to be such that folks will have to make a pretty serious decision as to whether or not they want to try to rebuild in Pinhook and be in compliance with National Flood Insurance requirements which requires elevations that they will have to verify with their local flood plain manager or make the decision to try and relocate the entire community of Pinhook as a whole and rebuild the community. After a flooding disaster, residents may get help relocating to safer ground through the Hazard Mitigation

> Grant Program, a FEMA-funded program administered by the State.[1]

Immediately, upon hearing this assessment, the displaced residents of Pinhook began the arduous task of filling out applications for block grants for restitution and funding to rebuild their town. Debra Robinson-Tarver, with the help of other displaced Pinhook residents, filled out mountains of paperwork, filed and refilled, revised and resubmitted hundreds of pages of grants for funding from FEMA. At first, they assumed they would be able to rebuild their homes on the original site of their town. Rather quickly, however, the Corps informed the citizens that because their town was located within the spillway, future flooding would likely destroy the town again. In addition, rebuilt structures would have to adhere to National Flood Insurance regulations, meaning they would all need to be elevated on twelve- to fifteen-foot stilts. As Aretha Robinson and George Williams both pointed out to us, building their houses on stilts was not a feasible plan for the townspeople. It seemed a ludicrous plan to them, one strategically engineered to fail. Their frustrations grew.

One year went by, then two, three, four, five, six, and now, seven years have passed.

Sometime in late 2014, we were informed by Debra Robinson-Tarver that FEMA had agreed to offer a buyout for the land owned by the Pinhook former residents. FEMA would work with them to rebuild some of their homes, she had been told, on land that was not within the spillway. While they were pleased to hear that FEMA was finally willing to talk about a buyout for their land in Pinhook, Debra described to us how devastating this proposition was for the Pinhook people. The town, as it sat centered within the fields they farmed together, was the heart of Pinhook. It sealed their community in time, place, and history. Working the fields only yards from their backyards provided a way for the community to work together and maintain their independence and sustain their way of life. Building a new Pinhook miles away from their farmland was another concession they were sad to accept. As if this was not already difficult enough, FEMA put the responsibility for locating possible town sites on the Pinhook residents themselves.

The demands were clear: find a place to rebuild and maybe we will provide the funding for a buyout. What ensued were months and years of heartbreaking negotiations. Debra and her people followed ads, contacted landowners, pleaded with those they knew to help them locate land they could buy—land that would meet all the funding criteria, which included enough acreage for the entire town, plots for each former resident who wanted to rebuild a house—land that would already have all necessary and legal water, sewer, and electricity requirements. At least twice, perhaps three times, they identified a plot of land that fit most of the FEMA requirements, but problems asserted themselves almost immediately. It was difficult for them to learn that area neighbors did not want to sell to African Americans intent upon building a town in their midst. This happened more than once. Eventually, other plots of land were identified, but FEMA found problems with each plot that was suggested—requirements were not appropriately in place, no electricity lines, inadequate water supply, inappropriate sewer, the list went on and on. More than once, we were notified that "big news" was coming, yet within weeks Debra would let us know the plans had fallen through once again.

* * *

We were cautiously surprised to get a phone call from Debra Robinson-Tarver in late July 2016, informing us that some of the Pinhook community members were poised to buy plots of land on the outskirts of Charleston, Missouri, just a few miles from the original Pinhook site. She told us a plot of land had met with the approval of FEMA as an appropriate site for the relocation of their town. On land provided by a possible community development block grant, she explained, some Pinhook residents were making plans to build new homes with the help of area organizations who had already pledged their assistance, including the Mennonite Disaster Service, Church World Service,[2] and other religious and social groups.

We were eager with new questions. Which of the former residents were buying the land and building new homes? How much land had been made available? How much money was FEMA pledging for the project? As she had done so many times before, Debra was reluctant to share many details with us. Certainly, she was happy to let us know her good news—that the funding would be coming through! Yet, the more we plied her with questions, the less we seemed to learn. A few weeks later, we still did not have very many details, but that was typical of our dealings with the Pinhook community. They wanted us to share their good news, but they had learned to temper their excitement because of promises broken, plans undone, and government officials not coming through. With the blatant discrimination and disregard this community has endured for nearly a century, it is no surprise they were less than eager to spill all the still precarious details. Perhaps it was superstition; more likely it was caution bred by past experience, disappointment, and rejection.

While we sensed Debra was truly hopeful that this time this opportunity would be approved, we were hesitant to believe this long-awaited conclusion to their story was actually going to happen. To our dismay, we turned out to be correct. The city of Charleston proved an unwilling partner with the people of Pinhook, voting not to extend city services to the potential parcel of land Pinhook residents wanted to purchase. Connecting the land to necessary utilities without the city annexing the property would have been too expensive for the Pinhook residents and thus, the deal fell through. Residents found another potential plot of land near another small town in Missouri later in the year, but that deal fell through as well. After years of endless, frustrating work, the displaced residents were no better off than they were when we first met them.

The Power of Community

In our time working with the displaced residents of Pinhook, we have learned valuable lessons about institutional injustice, discrimination, disregard and ignorance. None of this has actually surprised us. The state of racial tension and unrest in our country at the present time reminds us that the injustices experienced by the displaced African American residents of Pinhook are part of a larger system and not an isolated incident. On the other hand, we have learned even more in the past several years about community solidarity, persistence, and the power of struggle by documenting the actions of our Pinhook collaborators. It is the fact of their strength and perseverance in the face of institutional opposition that has actually surprised us.

Our attempts to understand the Pinhook community's frame of mind, as perhaps different from our own (as outsiders), have guided us to develop a theory of hope for racial justice that relies not so much on institutional commitments to justice for all, but one that hinges more upon the potential power that stems from community stability, traditions, resilience, and agency. Our reading of the counter-narrative of Pinhook, recounted to us through the stories of this community's experiences, resists critical race theory (CRT) founder Derrick Bell's famous image of people of color as those residing "at the bottom of the well," an image that posits vulnerable populations as powerless victims. While Bell admits that "our actions" against racism and injustice may be "of more help to the system we despise than to the victims of that systems whom we are trying to help" (198–199), he maintains that we must all let down our "ropes" to help each other, because "Only by working together is escape [from injustice] possible" (*The Derrick Bell Reader* 311). Such an approach to justice through community solidarity and action would not preclude our helping the people of Pinhook, and certainly it does not suggest that people of color should continue to struggle on their own without aid from others, but it does suggest that hope may best be realized when a community stands in its own power and demands justice, even while working within the very institutions that operate to limit its power and keep it from succeeding. As Bell explains, African American history itself is "a story less of success than of survival through an unremitting struggle that leaves no room for giving up" (*Faces at the Bottom of the Well* 200). The survival of Pinhook is certainly a part of that story.

Our admiration for this dedicated community of African Americans confirms what those writing within critical race theory have come to recognize—that the unified struggle is what is important and that even small victories won through solidarity can change the face of racial and social justice in the United States. The kind of solidarity and agency we have seen in the efforts of the Pinhook community affirm that despair does not have to prevail. Bell reminds us that,

> The civil rights movement is, after all, much more than the totality of the judicial decisions, the antidiscrimination laws, and the changes in racial relationships reflected in those legal milestones. *The movement is a spiritual manifestation of the continuing faith of a people who have never truly gained their rights in a nation committed by its basic law to the freedom of all.* (*And Are We Not Saved* xi, emphasis added)

Bell identified the civil rights movement as a "phenomenon of rights gained, then lost, then gained again—a phenomenon that continues to surprise even though the cyclical experience of blacks in this country predates the Constitution by more than one hundred years" (*And We Are Not Saved* xi). His encouragement to fight the good fight follows from the questions that must be asked: "With the realization that the salvation of racial equality has eluded us again, questions arise from the ashes of our expectations: How have we failed—and why? What does this failure mean—for Black people and for whites? Where do we go from here? Should we redirect the quest for racial justice?" (*And We Are Not Saved* 3). Bell, with Marc Lamont Hill and other CRT scholars, admits many people are currently asking these questions without offering solutions. While we recognize it is depressing to understand that full racial equality may not be realized in our time, those in the movement assure us that "tangible progress *has been made*" (*And We Are Not Saved* 5). Nearly hidden in his discussion of the struggle for justice, Bell's most hopeful line remains more a murmur than a shout from the rooftops: "The pull of unfinished business is sufficient to strengthen and spur determination" (*And We Are Not Saved* 5). There is much unfinished business in the Missouri Bootheel.

Debra Robinson-Tarver claims she has the best lawyer anyone could possibly have and there is no way to pay him except to trust that by standing together the Pinhook community will prevail. Debra has relied on the strength of her community and her belief in God to right the wrongs that have been perpetrated against her people. And she has been consistent in her belief that truth and justice will prevail. Her generosity of spirit has prevented her from bitterness and public recriminations. Indeed, no other than Dr. Martin Luther King noted that his "adversaries expected him to harden into a grim and desperate man" (330). When that did not happen, he identified the opposition's failure as its inability "to perceive the sense of affirmation generated by the challenge of embracing struggle and surmounting obstacles" (330). Seen in this light, the struggle of the Pinhook community has been both courageous and victorious, at least to a point, and it continues to be a struggle based on hope and confidence, strength and passion, largely because they have relied on community. They have rallied in the face of terrible odds; they have faced down powerful cultural and governmental institutions without rancor; and they have relied on their faith in each other and their faith in God to get them through.

For the past seven years, we have watched the displaced people of Pinhook hold to their dignity in the face of extreme difficulties. When they are called to speak in public about their situation, they respond in measured tones, unless they crumple in tears as Twan once did at a hearing. They are slow to anger and resist becoming strident, and they reject the invitation to be perceived as helpless victims. We sincerely hope our book honors their accomplishments and dedication to their community and their shared traditions, strengths, and faith. Even Marc Hill ends his rather depressing history of how African Americans have been, and continue to be, devalued in American life on a note of hope: "The People have asserted that they are, in fact, Somebody. In doing so, they offer hope that another world is indeed possible, that empires eventually fall, and that freedom is closer than we think" (184).

* * *

This case study of one African American town's plight in the face of what we are calling persistent discrimination, indifference, disregard, and environmental racism may not help prevent a repeat scenario anytime in the future, but we are committed to documenting injustices where they occur, to naming the offenders and the offences, and to take a stand that openly rejects all actions that suggest that some communities of American citizens are "less-than" others and therefore not eligible for the government's very best efforts at protection and assistance for their bodily safety, their happiness, and their preferred way of life. By exposing what happened to Pinhook, Missouri, and by highlighting the difficulties displaced residents continue to have in their efforts to rebuild their town, our intention is to keep governmental institutions responsible to all citizens, regardless of race, creed, class, or nationality. If people know the on-the-ground story of what happened to Pinhook, that story can be evaluated alongside the published stories propagated by the institutions with the most power. The voices of the displaced Pinhook residents in this book resonate with the truth that people of color matter, their lives matter, their experiences, and their stories, matter. Ethnographers such as ourselves are obligated to expose injustices and call for their restitution by publishing the counter-narratives of the people with whom we collaborate. We have been honored to hear the counter-narratives of the Pinhook community and share them alongside the public ones endorsed and distributed by the agencies involved. Our intention is to elevate the people's stories to the same narrative plane as that occupied by those in power.

Coda

On June 18 of 2017, Debra texted Todd. "There should be something in the semo paper about

Pinhook today," her brief message read. We had heard from Debra about a community development grant possibly coming through in the few weeks preceding the 18th. Debra had let us know that the possibility for displaced Pinhook residents to be able to relocate and rebuild their town together was growing smaller and smaller. There was still a chance, however, that individual families would finally get money to help them rebuild their houses outside the Birds Point–New Madrid Floodway.

The article in the *Southeast Missourian* Debra told Todd about announced that the state of Missouri had agreed to pay for the rebuilding of homes through a Community Development Grant. An agreement had been reached at a meeting in Charleston. Displaced Pinhook residents could purchase land and rebuild or they could purchase existing houses and renovate them. After seven long years, the people of Pinhook were finally getting something, even if it wasn't what they had been asking for. We, of course, saw this as just another way the government has treated Pinhook residents unjustly. The article in the *Missourian* even suggests that the reason Pinhook could not be relocated is because the residents themselves could not agree on a location. Statements by Missouri Department of Economic Development[3] spokesperson Amy Susan quoted in the article sound as if no one is responsible, as if things just didn't work out. The agreement residents would have had to come to to relocate the town "was never reached" (Bliss). This explanation flies in the face of everything we have been told by Debra in our ongoing communications with her.

Once again, it seems, the residents of Pinhook, a community of people we have come to admire and respect so much, have gotten a raw deal. They will get their money, but they will get it seven years too late. Some may be able to rebuild their houses, but they may not be able to do it together. Worse, the government will claim credit for providing this assistance to Pinhook even while it has never admitted its culpability in the town's destruction. As we have argued from the beginning of this book, what happened to the people of Pinhook was an entirely preventable disaster, one that was done by the hands of powerful entities unwilling to see the pain they would cause or right the wrong once they'd done it.

The people of Pinhook have shown us, however, that they will survive the injustice that has been done to them. They are an amazing community of people. And though we may never witness the triumphant reconstruction of Pinhook done nail by nail and plank by plank, maybe we have already seen something even more inspiring: how a community called Pinhook endured and survived when they blew the levee.

Notes

1. This quote was taken from a FEMA video of a question and answer session that happened in Charleston, Missouri, on June 7, 2011, just over a month after the levee breach. The video was posted on the FEMA.gov website for some time, but currently we can no longer locate the video or the excerpted transcribed comments which also appeared on the FEMA. gov website. A still photo of Kay Phillips and Pinhook resident Rosetta Bradley still exists on the site and on the National Archives website. It can be accessed at: https://www.fema.gov/ar/media-library/assets/images/59430.
2. We were always told by Debra that Church World Service, an international assistance organization, had committed to help with the rebuilding of residents' houses from almost

the very beginning. In fact, we met with and interviewed Barry Shade, a CWS representative, who was present at Pinhook Day the first time we attended in 2012. Church World Service was one of a number of agencies that had committed to help Pinhook with supplies or labor over the years. Their offers of assistance depended, though, on Debra and her fellow Pinhook residents securing land and being granted funding.

3 When we talked to Debra over the years about her efforts to secure financial assistance for the displaced residents of Pinhook to relocate and rebuild their town, she almost always referred to FEMA as the agency involved. The Community Development grant that will pay for Pinhook residents to individually rebuild their houses or buy new ones is being administered by the Missouri Department of Economic Development and the Bootheel Regional Planning Commission. Both are state agencies that sometimes work in partnership with FEMA. We have used FEMA in the book to refer generically to any agency responsible to the displaced residents of Pinhook largely because that is the way they themselves represented those agencies—county, state, or federal.

Bibliography

Bell, Derrick. *And We Are Not Saved: The Elusive Quest for Racial Justice.* New York: Basic Books, 1987.

———. *Faces From the Bottom of the Well: The Permanence of Racism.* New York: Basic Books, 1992.

———. *The Derrick Bell Reader.* Edited by Richard Delgado and Jean Stefancic. New York City: NYU Press, 2005. Print

Bliss, Mark. "Pinhook Reclaimed: State Grants Set to Help Former Village Residents Relocate." *Southeast Missourian*, 18 June 2017. Web. 18 June 2017.

Hill, Marc Lamont. *Nobody: Casualties of America's War on the Vulnerable, From Ferguson to Flint and Beyond.* New York: Atria Books, 2016.

King, Martin Luther. *A Testament of Hope: The Essential Writings and Speeches of Martin Luther King, Jr.* Edited by James Washington. New York City: Harper Collins Publishers, 1986.

Limbaugh, Stephen N. Personal Interview. 23 May 2013.

■ CHAPTER 6

The Symbolism of Big Technology and Political Power

Editor's Introduction

This chapter describes the symbolism of big technology within the context of power, wealth, and political authority. Josephson begins by examining symbols of state power in the medieval ruling elite. The author then describes the monumental skyscrapers constructed in the Soviet Union under Joseph Stalin. At the same time, the citizens of the Soviet Union lived in disadvantaged circumstances as a result of World War II. This example compares the monumentalism and power in physical structures to the power of the state, modernity, and national destiny. Furthermore, the example demonstrates how authoritarian regimes can use large-scale technology to reinforce power and create distraction. The United States has also recognized the ideological role of large-scale technologies, such as in the case of the Space Race. This reality raises the following questions: What is big technology's ideological significance for nation and state? Why did we choose the moon's conquest as our goal during the Cold War era? How do a country's achievements in big technology distract citizen attention from social and political problems?

READING 6 Big Artifacts: Technological Symbolism and State Power

Paul R. Josephson

Technologies of state power obviously include offensive and defensive weapons. Almost everyone is familiar with fighter jets and bombers; destroyers and aircraft carriers; and rockets. Yet even before the twentieth century, big technology served as a symbol of state power, wealth, political authority, or a combination of the three. In medieval towns, cathedrals, then clocks, were signs of prosperity that were visible from the surrounding countryside. The cathedral, a magnificent achievement of geometry, strength of materials, and construction know-how, was the house of God and confirmation of the infinite goodness of the church, a center of civic pride, a destination for pilgrimage, and a place to display artifacts. Gothic architecture represented the authority of the medieval ruling elite, their power, wealth, and proximity to God, and was intended to suggest the awe and admiration of citizens.[1] The clock tower indicated prosperity, perhaps yet to come. In the nineteenth century technological expositions celebrated the joining of state and economic power. The "Great Exhibition of the Works of Industry of all Nations," often referred to as the Crystal Palace Exhibition, held in Hyde Park, London, in 1851, catalogued the achievements of mercantilistic European powers, while the 1876 Centennial Exposition in Philadelphia celebrated not only the Declaration of Independence but "Arts, Manufactures and Products of the Soil and Mine."[2] These expositions demonstrated, in the minds of their promoters and those of the throngs of curious crowds, the epitome of advanced civilization, the power of its industry, and the legitimacy of the political regimes that created such things.

Large-scale technological systems became paradigmatic in the twentieth century as symbols of state power. The monumentalism of the National Socialist Third Reich was intended to demonstrate the racial superiority of the nation and its unassailable power in physical structures that would last a thousand years. Adolf Hitler's architect, Albert Speer, designed parade grounds for Nuremburg spread over 16 square kilometers that, although never built, included a stadium for 400,000 people. Joseph Stalin ordered seven major skyscrapers built around Moscow in the late 1940s to confirm the glory of his rule while people still lived in rubble left from the World War. In 1948 he approved the Stalinist Plan for the Transformation of Nature to subjugate nature itself to Stalinist grandeur through canals, hydroelectric power stations, multimillion-hectare irrigation systems, and forest defense belts. Brasilia in the center of Amazonia, built under President Juscelino Kubitschek, a man of planning and development in the late 1950s, served as a symbol of technocratic rule and was intended to indicate the power of the state to open the nation's rich interior to exploitation, modernity, national destiny in the hinterlands, and freedom from colonial past.[3]

Not only authoritarian regimes have recognized the ideological role of large-scale technologies. On May 25, 1961, President John F. Kennedy addressed a joint session of the US Congress calling for a very expensive and risky effort to put a man on the moon. He said, "[The moon's] conquest deserves the best of all mankind, and its opportunity for peaceful cooperation may never come again. But why, some say, the moon? Why choose this as our goal?

Paul R. Josephson, "Big Artifacts: Technological Symbolism and State Power," ***Fish Sticks, Sports Bras, and Aluminum Cans: The Politics of Everyday Technologies***, pp. 139-162, 196-202.

And they may well ask why climb the highest mountain? Why, 35 years ago, fly the Atlantic? ... We choose to go to the moon in this decade and do the other things, not because they are easy, but because they are hard, because that goal will serve to organize and measure the best of our energies and skills, because that challenge is one that we are willing to accept, one we are unwilling to postpone, and one which we intend to win, and the others, too." [4]

The genesis of large-scale technological systems in the complex interaction of economic, cultural, and political forces has been studied extensively.[5] Their ideological significance for nation and state also has served as the focus of analysis, for example, of the development of atomic energy in postwar France or the space race in the United States, the USSR, and in Europe.[6] Whether big technology is the most efficient way to accomplish some specific end has provoked debate. Achievements in big technology distract attention and budgets from social and political problems at the same time as they engender national pride. Yet most leaders, engineers, and citizens unquestioningly embrace big technology for economic, military, and other purposes, and as icons of national achievement—in the form of modern highways in Germany or the United States, hydroelectric power stations in India and Brazil, rockets and nuclear weapons for North Korea, and the industrial transformation in China.[7] This ideological significance might be called the "display value" of technology, that is, its cultural meaning beyond its technical importance.[8]

Not surprisingly, the government of the Russian Federation under President Vladimir Putin determined early in the twenty-first century to allocate extensive resources to large-scale technologies to shore up the nation's image and self-understanding as a superpower following the psychological shock of the breakup of the USSR. In addition to the military and economic benefits of big technology which Putin and his advisers underline, including annexation of Ukrainian territory in 2014 and reestablishment of army bases in extreme northern latitudes, they recognize the display value of these technologies to secure Russia's place among the leading scientific powers of the world and channel the thinking of the citizenry away from concerns about the present and political dissent and toward feelings of love for the motherland. Combined with state-sponsored programs to develop natural and mineral resources (timber, oil, gas, nickel, platinum, copper, and so on), Putin believes that big technologies indicate the success of his rule and provide the justification for tightening political power over any remaining opposition.

What is surprising is the similarity in the rhetoric surrounding Putin's various programs with those of the Stalin era, and even Putin's unabashedly direct reference to Stalinist programs and approaches to justify investment in the Great Northern Sea Route and Arctic conquest; the military-industrial complex, space, and jets; nuclear power; a kind of Kremlin silicon valley; and even skyscrapers and other extravagant displays of state power, many of whose roots date to the Stalin period.[9] What has been the role of big technology under Stalin and Putin?

Harkening to the Past: The Great Northern Sea Route

In the 1930s Joseph Stalin provided extensive financial resources, personnel, and such new technologies as modern icebreakers to underwrite the effort to secure the Soviet Arctic from Murmansk on the Barents Sea near Norway to Vladivostok in the Pacific Ocean. Scientists, engineers, and explorers journeyed northward at great personal risk, but in their widely published memoirs and public appearances noted their belief that Stalin personally was looking out for them.[10] Like cosmonauts and astronauts decades later, heroic pilots flew a series of bold missions—in this case over the North Pole—to demonstrate Soviet prowess.[11] Explorers wintered on the Arctic ice and studied ice regime, ocean currents, and water chemistry. Communist Party officials worked with leading specialists to establish an entire Arctic empire bureaucracy: the Main Administration for the Northern Sea Route responsible for Arctic economic development whose rapid growth accompanied ambitious national industrialization and militarization programs under the first five-year plans (1929–1941).

Powerful new icebreakers were the essential tool. With them, the "industrialization of the north" would follow. On the eve of the revolution, the Russians had some twenty icebreaking and ice-strengthened vessels operating in Arctic waters. Until the 1930s most of the Russian and Soviet icebreakers that came from British or other European shipyards were underpowered, and it was difficult to get parts for them. By the late 1920s the shipbuilding industry had recovered sufficiently to embark on modernization. They built motorboats for rivers, military vessels, lighters, freighters and icebreakers, although many vessels relied on coal power, which presented serious logistical problems.[12] The technological lag on the Northern Sea Route created significant challenges. Because of growing recognition of the limits of the fleet, in the mid-1930s the Soviet government determined to build new, more powerful icebreakers. Of course, the first ship to be launched was the *Joseph Stalin* in 1938, although two years later than planned. The Ordzhonikidze Shipbuilding Factory in Leningrad launched four ships of the "Stalin" class with length, about 107 m; breadth, 23 m; draft, 9.2 m; displacement, 11,200 tons; speed, 15.3 knots. They could navigate through ice almost 1.0 m thick.[13] In the postwar years, the USSR maintained its lead in and expanded on icebreaker technology with larger vessels, and eventually with nuclear-powered ships.

Stretching roughly halfway around the world, the Russian Arctic covers nine time zones from Norway to the Bering Strait. Approximately one-fifth of the Russian landmass is north of the Arctic Circle. Of 14 million square kilometers that comprise the entire Arctic region (along with the landmass of Canada, the Scandinavian countries, and the United States), Russia's share is roughly 3.5 million square kilometers, one-quarter of the total. (Canada has the largest arctic landmass.) Like Lenin and the early Bolsheviks who saw the Arctic in strategic terms, and after Allied intervention in World War I worried about invasion, Vladimir Putin saw these vast Arctic spaces through military and economic lenses. In a manner reminiscent of the Stalinist 1930s in terms of economic importance, hubristic plans, political legitimacy, and even his rhetoric, Putin reenergized Arctic exploration. Welcoming global warming as an opportunity to develop oil, gas, and other resources, his officials and Russian specialists saw the expansion of the Northern Sea Route as a key to the nation's future. Russia's industrial policy of pushing economic growth on the basis of extraction of raw materials was central to Putin's worldview. He has long believed the development of natural resources was crucial to economic growth and rebuilding Russia's status as a superpower.[14]

Symbolism and rubles have combined to secure the Russian Arctic. Reminiscent of the race between the Soviet Union and the United States to put a man—and flag—on the moon, in August 2007, Russian parliamentarian and explorer Artur Chilingarov engaged in what some observers called a publicity stunt by planting a Russian flag on the bottom of the Arctic

Ocean at the North Pole. The government supported the expensive expedition as part of the Russian contribution to the Third International Polar Year (2007–2008). All of the components of Russia's quest for strategic advantage, economic growth, and superpower symbolism were pre sent. A nuclear-powered ice breaker, *Rossiia*, cleared the way for a research ship, *Akademik Fedorov*, staffed by approximately 130 scientists, to get into position for Chilingarov's descent. President Putin welcomed Chilingarov's flag-planting expedition as confirmation of Russia's claim of the Lomonosov Ridge to extend its exclusive economic zone toward the North Pole and several vast oil and mineral deposits. Putin noted that Russia's distinguished history was closely linked to Arctic exploration. Tying these Russian efforts to the great power status of the USSR, he referred to Soviet efforts to build major facilities and cities in circumpolar regions and to the Northern Sea Route in the 1930s.[15]

Russian lawmakers, following the lead of the administration, passed legislation that emphasized Russian sovereignty, underlined the crucial economic importance of Arctic resources, and celebrated the symbolic significance of the northern sea route for Russia's great power aspirations in the twenty-first century. According to a 2001 bill that established Russian Maritime Policy through 2020, Russia reasonably asserted "sovereign rights in the exclusive economic zone for exploration." The policy referred to "the increasing importance of the Northern Sea Route for sustainable development of the Russian Federation." Maritime policy established such long-term objectives as "research and development of the Arctic to the development of export-oriented economic sectors, priority social problems," and "the creation of ice-class vessels for shipping, specialized vessels for fishing, research and other specialized fleets," all toward the ends of state defense and resource development.[16] The Russian Federation would invest billions of rubles to develop gas, oil, apatite concentrate, and many strategically significant nonferrous and precious metals (nickel, copper, cobalt, among others) through state and state-private ventures, with funding for infrastructure, military bases, and occasionally housing.[17]

As it had for Joseph Stalin, the 5,000-kilometer Northern Sea Route from Murmansk to Vladivostok along the Arctic Circle assumed mythic scale for twenty-first-century Russian leaders. In June 2010, then President Dimitrii Medvedev called for the modernization of both military and civilian shipbuilding to enable Russia to engage in the "recently toughening competition for Arctic resources."[18] On May 12, 2012, Putin issued an executive order about the need to modernize Russia's military-industrial complex. He referred without irony to the Stalinist legacy of building military industry in the 1930s with his instructions for "developing the Navy, first and foremost in the Arctic areas and in Russia's Far East with the aim of protecting the Russian Federation's strategic interests."[19] Stalin had developed the Arctic and Soviet industry far and wide. But at what costs? Were the dubious achievements of Stalin in building a military power in the 1930s worth the murder of half of the Red Army officer corps—50,000 men—arrested and executed at Stalin's orders? The creation of the Gulag labor camps and the millions of innocent citizens who toiled—and perished—in them? The 3 million Ukrainian peasants who starved during the collectivization campaign? The poorly functioning economy, especially its poor innovative capacities?

For Putin, however, the big science and technology of airplanes, satellites, drifting ice research stations, and, crucially, icebreakers, including a third generation of nuclear icebreakers, were key to controlling the Arctic. Russian shipbuilders, administrators, and officials evinced great nostalgia for the Soviet Union which created the world's greatest icebreaker fleet. Russia remains the only country to operate civilian nuclear-powered icebreakers, although the icebreaker fleet has aged considerably, and a number of vessels have reached the end of their service lives. Hence Russians of the Soviet generation reminisce about the *Lenin* icebreaker that was launched in December 1957 and sailed on its first mission in September 1959. In the celebratory exposés of the glorious Soviet heritage, contemporary journalists never mention the dangers involved in the rapid, and perhaps premature, embrace of nuclear icebreakers, but instead emphasize that Russians are a full quarter century ahead of the other nations. At the end of the 1950s "we left the Americans behind and first built a nuclear icebreaker," the chief engineer of the *Lenin* atomic icebreaker recently recalled,[20] ignoring the fact that the *Lenin* had two serious accidents in 1965 and 1967, both of which released significant amounts of radioactivity and led to illegal dumping of wastes and reactors at sea.[21]

On August 17, 2012, the nation observed the twenty-fifth anniversary of the sailing of the icebreaker *Arktika* to the North Pole, the world's first surface vessel to do this. The feat celebrated the Soviet subjugation of the Arctic.[22] *Arktika*, a second-generation nuclear icebreaker, was nostalgically retired on October 3, 2008, after thirty-six years of service. It was the fifth of five nuclear icebreakers built at the Baltic Shipbuilding Yards.[23] The others have reached the end of their service, while construction on the most recent addition to the fleet, the *Fiftieth Anniversary of Victory*, a commemoration of Soviet victory in World War II, commenced in the Soviet era, but the ship was not put to sea until 2007 after twenty years of construction owing to extensive construction problems, including a serious fire.[24]

Russian leaders showed only determination to recapture the ideological glories of the Soviet icebreaker. Russia will spend 37 billion rubles (roughly $1 billion) on its next atomic icebreaker according to a contract signed between the Baltic Shipbuilding Factory and Rosatomflot, a subdivision of the Russian nuclear ministry, Rosatom. The new icebreaker has the name *Arktika*, which determines its class (size) and historical tie to the past.[25] Andrei Smirnov, the deputy director of Rosatomflot, Russia's civilian nuclear fleet company, argued that icebreakers will give impetus to exploitation of difficult-to-extract fossil fuels, will enable a five-or sixfold increase in shipping along the Northern Sea Route, and called for an entirely new icebreaker fleet. Icebreakers make not only economic sense: Smirnov pointed out that traveling from Kamchatka to Murmansk takes but 7 days, whereas through the Suez Canal it would take 20 or 25 days, and while the northern latitudes had ice, the southern had something more dangerous—pirates—and pirates "cannot exist in the Arctic in principle: they will freeze."[26]

Technological Utopianism: The Rosatom Nuclear Renaissance

Nuclear power, both peaceful and military, is a more modern technology than the icebreaker with the full essence of superpower status. From the 1940s it served as the engine of the Cold War as the United States and the Soviet Union raced to build tens of thousands of the immoral weapons of mass destruction, joined by England, France, China, and later other nations. They also built nuclear-powered submarines and aircraft carriers, and experimented with nuclear airplanes, rockets, and even locomotives. Since the early 1950s, and President Dwight D. Eisenhower's "Atoms for Peace" speech at the United Nations (1953), it was also a source of propaganda competition as the Soviets and Americans, and later other nations, sought to apply the energy of the atom to industrial, agricultural, medical, and especially energy production purposes in massive nuclear reactors. In the embrace of the peaceful atom, nations of the world touted nearly unlimited energy, in fact "electricity too cheap to meter." The attitudes about cheap energy, declining capital costs for construction, and inherent safety of reactors permeated the thoughts of nuclear engineers throughout the world, including in Soviet Russia, where utopian beliefs about the present and future of nuclear power persist, although the record of peaceful—and military—programs is a frightening reminder of the dangers of elevating symbolism above reality.[27]

At the June 2012 AtomExpo exposition in Moscow, representatives of more than two dozen different nuclear companies, all of which grew out of the Soviet Ministry of Middle Machine Building (Minsredmash), met with potential customers to pursue expansion of nuclear sales. While a number of the companies are connected with operations in Kazakhstan and other former Soviet republics, the vast majority were located in Russia, a fact that reflected the resurgence of nuclear power in the twenty-first century under the leadership of Rosatom (the powerful Russian nuclear ministry). According to Rosatom, the industry is gearing up to bring the peaceful atom to overseas markets.[28]

Ten years ago, as part of state-building of the first Putin presidency, the federal government embraced a crash construction program for nuclear power stations as a symbol of Russia's status as a scientific superpower. At that time this was a dream since the industry was in decay. In the fifteen years since Chernobyl, Russia's nuclear establishment had fallen on hard times and reactor construction lagged. The public remained skeptical of nuclear power; a series of exposés filled the newspapers about past accidents and close calls, not to mention the grotesqueries of haphazard waste disposal that spoiled hundreds of square kilometers of land, especially in the Urals region with great and continuing public health costs.[29]

But Putin and Rosatom officials were determined to pursue a self-proclaimed nuclear "renaissance." Rosatom, a quasi-state corporation, operates thirty-two nuclear power reactors (versus 58 in France and 103 in the United States) with the overall installed capacity of 24.2 GW (gigawatts) at ten power stations. In 2014 they accounted for roughly 16 percent of domestic electricity generation, but were concentrated in western Russia. The share of nuclear generation in the European part of the country reached 30 percent, and in the northwest part of the country it reached 37 percent. A subsidiary of Rosatom, Rosenergoatom, is Europe's second largest utility after the French EDF. Nuclear specialists at the Kurchatov Institute for Atomic Energy, where pressurized water reactors (PWRs, in Russian parlance "VVER") and channel-graphite reactors (the Chernobyl-type RBMK) were designed decades ago, forecast 50–60 GW of installed capacity by 2030, that is, the construction and operation of at least 25 new 1,000-MW new reactors over the next eighteen years, a pace of construction, testing, licensing, and power generation never before accomplished in the world. Anything is possible given that the contemporary Russian nuclear industry constitutes a powerful complex of over 250 enterprises and organizations employing more than 250,000 people—three times the number in France. Nuclear power engineering thus resumed its role as a crucial engine of the Russian economy, a sign of energy independence and sales abroad, and of geopolitical virility.[30]

A great deal of continuity exists between Soviet and Russian nuclear programs, even twenty years after the collapse of the USSR. First, while acknowledging at times the high capital costs per kilowatt hour installed capacity, Soviet and Russian engineers claimed that nuclear power was the only alternative to fossil fuels. If not "too cheap to meter," as the world physics community claimed in the 1950s, then nuclear power, which avoids green house gases, will serve modern industrial society into the twenty-second century when peak oil and gas are part of the past.

Second, engineers have long had dreams of adopting standardized designs for reactors as a way to keep costs down, relying ultimately on "serial production" of reactor components, vessels, and plant facilities. According to their thinking, this would also help quality control in the field and lessen the chance of worker error. The French example provided hope; France produces nearly 80 percent of its electricity from standardized PWRs. Yet at each stage, French specialists have had to introduce safety modifications. The price has risen steadily to $6 billion per nuclear power station, and time horizons for construction have hardly diminished from ten years per reactor. Yet Rosatom specialists, like Minsredmash engineers before them, remain convinced that serial reactor production will succeed and costs will drop significantly, with Russia soon building two, three, even four reactors annually, and at costs significantly lower than those in France.

Builders in the Soviet Union never lacked enthusiasm for large projects, nor was it challenging to gain support for them. From Stalin's canals, metallurgical combines, and entire mining cities, built in part with gulag slave labor, and his grandiose 1948 Plan for the Transformation of Nature, also undertaken with slave labor, to Khrushchev's hydroelectric power stations in Siberia and agricultural programs, and to Brezhnev's new trans-Siberian railroad (known by its acronym "BAM"—the Baikal-Amur Magistral), planners, party officials, and managers found it easier to gather workers at huge construction sites, and everyone believed in economies of scale.[31] No surprise, then, that the nuclear industry built a factory, Atommash ("Atomic Machinery") in Volgodonsk on the Volga River in the 1970s to produce annually up to eight pressure vessels and associated equipment serially in a huge foundry à la Henry Ford. Atommash would ship the 1,000 megawatt electric PWRs by barge and railroad to reactor "parks" of up to ten reactors. But rather than maximizing on serial production and low costs, Atommash produced only three reactor vessels in all before a wall of the main foundry building collapsed in the muck. Apparently engineers failed to take into consideration the changed hydrology of soils on the building site brought about by the proximity to the Tsimlianskoe Reservoir.[32] Hubristic engineers have hardly changed since Soviet times; mass production remains the goal in Russia today. Will the engineers remember to carry out accurate surveys and site selection?

In spite of as yet unsolved waste disposal problems connected with the Soviet military and civilian nuclear legacies, Russia continues to embrace a utopian view of nuclear power as a panacea for energy and for geographic and geopolitical concerns. Sergei Kirienko, the head of Rosatom, and other spokesmen have repeatedly referred to a "renaissance" in the industry. According to Kirienko the nuclear renaissance had three components: perfection and modification of existing reactors, development of fast reactors, and eventually the construction of fusion reactors. "Today we have entered the period of large-scale construction of new stations. The problem is to build the entire system in order to put out one new block in one year, and then two [in one year]."[33] Kirienko asserted, not without foundation, that atomic energy had become safer over the previous twenty years as Russia has embraced International Atomic Energy Agency (IAEA) and International Nuclear Event Scale (INES) standards for operation of reactors.[34] Rosatom's public relations operations have become adept at handling public concerns. The annual "Miss Atom" contest seeks to demonstrate a more feminine side of nuclear power; the 2011 winner, Marina Kiriy, was a mother from the Bilibino Station in Chukotka. The station, the northernmost nuclear power plant in the world, well above the Arctic Circle and part of the country's effort to create a nuclear-powered Arctic and to bring a special kind of "fire" to the indigenous Chukchi reindeer and whaling people, consists of four graphite-moderated EPG-6 reactors, related to the RMBK design, each producing 12 MW electric and 62 MW thermal power (heat) that provides 80 percent of the region's electricity.[35]

Igor Kurchatov, father of the Soviet atomic bomb, pursued peaceful programs with vigorous visions of nuclear-powered utopias until his early death in 1960. He and other Soviet delegates astounded the attendees of the first International Conference on the Peaceful Uses of Atomic Energy in Geneva, Switzerland, in 1955, with the presentations on the Soviet peaceful atom, especially the work of Igor Tamm and Andrei Sakharov on controlled thermonuclear synthesis (fusion).[36] At the twentieth Communist Party Congress in Moscow in February 1956, best known for Nikita Khrushchev's speech condemning the murderous excesses of Stalinism, Kurchatov proposed an aggressive program for the commercialization of atomic energy and applications in industry, agriculture, and medicine that have been expanded and adapted to the twenty-first century.[37]

In patterns now being repeated by Rosatom, Soviet engineers gained government support to accelerate the construction of new nuclear power stations in "parks" of PWRs, RBMKs, and breeder reactors. Embracing technological enthusiasm without sufficient consideration of the risks, Soviet nuclear engineers sought to commercialize breeder reactors on the basis of 1,600 MWe units (the BN-1600).[38] Russia remains firmly committed to breeder reactors that have been costly to operate and waylaid by accidents and fires. The Rosatom goal is to bring the BN-800 on line to demonstrate a closed fuel cycle, and to commence serial construction of breeders in the period 2025–2030. The standard reactors will most likely be 800 MW units and located near the Maiak chemical nuclear fuel facility at Cheliabinsk to take advantage of huge plutonium stockpiles.[39] Russian breeders have the endorsement of President Vladimir Putin and the International Atomic Energy Agency because of the closed fuel cycle. On what foundation is unclear, but Putin claimed that fast reactors are "technically quite feasible." Iurii Kazanskii, a physicist involved in the startup of the BN-600 in 1980, called the completion of the BN-800 "a question of the leadership of Russia."[40]

The Northern Sea Route, Arctic gas deposits, and nuclear power have been confidently linked to one of the most troubling technologies to drift from Rosatom Arctic tides—floating nuclear power stations. Based on submarine reactors, and developed in Severodvinsk and other military R & D facilities to maintain high levels of employment in the nuclear shipbuilding industry, floating reactors (and floating nuclear-powered oil platforms still in the design stage) will provide electric energy and heat above the Arctic Circle. To achieve this "maritime" Bilibino, Russia has announced plans to build twelve floating nuclear reactors. The reactors will produce 90 MWe, but could also be designed for desalinization and industrial heat production. Rosatom plans to sell them for $335 million each; China, Algeria, Indonesia, Brazil, and other countries have indicated an interest in the plants. The first floating reactor was planned to be operational by the end of 2013, but apparently will not be operational until late in 2015, and will be moored near Petropavlovsk-Kamchatsky. The region is seismically active, but Kirienko dismissed Fukushima as irrelevant to the Russian experience concerns. He said, "I know Fukushima has sparked many inflammatory rumors and gossip, including on the floating nuclear plant. Some people say that if a ground plant could not withstand a tsunami, what would then happen with a waterborne nuclear plant. But nothing will happen. Everything will be just fine."[41] Everything will be fine, according to the inhabitants of Pevek, in the Arctic Circle, who have apparently welcomed the next floating reactor, whenever it arrives, for its promised heat and electricity.[42] Safety, proliferation, terrorism, tsunamis—all of these things have little place in Rosatom's world when heat and light will be the result.[43]

On March 18, 2010, on a visit to the Volgodonsk nuclear power station to promote the future of the "Russian peaceful atom" and reveal his modern leadership, Putin declared that Russia was prepared to claim one-fourth of the world's reactor market, and not just cap Soviet achievements in the domestic arena. In a distinctly Soviet ceremony, Putin himself pushed the "power" button in the control room and then gave state prizes to "outstanding" atomic workers, perhaps even more outstanding than the "heroes of socialist labor" Communist Party officials celebrated but two decades earlier. He was confident that within a short time frame Rosatom would bring online nearly as many reactors as were built during the entire Soviet period. Putin wistfully referred to the unlimited potential of Russian programs: "We are fully capable of taking no less than 25 percent of the world market in construction and operation of AES."[44]

In all of these ways, pride and technological momentum remain central aspects of the Russian nuclear industry since its founding in the 1950s. Nuclear power serves as a panacea for power production, transportation, and uneven distribution of resources and population. It warms and illuminates the masses. Engineers have no doubts they can design safe reactors with a variety of different applications, and use their original purposes interchangeably. They have the support of the president, the state, and a large branch of the economy. Leaders and ministers see nuclear power as a symbol of great power status and support billion-dollar expenditures accordingly.

Missile Envy: The Stalinist Military-Industrial Complex

It is not surprising that nuclear nostalgia triggered military envy. Russian leaders have been increasingly vocal in celebrating Soviet achievements—Stalin's joyous establishment of the nation as a military power in the 1930s, the first satellite, Sputnik, and man, Yuri Gagarin, into space, in 1957 and 1961, respectively, and, of course, various nuclear achievements—with the exception of Chernobyl. Space has been centrally important to Russian self-image and imagination.[45] Gagarin, for example, was a new kind of hero—a hero of the potentialities of Soviet society under Khrushchev, and of reborn faith in the communist future. Under President Putin, Gagarin's heroism has been reborn to serve the state.[46] On the fifty-second anniversary of Yuri Gagarin's flight into space, Putin unveiled a $50 billion drive for Russia to preserve its status in space, including the construction of a new cosmodrome at Vostochny in the Amur region of the

Far East.[47] As Stalin forced the nation to "reach and surpass" the West, so Putin announced that Russia will send manned flights from its own soil in 2018 from Vostochny to deep space as well as moon missions as part of the effort to catch up and overcome the gap in "so-called deep space exploration" and for Russia to "preserve its status as a leading space power." Then, following Brezhnev's lead, Putin congratulated cosmonauts on Russia's Space Exploration Day: "These are not just any greetings, these are greetings from the construction site of our future."[48] On April 12, 2014, Putin appeared at the Space Museum in Moscow to celebrate Gagarin Day and announced a plan to colonize and mine the moon.[49]

Russian leaders may well embark on this new space effort through the new "Angara" low-earth orbit rocket. The Angara project dates to the 1990s and represents an ongoing effort to be free from Soviet dependencies on Ukrainian missile construction facilities and Kazakh-based launches from the Baikonur cosmodrome that supported Gagarin and others. Unfortunately, to date, the Angara has yet to lift off successfully from Plesetsk in Arkhangelsk province.[50] Other rocket disasters belabor the industry.

Putin has also pushed Russia to recover the Soviet heritage of military and civilian jets. While the Russian government puts money into high tech, its low-tech infrastructure of mines, roads, railroads, ships, and Soviet-era passenger jets will have a hard time competing abroad. Much of the industrial base dates to the 1960s or earlier.[51] Nonetheless, the authorities have determined to pursue a passenger superjet in the tradition of the Tupolev, Iliushin, and other airplanes whose sardine-like cabins provided legendary discomfort for the passenger. In April 2011 President Medvedev called for Russia to "upgrade the civil aviation fleet. Passenger planes flying the main routes have an average age of 17 years, and regional planes are even older, up to 30 years. These are very old aircraft."[52] Russia can hardly make spare parts for its aging fleet, let alone compete with the European Airbus, the American Boeing, the Canadian Bombardier, and the Brazilian Embraer passenger jets. The Superjet 100, the only commercial airliner designed and built by Russia since the fall of the Soviet Union, was meant to generate sales and "to restore at least some of the prestige that Russian engineering had lost after the Soviet collapse." President Putin supported the Superjet "as a point of national pride."

When big technology fails, it fails in terribly costly and public ways—as the *Challenger*, *Exxon Valdez*, and Bhopal, India, disasters indicate.[53] Since it can no longer control access to news about technological failure as during the Soviet period, the government and its state-controlled high-tech agencies run the risk of public examination of any disaster, whether the sinking of the decrepit *Bulgaria* passenger ferry in the Volga near Kazan in July 2011 with the loss of more than 110 passengers,[54] forest fires in Moscow in 2010, floods in Siberia and the Far East in 2011 and 2014, or a modern Superjet. The crash of a Superjet in Indonesia in May 2012 indicated the problems and pitfalls of seeking state power through high technology. No sooner had the jet crashed than the Russian press published articles in which some unnamed xenophobic individuals suggested that the United States must have contributed to the accident by jamming the jet's communication system.[55] How else could this state program fail without some dastardly outside, ill-intended party acting, they posited, rather than allow for the fact that accidents unfortunately occur and that sometimes Russian engineers are responsible for them—as dozens of space failures, Chernobyl, and other airline accidents indicate.

Problems with the new Sukhoi indicate that the confidence of the Putin administration may be misplaced. In 2013, a Sukhoi Superjet aborted a takeoff from Sheremetevo Airport in Moscow after an engine failure. Aeroflot grounded four of its Superjets in February due to "technical problems," while a flight from Moscow to Kharkiv, Ukraine, was also aborted during takeoff because of engine failure. Sukhoi blamed the problem on Aeroflot maintenance, while Aeroflot refused to comment. But the president insists Russia will compete with Brazil's Embraer and Canada's Bombardier, and claims that Russian industry will sell $250 billion worth of aircraft by 2025 and then compete with US and European giants.[56]

The fight to resurrect the jet as a symbol of post-Soviet verve commenced under Putin with the merging of the Iliushin, Mikoian, Irkut, Tupolev, Iakavlev, and Sukhoi companies in the state-controlled United Aircraft Corporation.[57] In recent years the government has supported this corporation to modernize factories and lower the cost of serial production of airplanes. Russia's Tu-134, Tu-154, Il-62, and even the Il-18 were outdated, expensive to operate, used vast amounts of fuel, and needed repairs that required impossible-to-get parts.[58]

These design bureaus and their factories had a glorious past dating to the 1930s; Stalin's compatriots carried out a campaign to glorify pilots and planes and pursued technological hero worship. But the aerospace industry under Putin faced an uncertain future because of cost overruns, concerns over safety, lags in manufacturing capability, the need to rebuild capacity from design to manufacture, and lack of international interest. The company Antonov tried to introduce the An-148 to compete with the Boeing 737, but it was too expensive to operate. A cargo version, the An-178, had no market. Without a captive market and without the ability to subsidize aircraft as the USSR did during the Cold War, the Russian civil aviation sector may not survive competition with better-made and more modern Airbuses and Boeings—and their worldwide product support.[59] Fully 50 percent of the Russian industry is state-owned, versus 30 percent when Putin assumed power. Like Peter the Great and Joseph Stalin before him, Putin intends the Russian state to lead the way in modern science and technology in partnership with resource development programs directed by close oligarchic advisers. But the barriers to innovation and progress—including political control of capital, a closed political system, and the lack of a culture of innovation—are legion.[60]

Oligarchic Exploitation: The State of Oil and Gazprom

Another facet of technological display in modern societies comes from the combination of corporate strength, state authority, and vast quantities of capital. Many people identify "America" with such corporations as McDonald's, Coca-Cola, and Exxon. Such massive organizations actually date to the beginning of the 1600s and the British East Indies Company that came to control India through its private armies and the Dutch East Indies Company which gained the wealth and power to wage wars, establish colonies, and even imprison and execute convicts. In the nineteenth century they accumulated enough power and wealth to create monopolies, engage in price-fixing, and lead to the call for antitrust legislation. They remain massive and powerful into the twenty-first century; the US Supreme Court even gave them the status of "people" and rights of free speech.[61]

Similarly, there is no shortage of oligarchic state companies in twenty-first-century Russia, whose logos have become recognized throughout the world and whose wealth has few rivals. The most widely recognizable, Gazprom, a Soviet-Russian hybrid, with nearly 400,000 employees, self-consciously embraced display value.[62] Its logo fills posters throughout the nation, supplanting the once ubiquitous Soviet political posters. Two major artifacts of natural gas reveal both the promise and the challenges of playing up the symbolism of big science and technology in contemporary Russia: the Shtokman fields in the Barents Sea and the Gazprom Skyscraper in St. Petersburg. They make quite clear the unlimited power of industries connected with the Russian presidency.

Launched like the *Stalin*, *Lenin*, and *Arktika* icebreakers with anticipation of great economic benefits, but like many Soviet expeditions caught unexpectedly in the ice, the Shtokman fields have not opened in spite of the hundreds of millions of dollars thrown their way. Initially owned by Gazprom (51%), Total SA (France, 25%), and Statoil ASA (Norway, 24%), the Shtokman Development AG had a bud get that exceeded $800 million for 2008–2009,[63] based on a promise of access to reserves estimated at more than 4 trillion cubic meters of gas; an agreement signed in 2008 anticipated production beginning in 2013–14. But just four years later, the project was frozen. According to the Bellona Foundation, "The announcement from the Russian state gas monopoly indicates that even the Russian government cannot, for the time being, see its signature gas project yielding a healthy financial return." This was a disappointment for President Putin and his economic strategy, for Russian leaders saw liquefied natural gas for export as key to the country's financial growth. Both Total and Statoil have given up their shares of the field as too environmentally risky and expensive. It does not help that Russian laws make it difficult for Western companies to join any Russian project,[64] and that original estimates of costs have doubled, to $30 billion.[65] And it hurts that, in response to Russia's annexation of Crimea and war in Ukraine, the European Union and United States have embargoed vital oil equipment for future Arctic exploitation, and one-fifth of Russian oil and gas production is at risk.[66]

But Gazprom insists on being known as a success story with its stony blue-flame logo plastered everywhere. It also plans a grotesque skyscraper that is inappropriate by any standard to blight the St. Petersburg skyline. Like the monumentalist Stalinist skyscrapers and apartment buildings reserved for Soviet elites that demonstrated the omniscient glory of state power, so the planned Gazprom tower indicated that Russia's new elite class of resource developers have exclusive access to the Kremlin. The controversy over the extravagant Gazprom skyscraper reveals the determination of the huge conglomerates to paste their advertisements of wealth not only on billboards and soccer jerseys, but above the skyline, while ignoring the will of citizens to preserve history. Like the seven Stalinist "wedding cake" skyscrapers in Moscow that were symbolic of Stalin's glory, and were built when millions of people lived in *kommunalki* (shared apartments, including sharing kitchens and bathrooms with strangers), in the rubble, and in underground *zemlianki*, they indicate power run amok among oligarchs. Like a Soviet-era ministry with no checks on its programs and with legendary access to manpower and resources, Gazprom directors want to build Europe's tallest skyscraper in St. Petersburg, a city comprised mostly of five-and six-story buildings. Designers claim that the tower will "make St. Petersburg a world city" and be true to the city's history, for example, with a base "modeled on the pentagonal shape of the ancient Swedish fortress Nienshant[z] … to pay homage to the myth of St. Petersburg as a city built on water (the spiraling glass structure representing water)."[67]

The first skyscrapers bespoke the wealth of corporate owners, but also celebrated national culture, and capitalist ambition, energy, and enthusiasm. They grew from the Woolworth

Building (1913), to the Chrysler and Empire State Buildings of the 1930s, the World Trade Center and Sears Tower, to a veritable skyscraper-building orgy in China and the Burj Khalifa in Dubai, the twenty-first century skyscrapers that include luxury apartments for the wealthy to the glorification of state and economic power. Gazprom owners—the Russian state and Putin's oligarchs—intended the same. Gazprom directors were thrilled with the original plan to erect the structure across from the Smolnyi Institute, a women's school from the tsarist era, Vladimir Lenin's first seat of power, and where Sergei Kirov, first secretary of the Leningrad Party organization, was murdered on Stalin's orders in 1934, to create a business district near the downtown. It is not clear what Lenin would have thought of the juxtaposition of capitalist greed with political power. In any event, the tower's monstrous size was a violation of local sensibilities, commonsense aesthetics, and likely of UNESCO "World Heritage" designation for St. Petersburg. After its approval by Russia's State Expert Evaluation Department, in no way a zoning commission, the St. Petersburg Committee for City Planning and Architecture and the City Court approved the crystal tower. The City Council waived height restrictions to permit the project to go forward, but public outcry about the fact that the crystal shaft would destroy the skyline and distort the historical center of the city slowed the project, and President Dimitrii Medvedev, who served on the Gazprom board until he became president in 2008, announced his opposition. Surprisingly, Gazprom had to reconsider.

Not surprisingly, Gazprom returned with an even taller palace. In August 2012, President Putin made a fast-track decision to approve the new design, the so-called Lakhta Center, on the city's outskirts near the Gulf of Finland. If nothing else this decision indicates the power of the Kremlin to intervene arbitrarily. Gazprom took the decision on the new site two weeks before planned public meetings in order to prevent any input from citizens since the first project had been so roundly shunned. The spire, at 1,640 feet (500 meters), would include stores, restaurants and cafes, and is 300 feet taller than an earlier proposed skyscraper.[68] Gazprom officials and their handler, Mr. Putin, a Petersburg native, apparently find no aesthetic dissonance between an ugly crystalline phallus and the historic, human-scale buildings that fill Petersburg.[69]

While moving the tower out of the center to the northwestern edge of the city near the Gulf of Finland, its construction will lead to traffic, pollution, environmental and other problems,[70] and will fail to create a "business center" in Petersburg, which was one of its stated goals, although a "failed business periphery" is a real possibility. Boris Vishnevsky, a journalist and local legislature member of the opposition Yabloko Party, said, "Even nine kilometres [5.6 miles] from the centre, the building will be the most prominent object that an eye can see."[71] Vishnevsky referred to the excrescence as "Gazoskreb" (Gas-scraper). The question is whether various political parties, Russian NGOs, architects, journalists, and UNESCO have any chance to bring down the Gazoskreb before it goes up with the support of the city, Putin, and Gazprom.[72]

The Lakhta Center will be a traffic magnet and environmental disaster. It involves the construction of a new metro station, of course, but also of a new embankment along the Okhta River; the extension of Sverdlovskaia embankment; the construction of a multilayer modern flyover on Krasnogvardeiskaia Square and a tunnel underneath it; and the widening and extension of streets to the Ring Road. Parking garages and parks of 25,000 square meters (6.2 acres) will draw more smoke-belching vehicles to the region.[73] Petersburg's legendary traffic jams will extend to the Gulf of Finland. But the skyscraper will satisfy the interlocking interests of the state and gas industry for a project visible from the bedrooms of every citizen, reminding him or her where power lies.

Technological Display in Full Flower: Snow in the Black Sea

We have seen so far how, in modern technological societies, state power aspirations, industrial strength, corporate logo-ism, and utopian visions have come together in large-scale systems whose cost may far outweigh their benefits, but which have acquired significant value symbolically for the legitimators of those states, especially in aero-astro, construction, nuclear, exploration, and other technologies. Yet in authoritarian political systems perhaps technological enthusiasm goes even further, because there are few brakes on its embrace by the state. The public may have been emasculated by the police, or perhaps a vital civic culture never really formed, as in the case of Russia.

In the Sochi Winter Olympic Games, as in Hitler's 1936 Berlin games, Putin wedded state power, wealth (here petrorubles), and visions of gold medals—the latter achieved especially on the last day of the Olympics with a sweep of the gold, silver, and bronze medals in the men's 50km ski race—with the goal of demonstrating to the Russian citizenry the recovery of the nation from the embarrassments of the 1990s, including the breakup of the Soviet empire, an allegedly farcical leader, Boris Yeltsin, who drunkenly played into the hands of the American capitalists and CIA, the collapse of the economy, and the shock of a demographic crisis that left Russia the only industrial power with a declining population as deaths exceed births.

The Putin administration was determined to use Sochi to deflect public attention from those problems—and from its assault on personal freedoms and its newly passed homophobic laws—in a grandiose celebration of state power. The celebration required Putin's oligarchs to pay for his leadership. Throwing environmental caution to the warmer winds of the Black Sea resort, the government spent at least $50 billion, much of it going to corrupt projects and individuals, for buildings, stadiums, venues, and snow-making machines to build a winter wonderland of benefit to the wealthy in an inappropriate climate, and with significant environmental degradation the result.[74] Described by one observer as "outsized in scale and ambition," the cost exceeded the 2010 games in Vancouver, Canada, tenfold. A company owned by Vladimir Potanin, one of the wealthiest men in the world whose fortune includes Norilsk Nickel, complained that one of his companies had to pay out $530 million in extra work. Other oligarchs complained as well, but Putin determined that costs were no object because he wanted the Sochi games to project an international image. One of his spokesmen said, "All (rises in costs) there are justified. It is not possible to calculate everything in advance. New demands arise, including those from the International Olympic Committee, which require additional costs. There's nothing extraordinary about it."[75] Hidden not far from the Olympic village, the number of Russian people living in poverty continued to grow, human rights violations played out in the name of protection against terrorism, and activists were arrested, jailed, and sentenced to long prison terms.

The opening ceremony of the Sochi Olympic games was a bizarre self-referential celebration of the Russian past and present that glossed over the authoritarianism of the tsars and the murderous policies of Stalin while incorporating symbols of that Russian past: robot bears; a likeness of the "bronze horse men" statue of Peter the Great; the Soviet hammer and sickle (as historian Matthew Light wondered, how would people react to a swastika being displayed at an Olympics in Germany?); and castles, fortresses, and churches that reminded viewers that the Russian Orthodox Church has reunited with the Kremlin after the Soviet interregnum, the same church that joined Putin's United Russia political party in trying to dominate elections, happily saw the prosecution of the Pussy Riot rock group, and spearheaded the effort to tie conservative homophobic values to state policies. There were a few glitches: the Olympic torch, developed by a Siberian factory that produced ballistic missile parts, which traveled to the cosmos and back on the way from Athens to Sochi, self-extinguished a number of times and had to be re-lit with cigarette lighters; one of the Olympic rings failed to light during the opening ceremony. But four of five is a passing grade.

Of course, other nations have used the Olympic games to do more than showcase the world's greatest athletes. Adolf Hitler in 1933 instituted an "Aryans-only" policy for the Reich's athletic teams, although he convinced other world and Olympic leaders that his policies would have no impact on the games and avoided a boycott. The Nazi government presented a peaceful image of Nazism during the 1936 Berlin games, but used propaganda to draw parallels between the Reich and the Aryan purity of ancient Greece. So, too, on the eve of the Sochi Olympics, the Putin administration introduced laws enabling the prosecution of gays and lesbians, yet assured the international audience that these laws had no relevance for the Olympics. Three years after the close of the Berlin Olympics the Nazis invaded Poland, and two years later, Ukraine. Putin annexed Ukraine's Crimea three days after the conclusion of the Sochi Olympics. But, like Hitler, Putin himself said little at the Olympic games. Nor did the Russian people, who had been cowed into silence. But he smiled smugly, having achieved his goals.

The symbolism of new Russian imperialism figures as well in the rebuilding of St. Petersburg for the approaching 2018 World Cup Soccer championships. In Petersburg, as in Sochi, crumbling Soviet-era infrastructure must be fixed rapidly and new infrastructure must be built, but the government will focus on ring roads and football stadiums to the detriment of all other needed rebuilding and modernization in provincial Russia.[76] Russia is rebuilding and modernizing soccer stadiums, none more expensive than the new "Zenit" football club stadium at a cost of 44 billion rubles ($1.4 billion, which rivals the monstrously expensive Yankee Stadium in Bronx, New York, built with public funds).[77] Located along the waterfront on the way to the planned Gazprom skyscraper, the project has commenced apparently without contributions from Gazprom, Zenit's majority owner, which means the Kremlin owns the stadium. Yet the public has received the bill, and the price tag has increased sixfold since the cost was first announced, although the size of the stadium increased only 10 percent. Most shocking is the fact that Governor Georgii Poltavchenko of St. Petersburg asked the residents of Petersburg, in particular the fans of Zenit, to consider voluntarily working on the stadium to keep costs down in the good Soviet fashion of getting workers to give up weekend rest days to build socialism by cleaning, pruning, painting, and so on (*subbotniki*, days of "voluntary labor").[78]

Political Power and Technological Conservatism

Beyond ideological functions, large-scale technologies have many useful purposes: flood control, power production, increases in agricultural bounty, job creation. During the New Deal,

US president Franklin Delano Roosevelt spoke at several occasions on the importance of modern large-scale, government-supported projects for electrification, expansion of industry, and improving the quality of life of the people of America. Announcing the New Deal in July 1932, Roosevelt called for the "improvement of a vast area of the Tennessee Valley … to the comfort and happiness of hundreds of thousands of people and the incident benefits will reach the entire nation."[79] At the dedication of the Grand Coulee Dam on the Columbia River in Washington State in August 1934, Roosevelt spoke about the huge increment to power production for agriculture and industry and to the family home. The dams would enable the "men and women and children" to make "an honest livelihood and [do] their best successfully to live up to the American standard of living and the American standard of citizenship."[80] And at the dedication of the Bonneville Dam in September 1937, Roosevelt identified the dam with "the future of the Nation. Its cost will be returned to the people of the United States many times over in the improvement of navigation and transportation, the cheapening of electric power, and the distribution of this power to hundreds of small communities within a great radius. … As I look upon Bonneville Dam today, I cannot help the thought that instead of spending, as some nations do, half their national income in piling up armaments and more armaments for purposes of war, we in America are wiser in using our wealth on projects like this which will give us more wealth, better living and greater happiness for our children."[81]

In rhetoric and reality, scientific and technological prowess remained important as symbols of superpower status, the will of man and woman, the crucial place of indefatigable curiosity, and the inevitability of discovery. On June 26, 2000, US president Bill Clinton celebrated the completion of the mapping of the entire human genome (the Human Genome Initiative, or HGI) in a speech that likened the HGI to conquest of the New World. He said,

> Nearly two centuries ago, in this room, on this floor, Thomas Jefferson and a trusted aide spread out a magnificent map—a map Jefferson had long prayed he would get to see in his lifetime. The aide was Meriwether Lewis and the map was the product of his courageous expedition across the American frontier, all the way to the Pacific. It was a map that defined the contours and forever expanded the frontiers of our continent and our imagination. Today, the world is joining us here in the East Room to behold a map of even greater significance. We are here to celebrate the completion of the first survey of the entire human genome. Without a doubt, this is the most important, most wondrous map ever produced by humankind.[82]

Clinton celebrated the "combined wisdom of biology, chemistry, physics, engineering, mathematics and computer science" and the force of "more than 1,000 researchers across six nations" in the achievement. He reminded his audience—those present and the American people—that the HGI was "more than just an epic-making triumph of science and reason. After all, when Galileo discovered he could use the tools of mathematics and mechanics to understand the motion of celestial bodies, he felt, in the words of one eminent researcher, 'that he had learned the language in which God created the universe.'"[83]

Never one to mince words, if often to mispronounce them, President George W. Bush also drew on big science and technology to legitimize his presidency. In 2004 he called for NASA "to gain a new foothold on the moon and to prepare for new journeys to the worlds beyond our own." He proposed sending robotic probes to the lunar surface by 2008, a human mission by 2015, "with the goal of living and working there," and then "human missions to Mars and to worlds beyond." He recognized that it would cost billions of dollars, but had no doubts about the worth of the expense.[84]

Under Presidents Vladimir Putin and Medvedev, the Russian government has ventured directly into science and technology policy to preserve Russia's status as a scientific superpower. The government found billions of rubles for continuing space research, resurrecting atomic energy, expanding Arctic programs with a nonpareil nuclear icebreaking fleet, and moving into passenger jet service to complement the sale of military jets. The Putin administration selected these regions of modern technology to demonstrate that the nation had not only significant resource wealth, but also scientific and engineering excellence befitting a superpower. Additionally, Putin has resurrected the symbolic awards and ceremonies of the Soviet era to praise the men whose achievements radiate onto state power, including a reborn "Hero of Labor" prize.[85]

If, under Stalin, the trappings of Soviet gigantomania reflected state power and the omniscient power of the leader, then new Russian technological display grows out of that same state power tied to massive industrial resource combines—Gazprom, Lukoil, Rosatom, and others. The pronouncements of leaders and officials indicate the importance of big technology for contemporary Russia as proof that the nation remains a superpower at the cutting edge of technology, with military might as an added bonus. Space and nuclear power, for all of the risks and costs associated with their pursuit, are at the top of the list of crucial state programs. Perhaps with the blessings of the Orthodox Church Patriarch, the Putin administration can avoid such problems associated with technological symbolism in the Soviet era as technological failure. But the reliance on big technology is problematic in another way: Moscow has become a black hole of power and money, while towns and cities in many regions of provincial Russia have inadequate budgets for repair of infrastructure—roads, bridges, and public transportation. Yet in this environment, patriotic engineers who desire support for grandiose projects have unsurprisingly even rekindled a variant of the on-again, off-again project to "reverse" the flow of Siberian rivers to provide water for industrial and agricultural purposes in Central Asia and to replenish the Aral Sea. The environmentally unsound, grotesquely costly project will cost at least $40 billion and rival the pyramids as symbols of engineering hubris.[86] The question is whether President Putin wants such a canal.

Notes

1 Arnold Pacey, *The Maze of Ingenuity: Ideas and Idealism in the Development of Technology* (Cambridge, MA: MIT Press, 1976), and David Landes, *Revolution in Time: Clocks and the Making of the Modern World* (Cambridge, MA: Harvard University Press, 2000).

2 Royal Commission, *Official Catalogue of the Great Exhibition of the Works of Industry of All Nations, 1851* (London: Spicer Brothers, 1851), and Centennial Board of Finance, *Visitors' Guide to the Centennial Exhibition and Philadelphia. May 10th to November 10th, 1876* (Philadelphia: J.B. Lippincott & Co., 1876).

3 Albert Speer, *Inside the Third Reich* (New York: Avon, 1970), and Martino Stierli, "Building No Place: Oscar Niemeyer and the Utopias of Brasilia," *Journal of Architectural Education* 67, no. 1 (2013): 8–16.

4 John F. Kennedy, "Speech to Joint Session of the US Congress," May 25, 1961, http://

www.jfklibrary.org/Asset-Viewer/Archives/JFKWHA-032.aspx.

5 See, for example, Thomas Hughes, *Networks of Power: Electrification in Western Society, 1880–1930* (Baltimore: Johns Hopkins University Press, 1983), and *American Genesis: A Century of Invention and Technological Enthusiasm, 1870–1970* (New York: Viking, 1989).

6 For discussion of the European contribution to the space race, see John Krige and Arturo Russo, *Europe in Space, 1960–1973* (Noordwijk: European Space Agency Publications Division, 1994), and *A History of the European Space Agency. The History of ESRO and ELDO from 1958 to 1973*, vol. 1 (Noordwijk: ESA SP1235, 2000); also see Krige, Russo, and L. Sebesta, *A History of the European Space Agency. The History of ESA from 1973 to 1987*, vol. 2 (Noordwijk: ESA SP1235, 2000). On nuclear ideologies, see for example Gabrielle Hecht, *The Radiance of France* (Cambridge, MA: MIT Press, 1998).

7 Among the many studies that consider the ideological and social aspects of large-scale technologies, see Walter A. McDougall, … *The Heavens and the Earth: A Political History of the Space Age* (New York: Basic Books, 1985); Stephen Kotkin, *Magnetic Mountain* (Berkeley: University of California Press, 1995); Thomas Zeller, *Driving Germany* (New York: Berghahn Books, 2007); Alf Nilsen, *Dispossession and Resistance in India* (London, New York: Routledge, 2010); and Mark Reisner, *Cadillac Desert* (New York: Viking, 1986).

8 Paul Josephson, "'Projects of the Century' in Soviet History: Large Scale Technologies from Lenin to Gorbachev," *Technology and Culture* 36, no. 3 (July 1995): 519–59.

9 Loren Graham has written extensively about the political and cultural context of technology in Russian society, for example in *The Ghost of the Executed Engineer* (Cambridge, MA: Harvard University Press, 1993), and his recent *Lonely Thoughts* (Cambridge, MA: MIT Press, 2014).

10 Ivan Papanin, *Zhizn' na L'dine. Dnevnik* (Moscow: Pravda, 1938); M. Vodop'ianov, *Poliarnyi Letchik. Rasskazy* (Leningrad: Leningradskoe Gazetno-zhurnal'noe i Knizhnoe Izdatel'stvo, 1954).

11 See Kendall Bailes, "Technology and Legitimacy: Soviet Aviation and Stalinism in the 1930s," *Technology and Culture* 17 (1976): 55–81, and Scott Palmer, *Dictatorship of the Air* (Cambridge: Cambridge University Press, 2006).

12 V. K. Buinitskii, *812 Dnei v Dreifuiushchikh lLdakh* (Moscow: Glavsevmorput, 1945), pp. 15–23.

13 "Early Icebreakers," http://www.globalsecurity.org/military/world/russia/icebreaker-1.htm, accessed Sep. 22, 2014.

14 Putin addressed precisely these issues in his candidate thesis that he defended at the St. Petersburg Mining Institute in 1997. He argued that Russia's great natural resources were the key to remaking the country into a great economic power with a high standard of living based on the "fatherland's processing industry based on the extractive complex." See Harley Balzer, "Vladimir Putin's Academic Writings and Russian Natural Resource Policy," *Problems of Post-Communism* (Jan./Feb. 2006): 48–54.

15 On Soviet Arctic exploration see John McCannon, *Red Arctic* (New York: Oxford University Press, 1998) for the 1930s, and Paul Josephson, *The Conquest of the Russian Arctic* (Cambridge, MA: Harvard University Press, 2014). The Arctic has become transformed from a site of Cold War competition to one of fierce economic competition, and now perhaps again to military competition. See Lassi Heininen (with Heather Nicol), "The Importance of Northern Dimension Foreign Policies in the Geopolitics of the Circumpolar North," *Geopolitics* 12, no. 1 (Feb. 2007): 133–65.

16 President of Russia, "Maritime Doctrine of Russian Federation 2020," July 27, 2001, http://www.oceanlaw.org/downloads/arctic/Russian_Maritime_Policy_2020.pdf.

17 President of Russia, "The Basics of State Policy of the Russian Federation in the Arctic Region," Sep. 18, 2008, http://img9.custompublish.com/getfile.php/1042958.1529.avuqcurreq/Russian+Strategy.pdf?return=www.arcticgovernance.org, and http://www.arcticgovernance.org/russia-basics-of-the-state-policy-of-the-russian-federation-in-the-arctic-for-the-period-till-2020-and-for-a-further-perspective.4651232-142902.html. Russian leaders insisted years ago that they would accomplish these goals in the spirit of international cooperation through the maintenance of mutually advantageous bilateral and multilateral agreements and treaties, and through the sharing of information about the Arctic zone. But since the annexation of Crimea, Russian leaders have become more bellicose about the Arctic zone as well. For discussion of the relation between politics, investment, gas, and oil, see Per Hogselius, *Red Gas* (New York: Palgrave Macmillan, 2013). See also Marshall Goldman, *Petrostate* (New York: Oxford University Press, 2009).

18 President of Russia, "Security Council Meeting on Shipbuilding Development," June 9, 2010, http://eng.kremlin.ru/news/399.

19 President of Russia, "Executive Order on Implementing Plans for Developing Armed Forces and Modernising Military-Industrial Complex," May 7, 2012, http://eng.kremlin.ru/news/3777.

20 Evgenii Beliakov, "Arkticheskie Vezdekhody," Oct. 8, 2011, http://kp.ru/daily/25767/2751896/.

21 Andrei Ozharovskii, "Lozh' na Pervom: Po Mneniiu Zhurnalistov na Ledkole na Ledokole Lenin Avarii Ne Bylo," May 6, 2009, http://www.bellona.ru/weblog/andrey-ozharovsky/1241708613.5. For a map of other reactors dumped in the Arctic Ocean, see http://www.solovki.ca/danger/radiation_02.php.

22 Nataliia Antopkina, "Rossiia Prazdnuet 35-letie Pokoreniia Severnogo Poliusa Ledokolom 'Arktika,'" Aug. 12, 2012, http://www.kp.ru/online/news/1224536/, Aug. 16, 2012. Aerial research at the Arctic and Antarctic Research Institute on the Arctic ice regime facilitated the North Pole journey of the *Arktika*.

23 "Ledokhol 'Arktika' Otpravili na Pensiia," Oct. 3, 2008, http://kp.ru/online/news/148296/.

24 Trude Pettersen, "New Icebreakers Could Be Built Abroad," Dec. 12, 2013, http://barentsobserver.com/en/arctic/2013/12/new-icebreakers-could-be-built-abroad-12-12, and Yuri Golotuik, "Safeguarding the Arctic," in *Russia in Global Affairs*, Aug. 9, 2008, http://eng.globalaffairs.ru/person/p_1887.

25 "Est' Podozreniia, Chto Proekt Bol'she Sviazan s Osvoeniem Deneg, Chem s Polucheniem Rezultata," Aug. 24, 2012, http://kommersant.ru/doc/2007338?isSearch=True. The new *Arktika* "will differ from earlier atomic icebreakers by the fact that it is capable of working both in estuarial conditions which demand a small draft, and in deep waters which demand a large draft." Most people anticipate cost overruns, and funding already lags.

26 Beliakov, "Arkticheskie Vezdekhody."

27 In *Plutopia* (New York: Oxford University Press, 2013) Kate Brown chronicles the terrible human and environmental legacy of plutonium run amok in the United States and USSR.

28 "Rosatom Gears Up to Serve a Global Market," Aug. 21, 2012, http://www.rosatom.ru/en/presscentre/nuclear_industry/1f3573804c6d-425bae9eafda0118feee.

29 Among the dozens of excellent compilations and reports that indicate the extent of nuclear waste and other problems of the Soviet Cold

War legacy, see the Bellona Foundation reports: Nils Bøhmer, Aleksandr Nikitin, Igor Kudrik, Thomas Nilsen, Andrey Zolotkov, and Michael H. McGovern, *The Arctic Nuclear Challenge* (Bellona Foundation, 2001), and Igor Kudrik, Aleksandr Nikitin, Charles Digges, Nils Bøhmer, Vladislav Larin, and Vladimir Kuznetsov, *The Russian Nuclear Industry—The Need for Reform* (Bellona Foundation, 2004).

30 "The Russian Nuclear Industry," http://www.rosatom.ru/en/about/nuclear_industry/russian_nuclear_industry/, accessed Sep. 22, 2014.

31 On BAM, for example, see Christopher Ward, *Brezhnev's Folly: The Building of BAM and Late Soviet Socialism*. (Pittsburgh, PA: University of Pittsburgh Press, 2009). For an early variant of technological display, see Matthew Payne, *Stalin's Railroad: Turksib and the Building of Socialism* (Pittsburgh, PA: University of Pittsburgh Press, 2011).

32 On Atommash, see Paul Josephson, *Red Atom* (Pittsburgh, PA: University of Pittsburgh Press, 2005), pp. 97–108.

33 "Atomnaia Energetika Perezhivaet Nastoiashchii Renessans, i v Blizhaishie 15–20 Let Al'ternativy Ei ne Budet," April 15, 2010, http://www.atomic-energy.ru/news/2010/04/15/10481.

34 Ibid.

35 "Informatsionnyi Sait Bilibinskoi AES," http://www.bilnpp.rosenergoatom.ru/, accessed Sep. 16, 2014, http://miss2011.nuclear.ru/en/contestants/?id=1, and Josephson,

36 I. V. Kurchatov, "Nekotorye Voprosy Razvitiia Atomnoi Energetiki v SSSR," *Atomnaia Energiia* no. 3 (195): 5–10, and "O Vozmozhnosti sozdaniia termoiadernykh reaktsii v Gazovom Razriade," in ibid., pp. 65–75.

37 Kurchatov, "Rech' Tov. I. V. Kurchatova na XX s"ezde KPSS," http://vkpb2kpss.ru/book_view.jsp?idn=002416&page=601&format=html.

38 The breeders would produce plutonium from a fertile blanket of ^{235}U and ^{238}U, the latter of which would transmute into fissile plutonium for future generations of reactors, and the problem of nuclear fuel would be solved.

39 Josephson, *Red Atom*, pp. 47–80.

40 "Iurii Kazanskii: Reaktor BN-800—Eto Vopros Liderstva Rossii," http://www.atominfo.ru/news/air288.htm, accessed July 7, 2014. Breeder reactors are opposed by nonproliferationists of all stripes and by Russian ecologists. See Ana Uzelac, "IAEA Backs Controversial Neutron Reactor Plan," *Moscow Times*, Nov. 11, 2000, http://www.themoscowtimes.com/sitemap/free/2000/11/article/iaea-backs-controversial-neutron-reactor-plan/257496.html.

41 Claire Bigg, "Amid Nuclear Scare, Russia Pushes Ahead with Controversial Floating Reactors," April 22, 2011, http://www.rferl.org/content/russia_pushes_ahead_with_controversial_floating_nuclear_reactors/9502474.html. See also Yevgenia Borisova, "Floating Nuke Plant Drawing Opposition," *St. Petersburg Times*, March 16, 2001, and http://prop1.org/2000/safety/970930ru.htm.

42 See A. Nikitin and L. Andreev, *Plavuchie Atomnye Stantsii* (Oslo: Bellona Foundation, 2011), http://bellona.ru/filearchive/fil_Floating-npps-ru.pdf, and Atominfo, "Zhiteli Peveka Odobrili Plan Razmeshcheniia Plavuchei AES," Nov. 16, 2013, http://www.atominfo.ru/newsg/n0149.htm.

43 Bigg, "Amid Nuclear Scare."

44 Mikhail Antropov, "Atomnye Ambitsii Rossii," March 18, 2010, http://www.ntv.ru/novosti/188376.

45 Palmer, *Dictatorship of the Air*. On Russian hero building, see L. L. Kerber, *Tupolev* (St. Petersburg: Politekhnika, 1999); Nikolai Bodrikhin, *Tupolev* (Moscow: Molodaia Gvardiia, 2011); G. V. Novozhilov, ed., *Iz Istorii Sovetskoi Aviatsii: Samolety OKB imeni S.V. Il'iushina* (Moscow: Mashinostroenie, 1990); and P. Ia. Kozlov, *Velikoe Edinstvo: Dokumental'naia Poves'* (Moscow: DOSAAF SSSR, 1982).

46 Andrew L. Jenks, *The Cosmonaut Who Couldn't Stop Smiling: The Life and Legend of Yuri Gagarin* (DeKalb: Northern Illinois University Press, 2012).

47 For discussion of the political, social, and cultural importance of the space race to Soviet Russia, see Asif Siddiqi, *The Red Rockets' Glare: Spaceflight and the Soviet Imagination, 1857–1957* (Cambridge: Cambridge University Press, 2010).

48 Shaun Walker, "Putin Aims for the Stars with a £ 33bn Space Programme," April 12, 2013, http://www.independent.co.uk/news/world/europe/putin-aims-for-the-stars-with-33bn-space-programme-8570462.html. *Red Atom*, pp. 136–38.

49 "Is Vlad Keen on a Trip," April 12, 2014, http://www.dailymail.co.uk/news/article-2602291/We-coming-Moon-FOREVER-Russia-sets-plans-conquer-colonise-space-including-permanent-manned-moon-base.html.

50 "Russia Gearing Up for Launch of First Post-Soviet Rocket," *Moscow Times*, June 27, 2014, http://www.themoscowtimes.com/business/article/russia-gearing-up-for-launch-of-first-post-soviet-rocket/502608.html.

51 Simon Shuster, "Living and Dying with Russia's Soviet Legacy," July 12, 2012, http://www.time.com/time/world/article/0,8599,2082637,00.html.

52 President of Russia, "Security Council Meeting on Long-Term State Policy in the Aviation Sector," April 1, 2011, http://eng.kremlin.ru/news/1994.

53 Simon Shuster, "The Fatal Flight of Superjet-100," May 15, 2012, http://www.time.com/time/world/article/0,8599,2114872,00.html.

54 "Russia Fears 110 Dead as Boat Sinks on Volga River," July 11, 2011, http://www.bbc.co.uk/news/world-europe-14099637.

55 Will Stewart, "Undercover US Agents Brought Down Our New Superjet: Russia's Extraordinary Claim About Crash Which Killed 45," May 24, 2012, http://www.dailymail.co.uk/news/article-2149377/Undercover-US-agents-brought-new-Superjet-Russia-s-extraordinary-claim-crash-killed-45.html#ixzz3E49vBJjq.

56 "Problem-Plagued Sukhoi Superjet Fails Take-Off at Moscow Airport," Feb. 25, 2013, http://www.reuters.com/article/2013/02/25/uk-problem-plagued-sukhoi-superjet-fails-idUSLNE91O01120130225.

57 "United Aircraft Corporation," http://www.uacrussia.ru/en/, accessed Sep. 22, 2014.

58 "Soveshchanie o Formirovanii Goszakaza na Samolety Otechestvennogo Proizvodstva," October 4, 2012, http://kremlin.ru/news/16596.

59 "Antonov, Ilyushin and Tupolev Fading Away," https://www.strategypage.com/htmw/htairmo/20100614.asp.

60 Graham, *Lonely Thoughts.*

61 *Citizens United v. Federal Election Commission*, 558 US 310 (2010).

62 In *Wheel of Fortune* (Cambridge, MA: Harvard University Press, 2012), Thane Gustafson tracks the power, politics, and uncertainties surrounding Russia's oil and gas industry from the last years of Soviet power to the present.

63 "Gazprom Says Shtokman 2008–09 Bud get Over $800 mln," Oct. 20, 2008, http://in.reuters.com/article/2008/10/20/shtokman-budget-idINLK43254820081020.

64 "Russia's Giant Shtokman Gas Field Project Put on Indefinite Hold Over Cost Overruns and Failed Agreements," Aug. 29, 2012, http://www.bellona.org/articles/articles_2012/Shtokman_freeze.

65 Ol'ga Mordiushenko, Aug. 30, 2012, http://kommersant.ru/doc/2011009?isSearch=True.

66 Alexander Panin, "Western Sanctions Could Damage One-Fifth of Russia's Oil Production," *Moscow Times*, Sep. 21, 2014, http://www.themoscowtimes.com/business/article/

one-fifth-of-russia-s-oil-production-is-at-risk-due-to-sanctions/507474.html.

67 Alex McGrath, "Gazprom's Tower: Civil Society in the Venice of the North," http://petersburg.blogs.wm.edu/2011/10/04/gazprom%E2%80%99s-tower-civil-society-in-the-venice-of-the-north-by/#_ftn1.

68 Ibid. McGrath wonders if the Gazoskreb had any connection with Vladimir Tatlin's 1919 "Monument to the Third International," also "a spiraling mass of iron and steel that exemplified Russian Constructivist architecture and was to stand in the city's center," and also to rival and surpass the height of other European structures.

69 In an open letter to Governor Matvienko in June 2006, the Saint Petersburg Union of Architects wrote,

> The Construction of a high-rise building, which is sure to be visually connected to the historic center, we firmly believe, is absolutely unacceptable. … St. Petersburg is very uniform in height, so that its external appearance is dominated by the lines corresponding to the regularity of its plan. The low skyline of St. Petersburg makes its verticals particularly majestic, as they are almost always perceived against the sky. The preservation of the unique silhouette of steeples and domes is of great urban and spiritual importance. … The construction of a 300-meter tower will inevitably destroy the harmony of St. Petersburg's verticals, which has evolved for centuries, and will cause irreparable damage to the delicate silhouette of the city, practically making toys out of all the other verticals of the city … implementation of this construction will mean a complete break with St. Petersburg's urban-architectural tradition. (Alex McGrath, ibid., cited in Vishnevsky "Gazoskreb," 23)

70 UNESCO (the United Nations Educational, Scientific and Cultural Organization) officials rightly worry that the tower "might mar the historical panorama of the city's center and disrupt the architectural integrity of St. Petersburg." McGrath, ibid.

71 Ibid.

72 Ibid. Yury Volchok, architectural historian and professor at Moscow Architectural Institute, commented: "The situation with the Okhta Center repeats itself. The construction site was moved to the Primorsky District, which is not considered a part of the historical center, so it is easier to get the construction permit there. However, Russian legislation protects not only buildings but also city views." See "IuNESKO Mozhet Iskliuchit' Sankt-Peterburg iz Ob"ektov Vsemirnogo Naslediia," http://izvestia.ru/news/533615#ixzz24ScBI6f9.

73 "Lakhta Center," http://proektvlahte.ru/en/. "Okhta Center," http://www.ohta-center.ru/en/, has been closed down.

74 Anti-Corruption Foundation, *Sochi 2014: Comprehensive Report*, http://sochi.fbk.info/en/.

75 Thomas Grove, "Russia's $50 Billion Gamble on 2014 Olympics," http://www.nbcnews.com/id/50892025/ns/business-world_business/#.USfABh3BLmc.

76 Boris Nemtsov and Leonid Martyniuk, *Zimniaia Olipiada v Subtropikakh* (Moscow 2013), http://www.nemtsov.ru/?id=718789.

77 On the monstrous cost to taxpayers of privately owned stadiums in New York City, see "As Stadiums Rise, So Do Costs to Taxpayers," *New York Times*, Nov. 4, 2008.

78 Boris Vishnevskii, "Vsem Mirom—dlia 'Gazproma'?" *Novaia Gazeta*, Oct. 22, 2012, http://www.yabloko.ru/publikatsii/2012/10/22. The government was able to go $400 million over bud get to open a new Mariinsky Ballet and Opera Hall in May 2013, but critics generally find it to mesh harmoniously with the

Petersburg skyline and architecture. See Louise Levene, "Mariinsky 2 Opens with a Seamless Gala," May 3, 2013, http://www.telegraph.co.uk/culture/theatre/dance/10034976/Mariinsky-2-opens-with-a-seamless-gala.html.

79 President Franklin D. Roosevelt, "The New Deal," July 2, 1932, http://www.danaroc.com/guests_fdr_021609.html.

80 President Franklin D. Roosevelt, Dedication of the Grand Coulee Dam, Washington, Aug. 4, 1934, http://digitalcollections.lib.washington.edu/cdm/singleitem/collection/panoram/id/4.

81 Roosevelt, "Address at Bonneville Dam," Sep. 28, 1937, http://newdeal.feri.org/speeches/1937c.htm.

82 President Bill Clinton, "Remarks [on the Human Genome Initiative]," June 26, 2000, http://www.genome.gov/10001356.

83 Ibid.

84 "President Bush Offers New Vision for NASA," Jan. 14, 2004, http://www.nasa.gov/missions/solarsystem/bush_vision.html.

85 Andrei Anishchuk, "Russia's Putin Restores Stalin-era Labor Award," May 1, 2013, http://www.reuters.com/article/2013/05/01/us-russia-putin-medal-idUSBRE9400HL20130501.

86 Fred Pearce, "Russia Reviving Massive River Diversion Plan," Feb. 9, 2014, http://www.newscientist.com/article/dn4637-russia-reviving-massive-river-diversion-plan.html, and Energy Resources Group, "Moscow Actively Considering Diverting Siberian River Water for Profit," Sep. 26, 2010, http://groups.yahoo.com/group/energyresources/message/125152.

■ CHAPTER 7

Political Movements: Changing Political Tide

Editor's Introduction

Chapter 7 examines the rise of broad political movements in North America and Europe. This chapter describes the lives of individuals such as Ken, Alex, and many others who have faced divorce, suicide, broken families, homelessness, and mental health issues. These dramatic losses lead to lost faith in government and unions. Chen discusses the workers' ideological and critical perceptions concerning the changing political tide, which has turned against them, most obviously in America but also in Canada and other countries as well. The chapter raises these important questions: Why are grassroots organizations—coalitions of students, workers, church members, and others—upset with corporate greed and government inaction? Why are workers skeptical of government and union institutions designed to assist them during layoffs? Why are these workers turning their support away from these institutions and directing their support toward the upper class? According to Chen, it is easier for blue-collar workers to accept a *false consciousness* instead of fighting to maintain class consciousness for their economic interest. This false consciousness replaces hope with helplessness, desperation, a sense of guilt, and compliance with whatever will end the suffering. Lastly, the author offers a critique about government: Why is it that when corporations make a mistake, the corporation is paid billions to stay out of bankruptcy, but millions of workers are left to suffer?

READING 7 Vicious Circles: The Structure of Power and the Culture of Judgment

Victor Tan Chen

> The awful thing about life is this: everyone has their reasons.
>
> —Jean Renoir as Octave in *The Rules of the Game* (1939)

When he first got laid off, Alex Wynn waited two months before his first unemployment check came. The recession had struck, and Windsor firms were laying off workers in droves. The government agency in charge of the benefits was swamped with applications. Without any income, Alex had to tell his landlord—twice—that he couldn't pay his monthly rent. "He was visibly upset," Alex recalls. "He was just ranting and raving." Alex pleaded with him, pointing out that he'd never missed a payment before. "If I could have avoided this, you know I would have," he said.

The landlord let Alex stay. When the money finally came in, Alex paid up.

More than a year later, though, Alex is a month behind on his rent again—and this time, there's no check in the mail. His unemployment benefits have expired; a while back he burned through his retirement savings. Still unable to find a job, Alex has been doing construction projects here and there for a contractor friend of his, praying every month that the under-the-table cash will cover his expenses. Meanwhile, he and his wife Charlotte have separated. For the time being, she's living with her sister in another town. "It was hard on us, financially and everything else," says Alex, thirty-two. "She didn't make a lot of money." Charlotte had also lost her factory job, so Alex parceled out some of those retirement savings to help keep her afloat.

Their separation has also meant that Alex sees his stepson, eight-year-old Jasper, less often. "It kills me," Alex says. The two share a close bond. When the family was together, he'd spent every night after work hanging out with the boy. He describes Jasper as a sensitive boy—like his mother—and Alex worries about how he's processing the troubles of the adults around him. Jasper's grades have slipped, and he keeps asking his mother when Alex will be around next. "It's hard on him," Alex says. "He really starts to get broken down over that."

It's the first time in his life that Alex hasn't had a job. The son of a Ford worker, he got a job at the plating plant after a brief stint in college. He had developed a drinking problem while in school—at his worst, he could down two bottles of whiskey a day—but after struggling with it for a few years he went to rehab and cleaned himself up. The job at the plant kept him rooted. He made $21 an hour, enough to help out his cousin's family with cash here and there, and enough to pay for an apartment big enough to house his father and stepmom while they sorted their own issues out.

It's a two-bedroom apartment in a yellow-brick house, not far from a rowdy bar whose fistfights sometimes spill out onto the street. The rooms are decked out with mismatched and rickety furniture, including an ancient bookshelf filled with his grandfather's thirty-year-old encyclopedias. On the wall hangs a picture of Jasper, sporting sunglasses, in a frame printed with the words "Little Prince." Alex is tall and thin, his scruffy brown hair tucked under a cap, a light growth of facial hair circling his mouth. As he talks about his stepson, his hazel eyes begin to tear up. He takes off his glasses and wipes the reddened lids with his fingers. "It's very stressful," he says. "It can get to the point to where I just break down and cry some nights, you know. I got no choice—I got to let it out somehow."

If he could just get another job, perhaps he could—as Alex puts it—"regain the family environment we had." But in spite of the six dozen or so applications he's sent out, nothing has turned up yet. There are too many people searching, he says—"It's like a thousand vultures at one carcass, you know what I mean?" Nonetheless, he keeps plugging away. Unable to afford a car, he rides the city's unreliable public transit buses everywhere. "It's no picnic trying to go look for a job in the freezing cold."

These days, Alex takes whatever help he can find. His mom has bought him a few hundred dollars worth of groceries. His dad forks over packs of cigarettes and some cash to get him through the week. A friend let Alex borrow his propane stove when the electric company cut off his power for a week; another friend loaned him money to pay his bill and get the lights turned back on. Not everyone has been supportive, though. Recently, an aunt mocked him during a family get-together, telling him that he might have to go on welfare. Alex was incensed. "You're putting me down to that level already," he says, "and I haven't even reached that yet."

In fact, if Alex had his way, he'd have nothing to do with any of the government's inept bureaucracies. When his unemployment benefits got delayed, he tried calling around for answers, only to get fed up with the agency's feeble attempts at customer service. "The government hires a lot of people that barely even speak English," he says. "You get some of these guys on the phone—you can't even understand a word they are saying to you." He doesn't understand why the government won't devote more resources to the agencies that are supposed to help the many jobless workers out there. "They're cutting back so that they can try to save money or something," he says. But the delays spiral into further problems that end up costing taxpayers even more. "If you waited eighteen weeks to get your first unemployment check, well, how damaged are your bills? How damaged is your credit?"

If Alex can't count on the government, he doesn't have much faith in the labor movement, either. He thinks auto unions will continue to lose ground in the years ahead. "But I think that's a good thing, because they're gaining too much ground, to the point where they're almost becoming the auto industry itself," he says. "That's not what unions were intended for." The unions go "gung ho" too often, making unreasonable demands for higher wages and more generous benefits with every contract, he says. "You have to make allowances for the company, too." At the same time, Alex avidly supports his own union local. He is grateful for the sense of camaraderie it fostered at the plant. "There was a lot of brotherhood and sisterhood going on there." He starts to tear up again, and apologizes. "I do get very emotional, because that was my life in that place, you know. These were my friends." But now they're losing their homes, he says. Prolonged unemployment has sucked the life out of them. "A lot of these guys, they're not the same people."

Neither is Alex, for that matter. "Mentally it's draining, and physically it's boring," he says of his forced idleness. His body isn't used to it, and so on most nights, he can't sleep. He cleans his house and yard incessantly, trying to keep himself busy. He smokes more—a pack a day, twice what he used to. And he pays attention to the news less. Alex used to be a political junkie. He and Charlotte would flip through the cable news networks every night. Nowadays, he doesn't bother. "Unless they're gonna tell me that people are gonna start getting their jobs back ... what is the point?"

* * *

Following the Great Depression, North America and Europe saw the rise of broad political movements determined to transform an unfair economic system. They successfully fought for potent policies and bounteous contracts that swallowed many of the risks of the market for the average citizen. Strong unions promoted a "moral economy" by assailing inequality in public pronouncements, lobbying for progressive social policies, and negotiating rules favorable to workers. Activist governments lifted the floor on wages, opened up possibilities for workers to organize, and reined in capital and corporate behavior. The trauma of depression and war and the surging power of leftist organizations and ideologies helped bring about relatively egalitarian attitudes and more enthusiasm about collective approaches to society's problems.

After the Great Recession, the worst economic crisis in eight decades, the response was much different. Many governments responded with austerity measures. Countries on both sides of the Atlantic saw glimmers of populist protest like that of the Depression era—grass-roots coalitions of students, workers, church members, and others upset with corporate greed and government inaction—but they also raged with nativist and antigovernment sentiment.

Clearly, the political tide has turned on workers—most obviously in America, but in Canada and other countries as well. Unions have seen steep declines in membership, and left-wing ideologies everywhere have flamed out. Fortified by trends of globalization and automation, a pro-corporate movement has successfully pushed its message that unions and government are evil. As a result, the institutions that once helped bend public attitudes toward egalitarian ends have been severely weakened. While at times governments have been able to halt its momentum, the *long-term* thrust of the economy since the postwar period has been toward unfettered markets and away from any spirited efforts to reduce inequality and increase employment through union or government meddling.

In short, when seen across decades, the arc of economic policy has bent toward pro-corporate conservatism. Even in their moments of electoral triumph, American and Canadian administrations on the political left have largely hewed to this consensus, pressing for market means to achieve liberal ends.[1] In Canada, it was the Liberal Party that pushed forward reforms in the nineties that shrank the size of the state; in more recent years the Conservative Party has continued that work, attacking public-sector unions for good measure. In America, Democratic lawmakers since at least the nineties have focused more on policies that place a floor on the downward mobility of the working and middle classes—that is, helping the "deserving" and preventing the very worst outcomes in the labor market, rather than aggressively supporting unions and pursuing egalitarian outcomes through more explicit shows of government power. While important, the implacable opposition of their political adversaries can only explain part of this reluctance to do more.

Indeed, while the political Left has done relatively well in U.S. presidential elections over the past two decades, the economic liberalism of the Clinton and Obama eras is altogether different from that of labor's heyday. In his 1996 State of the Union address, Bill Clinton pronounced that "the era of big government is over," and his administration's policy approach toward the labor market made good on that promise. It entailed individual training accounts, lifelong-learning credits, and the earned-income tax credit—market-friendly efforts to help people help themselves, rather than vigorous interventions in the market. Barack Obama has pushed somewhat more successfully—within a narrow political space—for a stronger safety net and tougher "rules of the road" for business, but the situation remains a world apart from the postwar period. His administration's most obvious success in addressing income inequality—ending the Bush tax cuts for top earners—was merely a return to Clinton-era tax rates. In spite of all the White House's rhetoric about addressing soaring inequality at the very top, politicians in both parties have put forward few serious ideas, having given up on past proposals for assertive government action, such as policies to achieve full employment and a guaranteed national income—proposals that were once supported by Republican leaders like Richard Nixon.[2] At least among Americans, concern about inequality has grown somewhat. Yet inequality has grown much more, especially in the United States, but in Canada as well.

Perhaps public opinion has played just a small role in what has transpired in recent years. The Wall Street banks whose market manipulation contributed to the meltdown have not received much in the way of punishment, but that outcome may have less to do with any deficit of public outrage and more to do with the ways that the pro-corporate movement has captured the loyalties of elected officials and government regulators alike. Likewise, the largest economic disaster since the Depression did not lead to an egalitarian reordering of the economic system on the scale of the New Deal, but here, too, the attitudes of ordinary Americans and Canadians may have mattered less than the professional preference for less interventionist approaches that prevails among the elite circle of policy technocrats, who worry incessantly—and perhaps excessively—about the tradeoff between efficiency and equality. Further back in time, politicized rulemaking also appears to be a better explanation for the fact that union membership dropped in the latter half of the twentieth century in America but not (at least for a time) in Canada.[3] Changes in institutions, rather than public opinion, have often been decisive in these cases.

That said, institutions do not emerge out of thin air. It is hard to imagine that the overall ideological climate has not influenced the economic experts and political operatives who have enacted recent policy changes—even as these elites have molded the broader context, too. More importantly, it is difficult to see how a labor movement that gains its power primarily by organizing people rather than money can grow in the long run when a pervasive ideology turns a significant segment of the population against that movement's aims. The political partisans who dictate economic policy clearly express more extreme views than ordinary citizens, and yet I was surprised by the extent to which my unemployed workers—left-of-center in their politics and recently members of powerful unions—agree with the views that today's elites take as the norm. Much of the reason they feel this way is that they are just realistic: this is the way today's market works. But there was also a sense among some of them that this is the way it *should* work—a point of view with consequences for how they coped with their inability to find jobs anything like the ones they once had.

In this chapter I tackle three questions. First, are workers like mine skeptical of the collective institutions that are supposed to help them—thereby moving in the direction of the self-reliant white-collar professionals and managers described in notable studies of past generations? Second, to what extent are their views driven by an ideology of individualism and critical judgment, as opposed to a simple realism about how today's market works? Along these lines, one argument is that blue-collar workers fail to champion their economic interests because they have abandoned "class consciousness" for "false consciousness"—no longer identifying or siding with the working class and instead internalizing an antilabor and antigovernment ideology that serves elites.[4] Finally, given the widespread trends of globalization and government retrenchment, how do the views of Americans on opportunity and institutions compare to those of Canadians?

Both powerful ideas in the culture and weak institutions operating on the ground shaped the attitudes that my workers held about the labor market. Their experiences with other people and their exposure to mass media instilled in them a set of beliefs from the available, changing selection that society offers. These ideologies seemed to be connected to certain attitudes toward government and unions and certain responses to unemployment. In this way, perhaps, culture matters. And yet individuals do not simply parrot beliefs handed down to them. My workers were also responding to real-world circumstances, adapting their beliefs as the situation changed.[5]

Nothing to Fall Back On

Travel down East Grand Boulevard in northeastern Detroit and you will find—sprawling across two full city blocks—the empty, rotting shell of the once-famed Packard plant. Built at the beginning of the twentieth century, it was one of the most state-of-the-art industrial complexes in the world: seventy-four buildings spread out over 3.5 million square feet, the first structurally reinforced concrete factory ever built, designed by the city's preeminent architect, Albert Kahn. Packard was the country's top-selling luxury brand through most of the 1920s and '30s. But after a hiatus to build aircraft engines during the war, Packard frittered away its image with lackluster models, and the mass market deserted the brand. The plant assembled its last Packard on June 2, 1956. Never demolished, it continues to stand in its solitude of concrete and brick, its drab skin of graffiti almost as weathered as the old Packard lettering on the walls, its long banks of smashed windows fixed in a toothless leer—looking in its perfect decrepitude like some totem to a postindustrial god.

Ken Brennan's father toiled in the Packard plant for two decades. After the factory shut its doors, he never really worked. He developed tuberculosis, and had a lung removed, then developed cancer in the other lung. He died in 1978, when Ken was a teenager. Ken's mom struggled to support the family by herself. "I had six brothers and two sisters, so we had it rough growing up," says Ken, forty-seven. "No Christmases, no none of that." He was a troubled kid. When Ken was seventeen, a driver almost ran him over, and in a fit of wrath Ken smashed the car's windshield with a baseball bat. His record barred him from joining the Army when he tried to apply several years later.

In high school Ken met a girl named Sue. They fell in love and married young. Ken dropped out of school to work as a house painter. That job didn't last, so Ken bounced around other low-wage positions. Around this time, Ken's older sister was murdered. Her husband, a felon, had run afoul of prison friends of his. They came to the house and stabbed Ken's sister and two nieces, ages fifteen and nine, to death. The killers were caught, but Ken was devastated. "When her birthday comes around it's hard for me," Ken says. He motions to a photo of the nieces with his sister, twenty-seven, beautiful and ageless. "She would be in her fifties now," he says.

"You can't trust too many people out here," he adds. "Sometimes I'm scared to go out in the world. It's kind of cruel."

Ken and Sue settled down in their hometown. Sue worked at a cleaning company, for eight dollars an hour and no benefits, always just a few hours shy of full-time. ("If you were full-time you had insurance," Ken notes.) For a number of years, Ken worked at a parts supplier, where tensions between labor and management ultimately reached a tipping point over wages, benefits, and the outsourcing of work. A few hundred workers, Ken included, went on strike. "The company was being stubborn, and the union was being stubborn," Ken says. "And you're a union member. What are you going to do? If they go on strike, you can't go there and work." The strike became a lockout, and Ken and his coworkers lost their jobs. Afterward, as everyone struggled to get new jobs, a friend of his committed suicide.

More recently, Ken was working at a supplier that made solar panels for cars. He drove a forklift for $11 an hour. This time, there was no union.

One day, Ken had an accident at the plant. He was driving a forklift when someone pushed a ladder into his vicinity, out of his field of vision. He reversed and bumped into it, sending it hurtling down. Nothing was damaged, no one was hurt, but immediately afterward he could not shake the thought that he would be laid off. *I'm going to lose my house. My wife's going to be totally pissed off.*

"That's exactly what happened." Four days later he was fired.

Ken claims that his accident was just an excuse for the company, which had seen orders taper off and wanted to cut its workforce. He consulted a lawyer about a wrongful termination suit but was told he was an "at will" employee—which meant they could fire him for wearing the wrong clothes if they wanted. Ken says he is still baffled by what happened. He was never late, he did what he was told, he worked hard. But nowadays, you can't make any mistakes. "One accident and I'm gone."

When Sue heard the news, she was furious. "You shouldn't have had an accident," she told him.

"Well, that's why they call it an accident," Ken said.

Sue wanted him to get a job right away, and when nothing turned up, they bickered some more. It's not that easy, Ken tried to tell her. Eventually, she told Ken she wanted a divorce. He decided not to contest it. They had been arguing regularly over money. "She's tired of struggling, and she can do better by herself," he says.

Now Ken is waiting for the foreclosure to come. Without the two of them pooling their wages, there's no chance of keeping their home.

It is a small house with weather-stained siding, flanked by two leafy trees. The plants out front are yellowed, but the lawn is well trimmed (Ken mows lawns for extra cash). On the door hangs a decorative wooden heart with the words, "Welcome Friends." Next door is a sullen white bungalow with a faded realtor sign in the window; Ken says it's a short sell.

Ken's "new" car sits in the driveway, a slate-blue 1991 Oldsmobile with a rusted-out left taillight and 113,000 miles. After his wife left him and took their car, he bought this one so that he could get to interviews. But the brakes went out, and to fix them he needs another $200 he doesn't have.

Inside, Ken leads his guest to the kitchen table. Impeccably polite, he offers homemade pastries and coffee before stepping into the doorway of the laundry room to puff away at a cigarette ("I don't want to bother you," he insists). Nearby, a cabinet displays a crystal-studded pendant bearing his mother's silhouette and an urn with her ashes. Ken says he couldn't afford a burial. His mother died of congestive heart failure, two months after one of Ken's brothers, a truck driver, died of a heart attack. "They're probably in a better place," Ken says, almost enviously.

He has been thinking of his mother lately, and how she raised her kids on welfare and food stamps. He swore he would never turn to that, but the loss of his job and the end of his marriage have left him, he says, with no options. "I'm dependent on the government right now," he says. "That's degrading, but I gotta eat." Ken is quick to add that he worked for three decades. "I paid into it. I should be able. I've always worked." In any case, since he doesn't have kids, he can't get much in the way of benefits, he notes. Ken actually wanted to have children, but he and Sue weren't able to.

Besides prescriptions, the Salvation Army has furnished him with gas cards to fill up his car. Now that it's no longer running, he rides his mountain bike everywhere. Ken has applied for a hundred jobs so far, but he hasn't landed a single interview. "If you had a high school diploma a while ago, you could get a job," he says. "Now they want college." He maintains that he isn't being picky. "If I have to shovel dog crap, I would"—so long as he can get insurance, he adds. In the meantime, he waits—for employers to call back, for bureaucrats to get around to his case file, for his divorce to wind its way through the courts. At least he has something to do once a week: for his church's Sunday school he volunteers on the bus, singing songs and otherwise entertaining the children. "It helps to be around young people."

Ken says he can't blame the company for his accident. "I'm a man. I man up. I did it. What am I going to say, I didn't do it?"

Ken used to think of himself as, in his words, a "happy-go-lucky" guy. But his downward momentum has driven him to despair. For a time, thoughts of suicide drifted regularly into the prickly core of his consciousness. His ears would ring; his head would swim with sudden bursts of hatred. Ken has not able to see a therapist or psychiatrist because he can't afford health insurance. But he has seen his family doctor, who prescribed Paxil, an antidepressant. "I'm not going to try to fool nobody," he says. "I have depression." He can't eat. His weight has shrunk several pants sizes. But if he takes the pills, at least his frenzied mind slows down. Without the medication, the anger creeps up, the senses narrow, the reason blurs; the urge not to suffer anymore seizes him again.

Ken can't turn to his siblings for help, he says. They have their own financial woes. "It's your problem, little brother," they tell him. "Deal with it." In truth, he's glad that his family doesn't pry; he is ashamed to tell them what's going on. As for Sue, Ken knows their marriage is just ashes now. "We're tired of each other. People fall out of love, is all I can say."

They have known each other for so long. Ken threw her a party for her sweet sixteen. They adored each other, then. But the years have gone by, fruitlessly, and now the two of them are worse than strangers: fuming over the slightest infraction, at war over the few dollars in their bank account. Sometimes, Ken brims with resentment. "I'm done. I'm a free man. No woman is going to tell me what to do again." Then his mood becomes somber, almost plaintive. "She don't love me no more, so I can't make her."

Once in a while, Sue drops by the house to pick up clothes and other things. She heads to her room without speaking a word, slamming the door shut. The rage returns, itching in a corner of Ken's skull, and he has to struggle to master it.

Ken went to the state job center and asked about counseling services. There was a two-month waiting list for anyone to see him, he was told. "You can commit suicide tomorrow," Ken points out. But "it's the sign of the times of Michigan—they take who they can take."

His own story is also a "sign of the times," Ken says. From protected union employee, to at-will worker fired for no good reason. From a married man with a spouse and extended family to lean on, to a lonely bachelor living off government aid and what medicine and gas he can beg from the Salvation Army. From a hard worker whose decent blue-collar wage made him an essential breadwinner, to a laid-off-has-been of no use to his employed wife. He's not alone, Ken knows. When the plants began shutting down decades ago, when fathers like his started losing jobs that gave "too much" pay for "too little" skill, when mothers like his went on welfare and sons like him quit school to get a paycheck—perhaps it started back then, for Ken, for his generation, for the generations that followed.

Politicians get on TV and make lofty promises of "no worker left behind," but Ken knows better. He can't rely on the government. "[I'm] trying to get aid, but like I said, they ran out of Medicaid," he says. Desperate, Ken finally decides to start going to a local church for group therapy. The only sessions available are for Narcotics Anonymous. Ken doesn't have a drug problem, but he starts attending anyway. "They'll talk to anybody," he says of the program. "They'll let anybody in." At each meeting, he will tell the recovering addicts there about his struggles with depression. They seem to understand what he's going through, he says. "But nobody has an answer."

* * *

Unemployed workers like Ken have learned that government policies that are generous on paper differ in practice when you're dealing with their sluggish, strained bureaucracies. States and provinces frequently do not have the funding or staff to fulfill their promises. Churches and other private organizations at times step in to fill in these gaps, but the help is often inferior and ad hoc—in the case of Ken, a non-addict resorting to the off-label assistance of Narcotics Anonymous, it's a hammer when he needs pliers.[6] And so he relies on himself, hustling every way he can to make a buck. "I'm strong," he says. "I'll make it. I'll be all right. I'm not going to let nothing get to me. … I'm not ready to check out. I'm not ready."

I've described the numerous frustrations that my workers experienced dealing with poor government institutions. Clearly, the Great Recession placed huge strains on these agencies. Americans searched for public health care options in vain. The few programs that actually existed were overwhelmed and underfunded. Without any coverage, my workers were forced to endure the degrading treatment and labyrinthine procedures of the health care system for the uninsured. In Canada, unemployment benefits were delayed by weeks, leading to nail-biting waits as bills piled up and that first unemployment check still hadn't come. And in both countries, surging demand led to huge waiting lists and service cutbacks for government-funded retraining.

Nevertheless, the weak infrastructure and implementation my unemployed workers encountered cannot be blamed just on the economic downturn. Government bureaucracies have long been criticized for ineffectiveness, delays, and poor service. In America, the much-touted initiative during the nineties (headed by vice president Al Gore) to "reinvent" government was a tacit acknowledgement of the extent of the problem. In more recent years, government services have been outsourced to private firms. In-person assistance has been replaced by call centers and websites. And for-profit schools have swallowed up a larger chunk of the retraining dollars.[7] Whether these changes have succeeded in making government sleeker and smarter is debatable. For their part, my workers were not big fans. They were especially upset about how profit-hungry training centers snapped up their government tuition checks but provided a poor education in return.

Half of my workers on the American side had troubling experiences with another critical institution: labor unions. Many of my workers were simply upset by the union's failure to stop their layoffs. But some of them also pointed to specific instances of favoritism. Even in organizations like unions—groups that in theory are rooted in the egalitarian creed—some people are inevitably "more equal" than others, because of friendships, political connections, or cultural affinities. (This rift between the leadership and the rank and file has long bedeviled the labor movement.)[8] One ex-Chrysler worker points out that her union had its own pecking order. Although she was a good worker, she was never invited to the UAW's Black Lake retreat and golf resort in upstate Michigan. Only friends of the local's officers went, she says. "If you really weren't friendly with them, you didn't get the chance to go." The old boys' network didn't care that she was dedicated and reliable on the line. Another former Chrysler worker remembers working alongside a union representative who was flat-out lazy. "I had to do his work," she says. "He'd just leave when he want to, and here I am doing his job and two other jobs." The union let his behavior go on unpunished, she says.

Because most of my workers were not working, they had to deal with government bureaucracies for their benefits. Amid the collapse of the auto industry, they saw their unions in their weakest and least helpful state. It is worth noting that I also interviewed several workers who had found new jobs by the time I talked to them, and among this group the skepticism about government was less intense—though they shared many of the ideological concerns about unions that their unemployed counterparts had, as I will discuss later in this [reading].

Among the unemployed workers, however—especially those with particularly frustrating encounters with government and unions—it was striking how little interest they had in politics, union organizing, or other means to change either the labor market that had left them without jobs or the social safety net that floundered in helping them. As other researchers have found, unemployment does not necessarily lead to political engagement, much less radicalization.[9]

My workers' views of government tended to be less ideological, and more pragmatic, than their views of unions. But there was little sense, especially among the Americans, that government was there to take care of them, or that they could depend on those institutions in any substantial or sustained sense. In addition to the government-sponsored action centers, a handful of my Canadians got involved in politics—mainly through the workers' party, the New Democratic Party—and that provided another collective outlet for their energies. But on the American side, the country's political parties had no such following among my workers. Again, this speaks to their social isolation. It also may reflect the demise of local party politics—the party machines that had once integrated struggling immigrants and given them the power to defend their interests—as political reforms and the rising power of wealthy donors and self-financed candidates have shunted them aside.[10]

With no alternatives, my Americans explicitly focused on self-reliance: overcoming their bouts of unemployment through their own efforts. Vincent Formosa is fifty-three and unemployed. He says he lost interest in politics after he lost his job at the parts plant. He voted for Obama and the Democrats in 2008, but "they didn't do shit for us." The government bailouts enraged him—not just the bailouts of Wall Street banks, which let corporate executives stick around and receive "million-dollar bonuses," but also the bailouts of the Big Three. "There ain't no sense in getting all these big corporations all this money," he says. He is equally fed up with unions, which he feels just look after the interests of union officials. "You know what? If I didn't get another union job I wouldn't even care."

In any case, Vincent has more immediate concerns than what is going on in Obama's White House or the UAW's Solidarity House. Vincent is struggling to pay for his prescriptions and get seen by a doctor for several chronic health conditions. His family has been on food stamps since he lost his job, though the benefit was recently pared down because the government said he made too much money—which Vincent finds ridiculous. Whenever he receives a letter from the social services office, anger instantly grips his thoughts. "I know it's something they're nitpicking about—'We're going to cut you off for this, or we're going to cut you off for that.'"

The kind of help that the government provides comes ensnarled in bureaucratic strings, Vincent says. His hot-water tank broke right after he was laid off, and he didn't have $400 to replace it. He turned to the social services office for help, and they said they would chip in—provided he got three different estimates of the cost, and then waited a month. If he were fifty-five years old, they added, he would qualify sooner. "What's fifty-five got to do with me getting a hot water tank?" Vincent asked, incredulous. The caseworker tried to explain, but by now Vincent was seething. "I don't even want to hear it." He hung up, called his brother, and asked him to wire the money. "I'm not waiting no month."

Vincent is outraged by the long delays and hostility he encounters whenever he tries to get help. So instead, he relies on himself. He is vehement that he will find a way out of his family's predicament, with God's help and his own sweat. Hard work makes a difference, he insists. He points out that he was raised in poverty. But decades of grinding through shifts at Walmart, a furniture company, and then the auto plant pulled Vincent out of that trap. "It made me the person I am," he says. "I could have been dead, in jail." He holds on to that same faith today. What else can he do? "I ain't got nothing to fall back on," he says.

And yet Vincent, who worked hard for thirty-six years, can't find anyone willing to hire him. "The only thing I've got going [for me] is my work ethic. If you give me a chance to prove myself, then I'm going to do the best I can." He pauses. "I ain't run across nobody like that. … You can't really blame them. But then again, you say, 'What the hell?' Just give me a chance, that's all I ask."

When the institutions that are supposed to help them let them down, workers like Vincent come to the rational conclusion that they are really on their own. Their lived experiences show them they have no other option.

Family, nonprofit organizations, and religious institutions are potential alternatives to the self-reliance my workers turned to. The failure of government and unions, then, may simply lead to a greater dependence on other parts of the private safety net. As they were in earlier times, families and charities could become the proper—and, perhaps, preponderant—sources of support for the long-term unemployed, with the privatization of economic *assistance* advancing alongside a privatization of economic *suffering*—as the plight of workers becomes seen as a private concern, not a public one.[11] (This is the once-and-future scenario advocated by some on the right, including America's Tea Party.) Regardless, my conversations with my workers suggest that these options are no real replacements for strong government policies and strong unions. Inequality plays a role here, too: blue-collar, lower-income, and less educated workers in general are more socially isolated than white-collar, middle-class, and more educated workers, meaning that they get involved less in voluntary associations and other organizational alternatives to unions or political parties.[12]

Their extended families offered to help the families I got to know, but in most cases (especially for the black households) there was not much in the way of resources to give. In any case, asking for their assistance was degrading, my workers routinely said. One benefit of government benefits is that households can receive them on the down low. As for charities, Ken Brennan was fortunate enough to receive prescriptions and gas money from the Salvation Army, but the rest of my workers received little in the way of tangible help: mainly groceries from food pantries and the occasional holiday gift card from the union. The meritocratic ideology generated a sense of guilt here as well, undermining the value of any outside help they did receive. Several of my workers, for example, said they refused to go to a food pantry because of the stigma attached to it. Food stamps, on the other hand, could be used with a relatively inconspicuous swipe of a card at a checkout counter.

As for religion, many of my workers—my Americans in particular—spoke of their faith as a means of getting through their personal crisis. But few went to church regularly. Religion for them was mainly a matter of individual faith and self-reliance, rather than a collective struggle for social justice. "With God's help," they believed, "*I* will get through this." Even those who attended black churches—traditionally strong reservoirs of social-justice sentiment—did not draw from that aspect of their faith.

Fewer of my Canadian workers had unfavorable encounters with their unions or government agencies. The action centers funded by the province and their former employers made a favorable impression on my workers. Peer helpers who were their fellow union members provided personalized counseling, burnishing the union's image. The centers guided my workers through the maze of government bureaucracy and lobbied officials on their behalf, alleviating some of their frustrations and making what government assistance they did tap more effective.

If the action centers improved the experiences that my Canadian workers had, the differences between the two nations in this area should not be overstated. Social spending in both countries, I noted earlier, has converged, with the Canadians becoming stingier. The labor movement remains stronger in Canada, but unions in both countries have been losing power. Meanwhile, the pro-corporate movement has had success even up north in its campaigns to deregulate markets, defund government, and rationalize labor. These trends have degraded the institutions that workers encounter in their day-to-day lives, perhaps leading to more similar experiences and responses in the two countries. For instance, as dedicated as the peer helpers were, they could do nothing to alter the sluggish pace at which the government paid out its unemployment benefits. They could not alter bureaucratic decisions to tighten an overwhelmed training program's requirements and to exclude many workers. In these and other ways, there were limits to what determined individuals could do to address the frequent structural strains endured by fraying social safety nets.

Those of my Canadian workers who did not have much contact with the action centers felt much the same way as the Americans did. Tom Moon, a fifty-four-year-old Canadian and former Ford worker, got on public assistance after his unemployment ran out. His encounters with bureaucracies have been universally bad. The government offers no real solutions for people like him, he says. "Are they gonna step in and give me $3 or $4 million to make my life better? No." (And yet they give corporations billions not to go bankrupt, he adds with disgust.) Meanwhile, the help he does get is half-hearted. "Welfare doesn't give you enough to live."

Their exposure to faltering institutions gave my workers good reasons to be skeptical of government and unions. But more broadly, they also acknowledged that the economy has changed. It was only practical to change with it. In 2009 and 2010, the auto companies and unions were on the brink of collapse. Government agencies were broke and cutting payrolls and benefits. My workers were responding to this extreme climate. At the same time, in both countries they were also well aware that long-run economic and political trends have not been moving in their direction. Unions have grown weaker, and corporations have grown stronger.

Unions were once important, Tom says. They won good wages and benefits for their members when they had bargaining power years ago. But nowadays, he says, autoworkers are getting paid too much relative to what the market will allow. "You're at a point where you have to give something back. And now everybody's saying, 'The union is doing this, the union is doing that.' No, they're not. The company is deciding what they're gonna do." Unlike the workers I mentioned earlier, Tom wasn't mad at his union for specific instances of favoritism. He was just being realistic.

As for corporations, many of my workers angrily attacked their former employers for making poor or dishonorable decisions that led to job losses. (This was especially true among my parts workers, whose plants had already been shut down.) That was not surprising. What *was* surprising was that a substantial minority of workers in both countries—again, former members of powerful unions—stressed how important it was to see things from the company's point of view.

Tellingly, they prided themselves on their knowledge of what is necessary to run a profitable business. At the end of the day, the decision to close the plant made sense, says Allen Lee, an American ex-parts worker. He was upset with how the company treated its employees right after the layoffs, but he sees the wisdom of transferring production to more modern, integrated, profitable facilities. "I can't get mad with what they did, 'cause it was a good business move," he says. Other workers "hate" the company's owner for what happened, but he knows a "good businessman" when he sees one. "I know sometimes you gotta make decisions that everybody ain't gonna coincide with," he points out.

Workers like Allen have a folk understanding of economics.[13] To some extent, they have adopted the viewpoint of those higher up in the labor market's hierarchy, who point out that companies are in business "to provide a service or a product," not "to hire people."[14] They realize that companies cannot survive if their expenses exceed revenues. They appreciate the competitive constraints that companies operate under. They become skeptical of unions and other collective action to deal with the consequences of those "good business moves."

This kind of market realism could be seen on both sides of the border. Americans and Canadians alike talked about how companies had moved their factories overseas, how automation had excised certain positions and upped the skills required for others, and how their government and union leaders had been either unwilling or unable to stop the loss of jobs. Free trade, automation, and politics had led to this dire situation, and they were helpless to do anything about it. And yet because hard work and further education are always things that (supposedly) will lead to a good job, they could pursue this individual strategy—and perhaps suffer the self-blame that came when their failures piled up.

Their personal experiences and personal understanding of the changed economy pushed my workers toward one course of action: relying on themselves. For the most part, then, my workers do not exactly fit the concept of false consciousness. They are acting rationally.[15] Policymakers, with their ineffective and incompetent bureaucracies, have failed them. Unions, with their cronyism and powerlessness, have failed them. They can't count on these institutions. They can only count on themselves. Rather than do nothing, they should be hitting the pavement, looking for jobs. Rather than wasting their time retraining for careers in growing industries that probably won't hire the likes of them anyways, they should be sending out résumés, making phone calls, and praying that there are factories that still want them.

Morality Plays

With his faith in God and the support of his wife, Eddie Frank has so far been able to take his unemployment in stride. Thankfully, Maria has a good job as a restaurant manager. They go to church every Sunday, and Eddie firmly believes that God will handle whatever may come. "He been doing it all my life," says the American ex-autoworker. "Everything is even probably closer to Him now than ever." Still, at times the stress ramps up. Things can seem "gloomy," he says. "You got to pay everything on time, but at the same time, you got to spend."

It bothers him that he can't help support Maria and the kids. "A man's got an ego," he says. "So ... I'm a little bit more humble." If he could get even an $11-an-hour job, he says, he'd take it. But so far nothing like that has presented itself. Meanwhile, their tight finances mean that he and Maria have no margin of error in their spending decisions. "It's like a chess game," Eddie says. "You got to be cautious on what kind of move you make now."

Eddie is a muscular man in his thirties, with a neatly trimmed beard and close-cropped hair. He worked for almost twenty years in the industry, and has a ruined shoulder to show for it. Nevertheless, he counts his blessings. He compares his situation to those of many of his former coworkers, who didn't put money away, and whose partners, if they have any, are unsupportive or lazy. "It's like you just defeated the purpose of you working hard," he says. "If you don't have nothing to show for all that time, shame on you."

It's not that he doesn't see the desperation around him. When Eddie moved into his Detroit home, he lived in a good neighborhood. But hard times have brought it down. Now, many of the houses on his block and elsewhere are shuttered, abandoned by their owners. He and Maria have an alarm, a fence, and a guard dog protecting their home. "I never had an incident, thank God." But if you park your car on the street at night, he adds, "forget about it. You wake up in the morning, they broke the glass." People will rip off parts and sell them easily in this car town.

Eddie doesn't know how to even begin solving these kinds of problems. Workers need education to get jobs, but a lot of his former coworkers are already middle-aged, he points out. What are they going to do? Companies no longer have any patience for anyone but the most productive workers. "They don't care if you're struggling in your house," he says, "or you ain't got no money to feed your kids. The only thing they worry about is ... they don't want to lose no money." As for unions, they will be "gone in a minute," he insists. Corporations are steadily rooting them out. The recession just provided another opening for management. "They want somebody that's gonna go in there and work with their rules, you know, not with the union rules."

To some extent, he understands the companies' point of view. "As soon as you hire somebody that's in a union in a company, then you pretty much gave up your right as a businessperson, because they're gonna find that loophole for them to get less work and get paid more money." Unions helped a lot of people "back in the day," he points out, but nowadays they go "overboard." "As every year goes by, they renew their contract, they want more, more. How much more? ... And then, on top of it, what do they do? Sit and eat donuts in the local?" It's not fair that some unionized workers get paid better than people who spent their time and money getting an education, he says.

Since he lost his job, Eddie has been busy taking care of his kids and cleaning up the house while Maria works. Meanwhile, he waits. He'd like to get a commercial driving license, which would allow him to get a job as a truck driver. He applied for the state retraining program, which would foot the thousands of dollars in tuition. But the program ran out of funds. "So what am I gonna do, you know?"

He understands that times are tough. The government only has so much money to spend, he notes. He can't blame them for needing to economize their resources. Still, if it's not going to help out, it would be better if the government could at least step out of the way. Years ago he worked as a barber, and these days he cuts his friends' hair for extra cash. But state regulations mean that he can't make that into any sort of living. "You got to be licensed," he points out.

Maria describes her husband as a "workaholic." For two decades he was up before anyone else in the house and out the door, headed to work. "If there was overtime, I was getting it," Eddie says. "It was not a day that I was home saying, 'Oh, I don't want to work.' Even [if] I'm sick, I'm going to work because it's just—that's the kind of person I am."

If things are going to work out, he's going to be the one to make it happen, he says. As for the union, they're useless. "They call and say bad news." He laughs. "That's what they help me on."

* * *

National surveys have consistently shown that Americans endorse the virtues of self-reliance, willpower, and individualism. Past scholarship has dubbed this set of interconnected beliefs the "American belief system" and the "achievement ideology." But even as it spurs ordinary Americans to extraordinary accomplishments, the ideology has consequences for those who falter along the way. As other scholars have argued, it focuses attention on how individuals, rather than the system, have failed, leading people to criticize others—and themselves—when they stay stuck in poverty and unemployment. Success, in this view, is a sign of moral virtue, and failure a mark of sin.[16]

For a span of decades in the middle of the last century, there were powerful and persistent alternatives to this meritocratic viewpoint. Strong labor unions emerged, rallying working men and women under the banner of solidarity and collective struggle. More radically, leftist political movements captured much of the world's imagination. Communism ended up being brutal and oppressive of the people it was supposed to lift up, but for a time it did offer a worldview that glorified ordinary workers. Under the Marxist ideology, they could see themselves as key players in a broader historical struggle, rather than just cogs in the market economy's perpetual-motion machine. And under its threat, capitalist societies were forced to respond to their demands—ironically, more so than was the case in totalitarian communist societies, which were hostile to independent labor movements.

It is important to note that, in America at least, what blue-collar workers once had going for them was never a socialist wonderland. As Kay Lehman Schlozman and Sidney Verba point out, blue-collar workers in the 1930s were somewhat more class conscious than was the case four decades later, in that more of them—though never a majority—identified with the working class and supported aggressive government action to further their economic interests. When Schlozman and Verba conducted a survey in mid-seventies, amid stagflation and worries about American decline, they found that even the unemployed held persistently onto the American Dream ideology, and blue-collar and white-collar attitudes had converged, largely moving in a more conservative direction. Even during these years of relative union strength, blue-collar Americans had conflicting attitudes about success, and about who was to blame for the lack of it.[17]

Nevertheless, the power of their unions to win good wages—beyond what their educational credentials would have paid—was a source of pride. "You got people working in offices, they might consider themselves ... a little better than the workingman," says a shop steward in Robert Lane's 1962 study of the political beliefs of ordinary Americans. "But nine times out of ten, the workingman is making more money than he is." In his later study of plant workers, David Halle tells the story of a high school dropout whose daughter told her teachers how much he earned. "They didn't believe it, so I Xeroxed a pay stub for her to show them!" he gloated. An egalitarian combination of institutions and ideologies insulated these workers to a significant degree from the self-doubts and self-blame that accompany low status. It encouraged these workers, in turn, to take a collective response to unemployment. In the eighties, Katherine Newman found laid-off plant workers to be a "brotherhood of the downwardly mobile," who stood together against corporate downsizing. A culture of meritocracy did thrive then, Newman says, but it was relevant to elite white-collar managers, who justified the startling inequality that placed them on top by pointing to their own "sheer ability and hard work." A decade later, Kathryn Marie Dudley described white-collar professionals who welcomed the closing of a Chrysler plant in their community. They believed that economic advancement should depend on individual credentials, not collective bargaining. Nevertheless, Dudley's unionized autoworkers still defended the value of organized labor.[18]

Looking across the border, Canadians have traditionally been more collectivist than Americans. In many ways, the two nations share quite similar cultures that harken back to the frontier lifestyle of the New World. Nevertheless, as sociologist Seymour Martin Lipset famously described, Canada and the United States emerged from distinct sets of political values. Canada grew into a communitarian nation that envisioned society as a mosaic of groups, while America evolved into an individualistic country that emphasized laissez-faire competition and meritocracy.[19] America's racial diversity, its ideology of the American Dream, and its unfettered markets have long meant that its citizens espoused a more self-reliant view of opportunity and government.

In recent decades, however, as the flow of ideas across national borders becomes increasingly costless and effortless, the American Dream is becoming a somewhat universal dream, even as cross-Atlantic concerns about inequality also percolate into the American consciousness. (Interestingly, Martin Whyte uses survey data to show that meritocratic views are the very strongest today in China, where the Chinese leadership boasts about the so-called Chinese Dream.)[20] For this reason, the terms

American belief system and *American Dream* may be outdated. Scholars have proposed other, less insular terms. I build on the work of Katherine Newman and use the term *meritocratic morality*, defined in opposition to three other kinds of moral ideologies: egalitarian morality, fraternal morality, and grace morality.[21] But first, I want to discuss what, if anything, public opinion surveys can tell us about possible changes in attitudes concerning individual opportunity and collective institutions.

If we think of the meritocratic perspective *just* in terms of hard work leading to success, support for this view has fluctuated slightly but remains strong. For example, posed the question of whether individuals get ahead by dint of hard work or the intervention of luck or other people, two-thirds of Americans over the past four decades have told Gallup they believe "hard work" is responsible—a proportion that has drifted upward. The less educated believe more strongly than their well-educated counterparts in this idea, although the differences are not large. A Pew Research Center poll on the same topic finds similar results: a strong, and slightly growing, belief that success is within our control. (Contradicting these other surveys, however, the World Values Survey finds a decline in this way of thinking over two decades, though the survey is not conducted as frequently as the others.)[22]

However, whether someone believes that "people get ahead by their own hard work" is not the best measure for the meritocratic thinking I have in mind, which as I've explained involves a more complicated understanding of what we understand merit to be. In addition, those who believe that people get ahead through hard work may simply be responding to a labor market that is no longer shackled by high degrees of nepotism and discrimination. They may or may not believe that people *should* rise and fall based on their effort and ability, but here the question is asking them what actually happens in the labor market. Finally, the idea of "luck" as an alternative to hard work is a nebulous one, as sociologist Leslie McCall points out. When luck is put in more concrete terms, she writes, a "significant minority of Americans (just under half) say that things such as social connections and coming from a privileged background are essential or very important factors in getting ahead." McCall argues that the fact that Americans acknowledge these barriers means that they are—contrary to scholarly stereotypes—concerned about the lack of opportunity for all to succeed.[23]

A different measure of meritocratic morality is how much people believe that education leads to success. According to one international survey, Americans overwhelmingly believe that education is important in "getting ahead," regardless of the amount of schooling they personally have, and this proportion has increased slightly over the years. But when we look at the public's view of how important education and training "ought" to be in deciding pay, the trend is in the opposite direction. It is not clear what to make of this divergence. On the one hand, it may be the case that any *pay* advantage of education is less salient for workers like mine—"getting ahead," which implies being gainfully employed, is the more pressing concern. It is worth noting, too, that the less educated are equally or slightly more supportive of the view that education *ought* to matter in deciding pay—denying, it seems, their own deservingness.[24] On the other hand, these trends may suggest (at least for the U.S. population) that realism, rather than ideology, is at work here: people increasingly acknowledge that education *does* matter, though they increasingly think it *shouldn't* matter.

The picture is further complicated by Americans' complex attitudes toward inequality. In 2009, for instance, two-thirds of Americans believed that income differences in their country were too large, slightly higher than the proportion a decade earlier. That said, the public's concern about inequality peaked in 1992, at 77 percent, and has remained below that level since—in spite of the rapid income gains of the top 1 percent over this period of time.[25] McCall points out that during the nineties the economy boomed and shared its bounty widely, which may have dampened concerns about inequality. Given the recent explosion in inequality, however, the lack of a larger and clearer shift in public opinion is puzzling.

Furthermore, on some questions, the public's views are a bit incoherent. For example, a third of Americans in 2009 agreed that government should reduce differences in income between people with high incomes and those with low incomes. However, when the same survey used a question with different wording—instead asking about income differences between the *rich* and the *poor*—half of Americans agreed. (Clearly, question wording matters, and popular views are not always ideologically consistent.) On the first question, support for government intervention has declined, but on the second question, it has increased. Meanwhile, a little more than a third of Americans have consistently said that it should be the responsibility of government "to provide a job for everyone who wants one."[26]

How do the American public's views compare with those across the border? In their views on the importance of hard work, one international survey finds that the attitudes in each country have moved a bit closer to those held across the border. In the middle of the last decade, for example, 76 percent of Canadians approved of the statement "Hard work usually brings a better life," compared to 77 percent of Americans—a one-point gap, compared to a seven-point one in 1990. Very similar numbers of Americans and Canadians said that education was essential or very important in getting ahead, in the one year that a survey was conducted in both countries. In terms of how much it *should* affect pay, however, Canadians believed substantially less in the importance of education, though the gap has shrunk over time.

In both countries, a majority of the population is concerned about inequality. More Canadians than Americans agree that government should reduce income differences between rich and poor, but this belief in intervention has risen in both countries since the mid-nineties. In terms of unemployment policy, about the same proportion of Canadians—four out of ten—believe that government should provide a job for everyone who wants one.[27]

Overall, then, Americans and Canadians tend to have fairly similar views about the importance of hard work and education in getting ahead, but they differ on how much they think education *ought* to matter and how much government *should* get involved in addressing inequality. The fact that Americans believe more strongly that education should be important suggests that there is a bit more ideological support over there for the kind of meritocratic labor market I have described. At the same time, this view appears to have declined over time in America and Canada alike, while support for the belief that education *does* matter has risen—suggesting that today's workers may be responding more to changing realities than to a changing culture per se. In terms of policy preferences, Americans tend to be more skeptical about direct government interventions in the market, with the exception of providing jobs (which still gets the support of only a minority of people in both countries). McCall, however, points out that, in line with their strong belief in the principle of equal opportunity, Americans do support spending on education, and that support has grown.

* * *

The workers I interviewed tended to come from less privileged backgrounds. Their stated politics were overwhelmingly liberal or moderate. And they were unionized blue-collar workers—a group that has long represented the upper bound of class consciousness in both America and Canada. For these reasons, I did not expect to hear the narrow individualism and self-blame that many of them expressed. In fact, I had begun my research with a focus on social policy, and without any particular interest in meritocracy. But the rhetoric my workers used prompted me to expand my study to try to capture what was going through their heads.

Of course, other groups express more extreme meritocratic views than my workers do. The Tea Party movement that rose to prominence in the 2010 U.S. elections has been driven in part by an especially uncompromising form of the ideology, most apparent in the movement's disdain for those reliant on government assistance. Likewise, anthropologist Karen Ho has studied the radical individualism of Wall Street investment bankers, smug in their knowledge that they are the superior exemplars of the meritocratic creed: intelligent, hard-working, and extraordinarily talented.[28]

Tea Party members may have an enthusiasm for dismantling the welfare state, and Wall Street bankers may extol the ruthless actions of corporations, but my more liberal workers didn't put forward such hard-line views about government or corporations. In fact, the American and Canadian autoworkers largely expressed support for *stronger* policy interventions to improve the economy.[29] As I've described, if they personally turned away from government agencies, they had little choice in the matter: their personal experiences had taught them that they could not rely on its underfunded and faltering bureaucracies. In other words, realism, and not the meritocratic ideology, appeared to drive my workers' views of government. Likewise, my workers expressed disgust with corporate executives. They were universally mad that some CEOs were receiving million-dollar bonuses even when their companies were falling apart. They fiercely criticized the careless and half-witted business decisions of the Big Three and other corporations, which many said contributed to the auto industry's ruin. And they were outraged by the corrupt and selfish actions of Wall Street during the economic crisis.

At the same time, ideology did matter in other, more subtle ways. The prevailing culture of judgment forces less advantaged workers to adopt a defensive posture, regardless of whether they espouse its meritocratic tenets. In the case of my workers, the broader narrative about the evils of big government was very much on their minds. They were sensitive to the extreme meritocratic viewpoint, adopted by some conservatives, that there are two classes: the makers, and the takers. They expressed great shame about receiving government benefits. They constantly sought to refute any notion that they were freeloaders. The bank bailouts were overwhelmingly unpopular among them, and yet their support for the auto bailouts was surprisingly tepid. This defensiveness about government was common among my Americans and Canadians, parts workers and Big Three workers.

Likewise, my workers in both countries felt the need to attack their own relatively high compensation even as they attacked overpaid corporate executives. Both management and labor were to blame because they didn't "deserve" what they were getting: the virtuous link between skill and compensation had been sundered. "The fact that they're paying a lot of these auto executives millions and millions of dollars and offering CEOs millions and millions of dollars in buyouts—I think it's asinine," said a Canadian worker. But he felt that the workers at his unionized plant were paid too much, too. "They gave it to us because the executives were getting it. That money should have gone back into the company for product development and research."

There did seem to be a more ideological tinge to my Americans' views of corporations. On the Canadian side, plenty of anger was directed at the inequality that corporations promoted. James Channing, a forty-three-year-old former parts worker, thinks it ludicrous that companies can pay their bosses million-dollar bonuses and still get upset that their workers are making $23 an hour. "I'm not talking a line worker should be gettin' CEO money, but there's no reason for anyone to get a $10 million bonus ever, for anything," he says. On the American side, however, workers more often couched these criticisms in the narrower terms of meritocratic morality (if with a more politically liberal cast), arguing not that too much wealth or power was necessarily a bad thing, but that elites had done bad things that proved them to be undeserving. "When you screw up and you're making a million dollars a year or better, they don't fire you," says Johnson Cheney, a former union steward at Chrysler. "They just say, 'Well, okay, we'll give you ten million dollars and you go on home.'"[30]

The broader culture of judgment did not always convert my workers to a meritocratic view, but it did force them to plead their case against its criticisms. In his postwar study of autoworkers, Eli Chinoy noted that the "defensive measures" that workers adopted back then were only "partially effective" in stopping the ideological onslaught of "guilt and self-depreciation."[31] Since then, however, the situation has grown worse for ordinary workers, through the trends of growing labor weakness and heightened market competition I have described. They have to fight against the now commonsense notions that the free market should be allowed to work its creative destruction unhindered, and that workers with little skill should not be paid much. In the next section, I will explore how the prevailing ideology colored their views of a third set of institutions, ones that traditionally have been bastions of collective action: labor unions.

A Union of the Deserving Is Not a Union

Because he's a hard worker, Mitch Beerman sees no point to unions. "I can't see which way they've actually helped me in the past up until now," says the thirty-three-year-old Canadian. "If I could stay away from unions, I probably would." In his thirteen years at a feeder plant, Mitch had to turn to the union exactly twice—once because the company stiffed him on some hours, and another time because it wouldn't give him a modified work assignment after he developed tendonitis. Other workers were always getting suspended and having the union bail them out, Mitch points out. "I never miss time, nothing. I stay out of trouble. I go and do my job. I go home."

Mitch does not see unions surviving in the long term—and in fact, he is "kind of hoping" they will go down. "All they do is they fight for the people that actually need the union—the ones that always get into trouble," he says. "They're the ones that save their butts."

These days, though, Mitch could use someone to save him. When he lost his job at the plant a year ago, his wife Kendra picked up a second, part-time job to help support them and their two young girls. After a short while it became clear that she resented the situation—bitterly. She would come home from work and start yelling at him, unprovoked. He was lazy, Kendra declared. He needed to start paying more bills. The two eventually decided to split up.

"You deserve somebody better than me that ain't gonna yell at you every day for no reason," Kendra told him.

Four months ago, Mitch moved back in with his parents. They are both retired, and they say they don't mind, but Mitch hasn't lived at home for a decade. Staying there grates at his pride. Even though he pays $150 a month in rent, "I still feel like I'm intruding," he says. But he has nowhere else to go. He has already spent the $10,000 he had in retirement savings. His bank account has run dry.

Mitch is deeply depressed. His weight has dropped twenty-seven pounds. "I just eat enough to get me by," he says. He feels guilty using up his parents' groceries. Unable to sleep more than a handful of hours at night, Mitch will crawl into bed during the day. When his mood sinks to its lowest, he will find himself sitting in front of the TV, aimlessly flipping through channels, a monologue running through his head: *What am I going to do? My parents are only going to let me live here for so long. Am I going to lose my Jeep? Is the bank going to take my house? Why can't I find a job? Is there something wrong with me? Is it my résumé? Am I just not smart enough to do this?*

Mitch doesn't blame himself for losing his job, but he can't help being hard on himself as the employer rejections pile up. "It's never taken me this long to find a job," he says a year after his layoff. When he was younger and bouncing between menial positions, he never thought to go on unemployment. "I'm usually someone who is right back in it."

Even though he, a diligent worker, suddenly finds himself jobless, buried under debt, and struggling to pull himself up again, Mitch wholeheartedly agrees with the idea that hard work brings a better life. "I've always felt like that," he says. He doesn't point to any structural flaws in the economy that hinder his chances or those of other hard-working men and women; the economy is bad right now—and that's temporary.[32] Things will get better "sooner or later," he adds. "I truly believe it. Things will start to turn."

For the moment, though, things are headed sharply downward. Recently, the utility company shut off the gas in his former home because the bills had gone unpaid. He asked his parents for the money to get it turned back on so that Kendra and his daughters wouldn't freeze. Later, Mitch had to go to the hospital for a severe respiratory infection. His father paid for the Percocet painkillers that the doctor prescribed.

"I've never asked for help all the way up until this year," Mitch points out. "And it takes a lot for me to actually ask somebody for help, because I feel embarrassed."

He should be the one providing—to his kids, above all. He still upbraids himself for what happened this past Christmas. The only things he could afford to buy his daughters came from the Dollar Store: coloring books, crayons, colored pencils, puzzles, workbooks. "I didn't get my brother or sister anything. Nothing for Mom and Dad." His daughters didn't mind so much. "They were just glad they had things under the tree." But he felt like "crap," he says. "Still do."

* * *

In recent years, anti-union activists and their corporate backers have won a telling string of victories. Around the time of the federal bailouts of the auto industry, commentators blasted unionized autoworkers as the undeserving recipients of taxpayer assistance, their intransigent opposition nearly dooming the industry to liquidation. Public-sector unions—a rare bright spot in the modern labor movement—came under fire for their generous pensions and other benefits, which their detractors said had put unsustainable pressures on government budgets.[33] In both countries, a significant segment of the population expressed support for these criticisms. In 2011, 48 percent of Canadians said that strikes by public-sector unions should be banned and settlements imposed by arbitrators, in step with recent efforts by the federal government to exert greater control over when those unions can and can't strike. That same year, 39 percent of Americans told Gallup that they supported the governors in Wisconsin and elsewhere who sought not just to force concessions from public-sector unions but to hobble their very ability to negotiate. And a year later, the unthinkable happened: Michigan—the home turf of the UAW—successfully passed a right-to-work law, the twenty-fourth state to do so. One poll before the vote found that the state's residents were evenly divided (47 percent in favor, 46 percent opposed) on the new law, which dilutes organized labor's power by allowing workers in unionized workplaces to refuse membership.[34]

In 2014 organized labor took another beating—this one involving the UAW itself. Employees at a Volkswagen car plant in Tennessee agreed to a vote on whether to unionize. Volkswagen, which was used to working with Germany's strong unions, pledged neutrality. With the employer standing aside, the Volkswagen drive represented perhaps the UAW's best opportunity ever to break into the labor-unfriendly South, where in recent decades foreign-owned plants employing nonunion workers have multiplied. But in the end, the UAW could not beat back an aggressive and well-funded opposition led by conservative lawmakers and lobbying groups. The plant's workers rejected the union.

We should not read too much into these recent defeats. To some extent, the public's disdain for "overpaid" government workers has to do with naturally tightfisted (but temporary) attitudes during a period of economic turmoil.[35] Likewise, the legislative victories of anti-union activists may say more about how much money today's pro-corporate movement is willing to pour into their cause, rather than any long-lasting groundswell of public opinion in their favor.

That said, current trends in public opinion cannot be very comforting for the labor movement. During the Great Depression and war years, unions were widely seen as champions of the underdog.[36] When the Gallup polling organization first asked about them, in 1936, only 20 percent of Americans disapproved of unions, while 72 percent approved. Aggressive strikes amid labor shortages gave even management a grudging respect for them—so much so that in the 1940s the president of the U.S. Chamber of Commerce could venture to say, "Labor unions are woven into our economic pattern of American life, and collective bargaining is a part of the democratic process."[37] A decade later, public approval of unions stood at record highs in both countries: 75 percent in America, and 69 percent in Canada.

Today, majorities continue to approve of unions, and surveys indicate that Americans and Canadians alike desire more representation at work than current union membership rates might imply.[38] Yet, in America at least, public approval has dropped significantly since the middle of the last century. The rate began to fall in the 1960s, recovered some of its lost ground around the turn of the century, and then collapsed dramatically in the years after the recession—when, for the first time, less than half of the country approved of unions.

Furthermore, the public's *disapproval* of unions has risen even more sharply than approval has fallen. This is because fewer people today, when polled, express "no opinion" of unions.[39] Since its peak in 2009, anti-union anger has simmered down, yet not enough to bring it back to its level just a decade ago. In Canada, comparable data doesn't exist for more recent years, but what is available paints a similar picture—indeed, approval rates in the two countries have largely moved in lockstep.[40]

As for my workers, a little less than half of them expressed ambivalent or hostile attitudes toward unions. The discontent was slightly higher in the United States, and much higher among the parts workers. To some extent, the fact that my workers were *former* autoworkers explains these harsh assessments. For my parts workers, the closure of their plants soured their views of the union. And losing their jobs during the worst economic crisis since the Great Depression added to a sense of bewilderment and fear that made them question institutions in general. Nevertheless, I did not expect to hear such intense discontent in my interviews. I found most of my workers with the help of the unions. If anything, I had expected them to be pro-union. Even more surprising, these men and women had recently been members of two of the most powerful labor organizations in North America, unions with proud histories of organizing and agitating on behalf of worker rights. Yet, a substantial number of them were skeptical about the very organizations that had won them years of good wages and benefits.

Earlier in the chapter I talked about how much of my workers' skepticism of unions was practical rather than ideological. A few of them pointed out that organized labor has a problem with corruption. They might not oppose unions in principle, but when they came across instances of blatant favoritism, it was hard to feel any loyalty to the cause. In this way, fraternal and self-serving pressures ruptured the union's egalitarian ideal. At the same time, other workers said the labor movement has too *little* power. They questioned whether, in today's economy, unions could continue to defend their interests given the steep declines in membership in both countries. If the views of my workers were likely colored by the fact that they were union members—or, contrarily, the fact that they lost their jobs during a severe downturn—in these areas they expressed attitudes not much different from those of the rest of the public. Majorities of Americans and Canadians have said that there is too much corruption in unions, and that unions are becoming weaker.[41]

Such assessments might imply that the problem is one of implementation. With honest leaders, unions could be governed better. With the right strategy, organized labor could claw back more power from corporations. However, my workers' criticisms sometimes went beyond a sober recognition of the weaknesses of today's labor movement. It was not just that unions are powerless, but that they are inefficient. It was not just that they happen to be corrupt, but that they—almost by definition—help the undeserving. Unlike the realism I discussed earlier, this perspective seemed to have less to do with the ups and downs of the market, and more to do with ideological conviction, or defensiveness, in the face of a dominant, anti-union narrative.

The public's focus on corruption is not surprising, given the long history of organized crime's dealings with organized labor—vividly dramatized in the late fifties by the McClellan Committee congressional hearings, with their endless procession of taciturn labor leaders invoking the Fifth Amendment. But the mafia organization most entangled in unions, Cosa Nostra, has seen its power wane from its peak in the sixties and seventies. Since the McClellan hearings, the U.S. government has monitored the activities of unions more closely and prosecuted corrupt leaders. And organized crime never had as strong a labor racketeering operation in Canada as it did in America.[42] So if there are modern-day concerns about union corruption, perhaps they have more to do with the kinds of minor-league corruption my workers experienced—episodes of union leaders looking out for themselves and their buddies.

Or, there may be deeper concerns at work. "Corruption" tends to be a catch-all term that people use to express any kind of disenchantment with public institutions. Meritocracy is the moral right; corruption is the moral wrong. This is the standard narrative of muckraking journalists: officials of a particular institution defy the law or bend the rules for the benefit of themselves and their friends.[43] As media scholar Jay Rosen observes, among news professionals the romantic image of the journalist is the "hard-boiled detective, ferreting out lies and corruption and moving on to the next town"—that is, not the pointy-headed commentator examining the workings of institutions and the sweep of social trends. In other words, the problem with focusing on corruption is that it distracts us from structural problems—problems with the system itself, rather than the people or groups who currently run it.[44] We root out the bad apples rather than tending to a sickly tree. In their criticisms of corporations, as I noted earlier, my American workers tended to adopt this narrower viewpoint, leveling their displeasure at corrupt business leaders rather than the larger structure of corporate power. In a similar vein (though a completely different domain), they would sometimes complain about union "corruption," but what they were really talking about was the way their own values clashed with the union's egalitarian spirit.

When meritocratic morality is taken to its logical conclusion, it leads to a particular viewpoint: I'm a hard worker and responsible for my own success, so why do I need a union? Burak Oya, a Canadian and a former Ford employee, has a more colorful way of expressing this view. He believes that the union's egalitarian rules penalize hard workers. "If you and I are doing the same job, but I'm busting my ass and you're not, why are you and I going to make the same pay?" he says. "Union thinks everyone should be paid in accordance with their job description, but there's a lot of dog fuckers out there, and I don't want to carry their ass." By clinging to unfair seniority practices and inefficient work rules, unions contradict the meritocratic society's essential principle: that people should be judged on their effort and ability.

Some of my workers said that they didn't "need" the union because they were just good workers, the kind that management respected and retained. They saw their union membership purely in instrumental terms—help when you're in trouble—and since they were never in trouble, there was no point to it. Others maintained that the union was important but that they wanted a union of workers who "deserved" protection—not the reprobates and malingerers and lackeys who were currently free-riding on the backs of dedicated workers. "I'm not so sure if it is good to have a union all the time," says a Canadian former parts worker. "Because there's a lot of people that take advantage of it ... and the union allows that." Unions these days are antiquated, he adds, because education is more widespread and important. "If you're hired by a company that has a well-educated management, I think you don't need a union." A few of the people I interviewed who had found new jobs shared these critical views of organized labor. Though she supported the UAW, one (now white-collar) worker said, it drove her crazy that the union would defend those of her coworkers who missed work. "That was the only thing I didn't like about the union," she says. "It did protect the bad workers as well as the good workers."

Johnson Cheney, the former union steward, told me about how he had had to defend lousy, incorrigible workers—the "fuck-ups," as he calls them. It bothered him that he spent his time helping them instead of workers who did their jobs well. ("I've got to treat everybody the same, you know?") So did the fact that some workers managed to get plum assignments that paid more, even though they didn't put much effort into their jobs. "The harder you work, the less you make, right? And the less you do, the more you make," he says. Even for those who ascend into the lower ranks of the leadership, unions can be double-edged swords, cleaving an arbitrary line between favoritism and fairness.

Part of what bothers these workers, both Americans and Canadians, is the fundamental nature of the union—the fact that the union protects *everyone,* and not just those who "deserve" it. But in criticizing organized labor, they neglect a simple strategic reality: a union of the deserving isn't really a union.[45] There is a reason that unions operate mainly according to rules of seniority, and not job performance. Any cracks in solidarity mean that the union's only power—its power of numbers—will come crashing to the ground. Yet, under the meritocratic perspective, critics of the union often ignored or dismissed what their unions had accomplished, and instead focused their ire—narrowly—on fellow workers who had violated the moral code of the workplace. To this extent, they exhibited false consciousness.

This disdain for protecting the unworthy may explain part of the public's perception of unions as "corrupt." Helping the undeserving is favoritism in the eyes of meritocrats, but solidarity in the eyes of a union, whose very legitimacy and influence are derived from the sum of all its members. In other words, undeservingness is to egalitarianism as inequality is to meritocracy (or as favoritism is to fraternity, or as permissiveness is to grace)—an unavoidable price of doing business.

Another of my American workers, Laura Leistikow, says it was infuriating to witness the lackadaisical attitude of her coworkers at the Chrysler plant. "A lot of people would take that pay and benefits for granted by not wanting to do their job, or screwing around, not coming in on time, because they had that 'buddy-buddy' system going on in the union," she says. What's more, her coworkers "trashed" the plant, and the janitors (also unionized) cared nothing for the quality of their cleaning. The bathrooms in particular were filthy: "You walk in there and you almost want to have a hazmat suit." Once, she found a janitor asleep on the job. "I'm telling you, you can't know how many times I've almost called. But if you call the Health Department, then you're ratting on a union brother or sister." With brothers and sisters like these, it was hard to feel a sense of solidarity.

What made Laura's view particularly interesting was that she also had problems with her black coworkers. Asked whether there was favoritism in the union, Laura, who is white, volunteered an explanation. "Definitely! Black favoritism. I'm being totally honest." African Americans were a third of her plant's workforce and were represented high in the union's leadership. Several times she heard her coworkers make racial comments that convinced her she was not really a union sister in their eyes. What's more, the union members who were black were able to leave their posts on the engine line for stints of training, she claims. "I always had to stay on the line while everybody else, it seemed like, was moving."

It is difficult to build group solidarity in a multiracial setting—a hurdle that American unions in times past sought to sidestep by excluding (and even demonizing) nonwhites. Some research suggests that a diverse populace is less likely to support policies to assist the poor: the "undeserving" become all the more so when they have different-colored skin.[46] Race can twist notions of deservingness in the workplace as well, making it harder for workers to see the union as their champion—or, for that matter, to acknowledge their coworkers as true "brothers and sisters" worthy of help or cooperation.

* * *

The meritocratic ideology fed a particular narrative that explained the travails of today's labor movement. If unions are weak, some of my workers said, it is because they were once too strong. They overreached. They asked for too much, more than the market would allow. If this view is somewhat self-contradictory, it speaks again to the ability of human beings in general to be of two minds (or multiple minds) on the same topic.

Market logic leads to the view that unions are anachronisms in today's dynamic economy. The only reason that union members turn to labor power is that they can't get ahead on their individual merits. According to a detailed 1996 survey of public attitudes toward unions, majorities in both countries agree that the "wage demands of unions don't reflect economic reality" and that "unions enable workers to get away with being inefficient."[47] In other words, the criticism of unions is in part pragmatic—what they ask for does not "reflect economic reality"—and in part judgmental—they "get away" with doing less than they "should."

If the public truly believes that union members are overpaid, that view may be in part a reaction to the excesses of the old (and disappearing) "labor aristocracy" and their "gold-plated" contracts. Private-sector unions are virtually nonexistent in the United States, which means that UAW-level wages and benefits seem all the more ludicrous in comparison to those elsewhere. Based on this logic, Perry Lew, an American and ex-Chrysler employee, vehemently disapproves of the benefits that his former union won over the years. "It's messed up because our parents messed it up," he says. "It got too plush. You know, the Jobs Bank—what is that? There's no work, go home. ... I'm paying you the same price, and you sitting in a break room watching movies, reading books, and playing cards?" As Perry sees it, the union's reckless persistence led to its downfall. And rightly so, because Big Labor failed to live within its means.

Even a few of my workers who call themselves staunch union supporters express misgivings that their unions did *too* good a job: winning wages and benefits that were ultimately unsustainable. Katherine Sergio, a Canadian, says she is fed up with the way certain corporate executives made out like bandits during the financial crisis. All the bank bailouts did, she says, "was line the executives' pockets." As for the auto industry, free trade "killed" it. And yet this self-described "union girl" also believes that organized labor bears some blame, too. "Unions put us in this predicament because of higher wages that are unreasonable," she says. "That [cost-of-living] percentage got put onto your wage before you even negotiated a new wage. Some companies were going up six bucks an hour." Katherine recognizes that the company needs to live within its means, labor costs included, if it's not to go bankrupt—like two out of the Big Three actually did. "You're not going to get retiree benefits anymore. We're all gonna have to pay for them, because companies that do have that turn out to be like GM." This is the way the market works, she points out. You have to be realistic.

As she continues talking, however, it's clear that Katherine is doing more than stating the new facts of life. Thanks to the economic crisis, the auto industry will never be the same, she says—and that may actually be a good thing. "There's not gonna be the twenty-one-dollar-an-hour job. We're gonna get back to reality and basics. We don't need the money for our boats and Ski-Doos. We need the money for our food and our homes and our utilities." Meanwhile, she empathizes with the company to some extent. "If anything, we probably owe the company because we robbed a lot of overtime hours out of them."

By calling for moderation, my workers are commenting on the modern-day limits of the union's ability to advocate for much higher wages. And yet their perspective is not just about realism. To some extent, it is also about ideology. They are falling in line with a specific, commonsense notion of what workers like them really deserve. It doesn't matter that a labor union's very reason for existing is to fight relentlessly for the best deal. By asking for too much, their unions violated the accepted moral standard of what workers like them merited in pay—the "natural" wage derived from the workings of the free market. In this way, a culture of meritocracy changes the moral calculus, shifting its focus from what decent wage employers should pay you and your coworkers, to whether you were "smart" enough to get enough education or experience to be valued in the labor market. Human capital replaces worker solidarity as the main, *moral* means of leverage in the workplace.

Ironically, though, the fact that they didn't just let the free market have its way is the very reason that these unions brought about egalitarian outcomes. For decades, they had successfully distorted the market in favor of higher wages for unskilled work, corroding the link the market forges between an educational credential and a job. The power of collective bargaining—and the threat of the strike weapon—in this way gave many ordinary workers access to the good life. And yet, to some extent, unions also allowed workers to be more inefficient, as the public widely believes.

It is important to understand that the choice of this one segment of experience to harp on—worker productivity and its effect on company profits and losses—is fundamentally ideological, too. I do not see the influence of ideology as necessarily a bad thing; it inevitably plays a role in any endeavor, for one thing, and in any case the structure of our economy should reflect the values we believe in. However, in this particular case the prevailing ideology promotes a narrow concept of efficiency that excludes other senses of the concept—for example, "efficient," or healthy, households and communities, ones that avoid falling into costly dysfunctions thanks to the stabilizing presence of employed people with good jobs.

If union disapproval was strong on both sides of the border, the other half of my workers followed large numbers of their fellow Americans and Canadians in supporting their unions. They pointed out the ways that unions could be a check on management's own penchant for abusing power. However, their defensiveness was, again, telling.

Even in a blue-collar city like Windsor, anti-union sentiments have trickled down so deeply that the public thinks today's autoworkers are "only getting what was coming to them." "We had so many people in the opinions column in the *Star* going, 'Haha! … It's about time you guys lose your thirty-two-dollar-an-hour jobs. Now you're really gonna know what the real world's like,'" says Liz Jung, a forty-six-year-old ex-Ford worker. The union never wished this kind of fate on the people now sniping at it, she points out; it wanted to pull all workers up, not push others down. For her part, Liz believes she and her coworkers earned every dollar that the union negotiated for them. "People always say, 'Well, you guys have it so easy, you make so much money,'" she says. "And [I'm] like, 'Yeah, come and play for a while and see how wonderful it is.'" Despite the union's ardent objections, people in the community continue to bash autoworkers, blaming them for the region's economic woes, and it is hard to ignore the critical chorus, Liz says. "When you have a city beating up their own, I think that's where the guilt comes from. Because you're always defending yourself."

"Even though it's a union town, it's not a union town anymore," says Ziggy Dordick, another former Ford worker. These days, Ziggy tries to steer clear of conversations about politics with acquaintances or even family, because inevitably they will start fulminating against unions. They work nice office jobs; they think union members are lazy and uneducated. "They've been lucky or whatever it is," says Ziggy, forty. "But at some point, they're going to feel the same thing." It bothers him that white-collar professionals want job security, too, but just don't want to give it to the "little guy." "If we didn't have unions, what would we have? We'd all have to have lawyers?"

James Channing, the unemployed parts worker, is separated from his wife and struggling financially after a year without work. He says being unemployed makes him ashamed. Yet he doesn't believe that good wages should go only to the well-educated. A former CAW member, he insists he is not "a big-time union supporter," but he thinks that the wages unions have won are fair. If the workers had not been organized, he says, it would have been "hell" at his feeder plant, because an unchecked management would have gone wild. "People talk about autoworkers like we were a bunch of greedy pricks. Like union people killed everything. Meanwhile, if it wasn't for unions, it would just be turnover—you know, 'You're fired. You're fired. You're fuckin' fired. Get out of here.'"

Though his factory job is long behind him, James Channing still bristles at the public's judgment of union members. "When we were in negotiations for contracts, if they couldn't afford to give us that money, they wouldn't have gave it to us. So now people are saying, 'Well, you know, you made too much money.' Well, what do you mean? What is too much money? You want everybody in Canada to make $8.50 an hour? Everybody's gotta make minimum wage? That's not right."

Even those workers who were critical of unions did not want minimum-wage jobs, of course. Like everyone else, they wanted decent jobs with decent pay. But their pragmatism and the broader meritocratic ideology made many of them question their unions. Among the half who were critical, some felt that less educated workers did not deserve the flush contracts their leaders had negotiated. Some felt that the union rewarded the undeserving. Almost all of them pointed out that times had changed—and unions, wrongly, had chosen not to change with them.

* * *

The attitude that unions let workers "get away with" bad behavior has consequences, in turn, for organizing. The battle over popular opinion that unfolds with every strike action becomes harder to fight if the public views union members as privileged "haves," their wage demands as unfair, and their very status as members of the middle class—attained through bargaining, not education—as undeserved.[48] Indeed, as they described how today's unions are too well-fed and contented for their own good, a few of my workers explicitly compared their union's rousing past with its more picayune present—which suggests they don't have a problem with unions per se, just with the lavishly appointed ones they happened to join. A century ago, when the UAW was waging bloody strikes to win recognition and living wages, there was an idealism and purpose to the struggle, they say. It is not just that earlier generations had it tougher in the plants; it is also that they were out there striking in droves, crowding the picket lines, scuffling with the police and Pinkerton detectives. "People died for our benefits," says Laura Leistikow, the American ex-Chrysler worker. "They actually laid their lives on the line to give us the privileges that we had." When autoworkers like her look back at those storied days, today's labor struggle seems bureaucratic and pedestrian in comparison, the benefits of union membership less clear, the dues subtracted from each paycheck more loathsome.

The generation that fights the good fight develops a devotion to its cause through the baptism of political struggle. Later generations find it harder to keep that faith.[49] "There's no real, 'One for all, and all for one,' anymore," Laura says. "It's part of that buddy-buddy system now that doesn't work for everybody, it just works for certain people." The UAW's long string of successful contracts over the decades may have come at the price of complacency and internal divisions, along with the loss of the underdog status that once won it widespread public sympathy. Without shared experiences of struggle and community, it is harder for workers to maintain an ethic of egalitarianism, and it is easier to dismiss the labor movement as irrelevant to their lives.

If unions continue to vanish, perhaps the public will eventually come to miss them. Any past of perceived excess will recede from the public consciousness. How much workers value unions may grow in response. Right now, though, public opinion polls give us little reason to believe this will happen any time soon.[50] Even as union membership in both countries continues to fall, large numbers of Americans and Canadians express the view that Big Labor remains too big. In 2011, six out of ten Canadians agreed that unions had too much power. That same year, four in ten Americans believed the same—a startling number, considering that today only one in ten American workers is unionized.[51] While the labor movement remains stronger in Canada, since the nineties even unions there have seen large membership declines. Meanwhile, Canada's networks of progressive advocacy organizations and think tanks have suffered from cuts in government funding. As a result, even up north there are fewer prominent voices making the case for collective solutions to society's problems.[52]

In fact, an alternative view is that organized labor's declining power does not make unions more enticing, but simply digs a deeper hole. After all, if UAW members in earlier times were truly principled, steadfast adherents of the egalitarian faith, a strong union organization helped make them so. The labor movement heralded norms of equity throughout the industrial and political realms, altering policies and also culture. It gave ordinary workers dignity and decent livelihoods, as well as opportunities to be leaders and agents of historical change. It is striking that in the late 1930s, a time of growing labor militancy, there was a stronger relation between the objective circumstances that the unemployed experienced and their expressed political attitudes. Engaged unions may have provided the institutional means to channel disparate frustrations into concrete political views and on-the-ground mobilization. But today's labor movement is bleeding membership. As its clout continues to weaken, so too does its ability to engage the imagination of broad segments of the workforce. In this climate, unions find it harder to foster solidarity among their members and also among the broader public. That cannot bode well for their popularity or membership rolls into the future.[53]

For their part, many of my workers—critics and supporters of the union alike—responded to the hostility of the surrounding culture by hunkering down. In this they were not unlike the black job seekers that sociologist Sandra Smith studied in poor Chicago neighborhoods, who avoided reaching out to family and friends for help.[54] What Smith calls "defensive individualism" is a survival strategy, a way to maintain pride and manage expectations in the face of daunting odds. But for Smith's workers as well as mine, this method of coping is tragically flawed. It means that some workers lose their faith in government or union solutions. It means that others ignore the structural barriers to their success and direct the blame for their long-term unemployment at themselves. The irony is that these are some of the workers who should be the most upset by the structure of today's economy. As the great transformation of our economy and culture has progressed, they have fallen farther than most.

The Cultural Contradictions of Self-Reliance

My research draws mainly from interviews and observations during the recession, and therefore it cannot make any strong claims about any historical change. The patterns I observe can only be suggestive and must be tested further. As I have described in this chapter, a mixed picture arises from the limited survey data now available. The international surveys find a strong (and realistic) sense that education matters in the labor market, in America especially. They describe some concern in both countries about inequality, though it is still below its peak levels—a somewhat curious finding given the spectacular rise in the top 1 percent's income and wealth in recent years. And they reveal the public's ambivalence about labor unions, in spite of the drastic deterioration of the U.S. labor movement in particular. That said, these various surveys do not fully capture the shifting cultural understandings of merit that are key to my argument about change over time. More exhaustive analysis of the available survey data and historical records is needed.

Being unemployed during the Great Recession clearly made my workers more cynical about government and unions in special ways. But they also understood that these institutions faced considerable challenges in a market economy that relentlessly cuts costs. Their personal experiences, too, reinforced a perspective of hardheaded realism. They were desperate for help, but many of them—especially the Americans—found little support from tottering unions or starved bureaucracies. Even though their social safety net and unions have also grown weaker in recent years, my Canadians' peer-staffed action centers improved to some extent their encounters with government and unions.

A rational appraisal of their situation led my workers toward self-reliance and away from the collective strategies of government and unions—pushing them a few steps in the direction of Newman's white-collar managers of old, and Lane's tech workers of today. Rather than relying on government or unions, they emphasized how their own courage and determination would get them out of the hole that the loss of their jobs had pitched them into. In today's labor market, a stunted meritocracy purged of labor unions and activist government policies, this course of action makes much sense. Clearly, over the past several decades the dominant institutions have changed in pivotal ways. Ordinary workers have lost the protections that once established sheltered (if sometimes sluggish) markets, and the social norms that once encouraged sheltering (if sometimes oppressive) families. The pro-corporate movement has gained in strength. Countervailing institutions—not just unions and governments, but also political party machines and church-led social movements—have seen their influence wane. With them has gone the ability to offer alternative visions of the economy and society.

With resignation, workers like mine recognize that corporations have the upper hand, and there is not much to be done about it. As management has gained power at the expense of labor, and as offshoring and automation have ramped up, they no longer have much faith in organized labor's ability to prevail at the negotiating table in any sustainable way. They come to the conclusion that they, and unions, can no longer ask for much. Instead, they have to sink or swim on their individual merit, a merit captured in the résumés that measure their accumulated experiences and skills—or lack thereof. Faced with systemic problems, they look, either falsely or just fatalistically, to individual solutions.

While past research has looked at how, for example, social networks and race shape views about opportunity, in this chapter I have focused on another, less studied domain: the effects of personal interactions with formal institutions of government, unions, and corporations.[55] Policy-makers tend to look at these institutions from a bird's-eye view. I showed how they are experienced on the ground, from the point of view of the unemployed. This kind of approach focuses our attention on an important but neglected policy dimension: implementation. In addition to benefit levels, we need to consider how well-meaning government policies are actually implemented. In addition to membership numbers, we need to look at how well-intentioned unions are actually organized. More broadly, the strategy that leaders adopt in response to economic and political trends also matters. In the face of globalization and automation and a powerful pro-corporate movement, the U.S. government long ago decided to turn away from robust interventions meant to bring about full employment, redistribution, and income security. In more recent decades, the Canadian welfare state has retreated as well. These high-level decisions have, among other things, impoverished and diminished the institutions encountered by ordinary workers.

At the same time, the broader culture of judgment acts to worsen the situation of ordinary workers. From the perspective of meritocratic morality, success in the labor market depends on acquiring skills and education, not on winning "undeserved" high wages through "unnatural" collective bargaining. When taken to an extreme, meritocratic morality conceals the collective nature of the problem of inequality and weakens the very institutions that could do something about it. To the extent that they adopt it, workers do not stop to consider whether organized labor's willingness to ask only what it "deserves" entrenches inequality. What they lack, in other words, is a sociological understanding to go along with the economic mindset: an awareness of how our culture's prevailing attitudes shape our expectations about what is the "right" wage—and what is the "right" way to get it. Nowadays, as waves of outsourcing start to threaten jobs at Silicon Valley tech firms, hospital radiology departments, and corporate law firms, this go-it-alone strategy is becoming questionable even for those elite workers at the very top of our stunted meritocracy. But that is the implicit consequence of an absolutist ideology of individualism: the right to rise, yes, but also the right to fall.

I must emphasize that a significant gap remains between the views of workers like mine and those of elite workers and conservative activists. My left-of-center union members did not attack government dependency and did attack corporate malfeasance. They did not necessarily internalize the meritocratic viewpoint. But ideological criticisms trumpeted by the media and the people around them put my workers on the defensive and overwhelmed their sense of worth. While my Americans and Canadians alike generally supported government intervention in the economy, they were ashamed about receiving benefits and sensitive to the critiques of government largesse. The Canadians expressed more concern about growing inequality and corporate power, while the Americans, if also quite critical of corporate executives, tended to focus in a meritocratic fashion on management's poor decisions. Both, however, recognized that the economic vitality of corporations was important to their own well-being. Meanwhile, though a good number of my Americans and Canadians believed that the labor movement faces daunting, even overwhelming, odds, some of their skepticism was more pointedly ideological, revolving around their sense that their union brothers and sisters were undeserving, and that their own unions had overreached.

To the extent that my workers attacked the guiding philosophy of unions, rather than just acknowledging their weaknesses and foibles, and spurned the possibility of collective action, rather than recognizing their common interests, false consciousness exerted its influence on them. That said, it is difficult to disentangle true adherence to the meritocratic perspective from simply a sensible assessment of the weakness of particular institutions. Their realism was particularly striking among my workers, especially the Canadians, but to some extent what factor is dominant—experience or ideology, realism or morality—is also in the eye of the beholder. And that is the point: both realism and ideology are at work here, interacting with each other in a feedback loop. Their real-world experience and knowledge convince workers that institutions are powerless or inadequate to their needs, and that they are better off on their own. In this way, the failures of government and unions push unemployed workers toward a disenchantment and self-reliance that fits well with the meritocratic ideology. That ideology, in turn, instills a market logic that channels their frustrations toward one set of the possible responses to institutional failure—that is, an individualistic approach of self-blame, skepticism of unions, and rationalization of the actions of corporations. These two mechanisms build upon each other, in an interactive and iterative process.

In this sense, the recent decline of unions and retrenchment of government present us with a vicious circle. A weak infrastructure of institutions leads to alienating personal encounters at union locals, state job centers, and other key bureaucratic contact points. These negative experiences lead to disenchantment and hostility toward government and unions, helping to support a reactionary politics that defunds and weakens those institutions further.

The meritocratic perspective, in turn, makes any opposing political force harder to sustain by sowing divisions within the broader society. Amid the attacks on the "undeserving" recipients of redistribution, the public looks not with sympathy, but with schadenfreude, on the plight of unionized workers, those once-favored sons and daughters now being laid off in droves. They are suffering, but their suffering is deserved because they received pay that was too high given their education. Meritocratic morality places the burden of responsibility squarely on the individual. With its perspective narrowed so, the public fixates on how government and unions stand in the way of liberty. With its ire directed at a dissolute and parasitic underclass, it has less enthusiasm for having public funds go toward building a stronger social safety net, much less intervening directly to create jobs for the jobless. It dwells on the moral decay of the "dispossessed" masses—the cable TV subscriptions and out-of-wedlock children of this or that poor family, the credit card debts and high school educations of this or that laid-off factory worker—but not, as Daniel Bell noted, on the "calculated chicanery" of groups of political and economic elites.[56] In this way, meritocratic morality deflects anger downwards, toward those least able to bear it—and away from the man behind the curtain.

* * *

When he started working at the plating plant in the late nineties, the first thing that Sarmad Dakka noticed was the stench. The carbon that filtered the liquid nickel filled the factory air, a dark cloud of dust. When he sneezed, black soot would come out of his nose. He had a mask, but it barely helped. After he had been there a while, his sense of smell and taste disappeared.

At the time, he lived with his parents, immigrants from the Middle East who had come to Canada to escape war. One day he found his mother crying in the laundry room. "Mom, what the heck is wrong with you?" he asked.

"I see what you go through," she replied, gazing at his dust-stained shirt, pants, and socks. "I feel so bad for you."

"Mom, it's not that bad of a job."

But it was, Sarmad admits. The plant was filthy. His friends asked him why he did it. It was the best option he had had after dropping out of college. Burdened with student loans, he signed up with a temp agency and got a job at the plant. It was just a ninety-day assignment, with the expectation of being rotated out, but one day he buttonholed his manager and begged for a real job. "I had my back to the wall," Sarmad notes. "I'll never forget how badly I wanted to have that job there. That's something I won't forget, that they let me work there."

He pauses. "Maybe they weren't doing me a favor, though."

Thirty-one, Sarmad has a boyish charm about him, expressed effortlessly in his easy smile, bright eyes, and smooth way of speaking. At the plant his people skills landed him a position as a union steward. He enjoyed the job, but the troublemakers he had to deal with every week—his feckless coworkers—wore down his nerves. "Nine out of ten times I was dealing with the same six or seven employees," he says. It made him wonder whether unions were doing right by their members. "A lot of times they're just defending the losers, the bums, the vagrants—the people that didn't deserve a job, the people that didn't need to be defended, the people that didn't appreciate it," he says. "A good employee that did what he was told was the minority, and in the meantime they could bypass him, or use him." It felt at times that the union was "helping the wrong people," he says.

When the company announced that the plant was closing, most of the workers were upset but went on with their work. A few of them, however, took their anger a big step further. "Some of the crazies vandalized things and smeared feces on the bathroom wall," Sarmad says. Workers sabotaged the line, trashed the union office, and stole curtains, files, even a modem. Sarmad was angry, too, but the vandalism was beyond stupid, he says. "They thought that this was a decision that a manager made. ... It's completely out of his hands. It was the economy."

After he lost his job, Sarmad went to the local job center to talk to a career counselor. "They're overwhelmed," he says. "I think I talked with her for seventeen minutes, and she had forty-three messages waiting for her in those seventeen minutes." Sarmad wanted to pursue a one-year training program for border security officers, but the counselor kept insisting he consider woodworking or welding. She was perfectly nice, Sarmad adds, but "she just saw a blue-collar guy sittin' in front of her."

He ended up enrolling anyway. What's allowed him to go back to school, he says, is a federal pilot program that has extended his unemployment benefits until the end of his course of study. It's made a huge difference for him and his wife Carolyn, who can't support them by herself with her income as a hair stylist. While he's grateful for the help, Sarmad wonders how many other people who could have used this benefit didn't know or didn't bother. There was only a short window in which to apply, and the program wasn't well-advertised, he points out. Self-reliance, self-initiative, and luck made all the difference here. Maybe the government didn't want the program to get overwhelmed, he says, but still, it makes no sense that a rich country like Canada can't do more to help its own. "In writing it looks great, but how many people did you really help?"

Although being back in school helps his mood, Sarmad deals with depression from time to time. "I'm still a young guy," he says. "There's still a lot of things I wanna see in the world and none of these things are available to me now because I'm not employed." Sarmad has what he needs—their financial situation is stable right now, he points out—and yet he doesn't have what he wants: the trappings of middle-class propriety, the level of affluence and opportunity whose bar rises with every generation. He thinks about the days when he and Carolyn could travel: Mexico, the Dominican Republic, Las Vegas. "It's nice to be together, to experience things together as husband and wife," he says.

He looks back on his decision to drop out of college with regret. When he was eighteen, he wasn't mature enough to realize how important his education was, he says. And it's not enough these days just to have a good work ethic. Yes, working hard in school pays off, he says. "But simply being a hard-working line operator? No, that will just leave you as a line operator."

Notes

1 Keith Banting and John Myles, eds., *Inequality and the Fading of Redistributive Politics* (Vancouver: UBC, 2013); Thomas Frank, *What's the Matter with Kansas?* (New York: Metropolitan, 2004).

2 The antipoverty policies that have been enacted in recent decades have mainly been targeted toward specific constituencies—the elderly and children above all. Meanwhile, the Federal Reserve has downplayed the goal of full employment codified in the Humphrey-Hawkins Act of 1978, focusing instead on inflation. Josh Bivens, *Failure by Design: The Story behind America's Broken Economy* (Ithaca, NY: ILR, 2011).

3 Public opinion regarding unions moved across similar trajectories in the two countries in those decades, but America's National Labor Relations Board and its labor laws both took a sharp rightward turn, making it harder to form unions. Martin Gilens and Benjamin I. Page, "Testing Theories of American Politics: Elites, Interest Groups, and Average Citizens," *Perspectives on Politics* (Fall 2014); Bivens, *Failure by Design*; Dan Zuberi, *Differences That Matter: Social Policy and the Working Poor in the United States and Canada* (Ithaca, NY: Cornell University Press, 2006), 52–54; Henry S. Farber and Bruce Western, "Accounting for the Decline of Unions in the Private Sector, 1973–1998," *Journal of Labor Research* 22 (2001): 459–85; Daniel Tope and David Jacobs, "The Politics of Union Decline: The Contingent Determinants of Union Recognition Elections and Victories," *American Sociological Review* 74 (2009): 842–64.

4 Frank, *What's the Matter with Kansas?*

5 Margaret R. Somers and Fred Block, "From Poverty to Perversity: Ideas, Markets, and Institutions over 200 Years of Welfare," *American Sociological Review* 70 (2005): 260–87; Jonathan Rieder, *Canarsie: The Jews and Italians of Brooklyn against Liberalism* (Cambridge, MA: Harvard University Press, 1985).

6 Off-label uses of government policies are quite common, too—for example, Medicaid, which has become a supplemental form of insurance for (once) middle-class patients whose nursing-home stays are not covered by Medicare.

7 Jody Freeman and Martha Minow, *Government by Contract: Outsourcing and American Democracy*

(Cambridge, MA: Harvard University Press, 2009); Suzanne Mettler, *Degrees of Inequality: How the Politics of Higher Education Sabotaged the American Dream* (New York: Basic, 2014).

8 Dana Cloud, *We* Are *the Union: Democratic Unionism and Dissent at Boeing* (Urbana: University of Illinois Press, 2011).

9 Kay Lehman Schlozman and Sidney Verba, *Injury to Insult: Unemployment, Class, and Political Response* (Cambridge, MA: Harvard University Press, 1979); Carrie M. Lane, *A Company of One: Insecurity, Independence, and the New World of White-Collar Unemployment* (Ithaca, NY: ILR, 2011).

10 In the past, political parties, like unions, offered a nonmeritocratic, fraternal alternative, through patronage jobs and clientelism more broadly.

11 Katherine S. Newman, *The Accordion Family: Boomerang Kids, Anxious Parents, and the Private Toll of Global Competition* (Boston: Beacon, 2012); Michael B. Katz, *In the Shadow of the Poorhouse: A Social History of Welfare in America* (New York: Basic, 1996).

12 Nan Lin, "Inequality in Social Capital," *Contemporary Sociology* 29 (November 2000): 785–95.

13 Victor Tan Chen and Katherine S. Newman, "Streetwise Economics," in *Chutes and Ladders: Navigating the Low-Wage Labor Market,* by Katherine S. Newman (New York: Russell Sage and Harvard University Press, 2006).

14 Lane, *A Company of One,* 39.

15 Rieder, *Canarsie.*

16 Jennifer L. Hochschild, *Facing Up to the American Dream: Race, Class, and the Soul of the Nation* (Princeton, NJ: Princeton University Press, 1995); James R. Kluegel and Eliot R. Smith, *Beliefs about Inequality: Americans' Views of What Is and What Ought to Be* (New York: Aldine de Gruyter, 1986), 37; Michèle Lamont, *The Dignity of Working Men: Morality and the Boundaries of Race, Class, and Immigration* (New York: Russell Sage and Harvard University Press, 2000); Jay MacLeod, *Ain't No Makin' It: Aspirations and Attainment in a Low-Income Neighborhood*, 3rd ed. (Boulder, CO: Westview, 2009).

17 Eli Chinoy, *Automobile Workers and the American Dream,* 2nd ed. (Urbana: University of Illinois Press, 1992); Richard Sennett and Jonathan Cobb, *The Hidden Injuries of Class* (New York: Norton, 1972/1993); Schlozman and Verba, *Injury to Insult.*

18 Robert E. Lane, *Political Ideology: Why the American Common Man Believes What He Does* (New York: Free Press, 1962), 66; David Halle, *America's Working Man: Work, Home, and Politics among Blue-Collar Property Owners* (Chicago, IL: University of Chicago Press, 1984), 61; Katherine S. Newman, *Falling from Grace: The Experience of Downward Mobility in the American Middle Class* (New York: Free Press, 1988), 77; Kathryn Marie Dudley, *The End of the Line: Lost Jobs, New Lives in Postindustrial America* (Chicago, IL: University of Chicago Press, 1994).

19 Seymour Martin Lipset, *Continental Divide: The Values and Institutions of the United States and Canada* (New York: Routledge, 1990).

20 In a 2004 survey, Whyte finds that "Chinese respondents tend to stress individual merit rather than unfair external or structural explanations of why some people are rich and others are poor." With the partial exception of Japan, this tendency is stronger in China than in a host of capitalist societies—the United States included—and post-socialist transition societies. For the Chinese public, Whyte argues, greater inequality can actually be seen as more "equitable" when contrasted with the rigidities of the previous nonmeritocratic system. Martin King Whyte, *Myth of the Social Volcano: Perceptions of Inequality and Distributive Injustice in Contemporary China* (Stanford, CA: Stanford University Press, 2010).

21 For example, Dudley (*End of the Line*) uses the term *social Darwinism*; Lamont (*Dignity*

of Working Men) uses *disciplined self* to describe the mindset of white working-class men, who value hard work and responsibility in the face of economic uncertainty. My emphasis, however, is on the ways that workers judge themselves and others according to (changing) notions of merit.

22 For tables and charts describing the survey data in this chapter, please go to my website, victortanchen.com. *First survey*: General Social Survey, 1973–2012. Americans' belief in hard work rose from a low of 61 percent in 1974 to 70 percent in 2012. In 1974, it was 60.7 percent among those with a high school degree or less education, and 59.9 percent among the more educated; in 2012, those figures were 73.0 percent and 64.3 percent, respectively. The unemployed and union members were less likely to believe that hard work leads to success.

Second survey: Pew Research Center for the People and the Press, *Trends in American Values, 1987–2012* (Washington, DC: Pew, 2012). Asked whether "success in life is pretty much determined by forces outside our control," 55 to 70 percent of Americans over the last three decades have said they *disagree*. The proportion of those disagreeing rose from a low of 56 percent in 1988 to a high of 67 percent in 1999 and 2003; in 2012, it was 63 percent.

Third survey: World Values Survey, 1990–2011. The question used a ten-point scale, with 1 representing agreement with the statement, "In the long run, hard work usually brings a better life," and 10 pegged to the statement, "Hard work doesn't generally bring success—it's more a matter of luck and connections." The percentage for answers 1 through 5 (belief in hard work) was 83.0 in 1990, 79.1 in 1995, 75.0 in 2006, and 74.3 percent in 2011—a steady decline. For answers 1 to 3 (strong belief in hard work), it was 60.1 in 1990, 56.5 in 1995, 47.0 in 2006, and 52.2 in 2011. In 2011, 71.4 percent of the less educated believed that hard work brings a better life, compared to 76.7 percent of the more educated.

23 Leslie McCall, *The Undeserving Rich: American Beliefs about Inequality, Opportunity, and Redistribution* (New York: Cambridge University Press, 2013), 225.

24 The percentage of Americans who said education was "essential" or "very important" in getting ahead was 84.0 in 1987, 87.1 in 1992, and 88.8 in 2009. Among those with a high school degree or less, the percentage rose from 81.1, to 85.0, to 87.7 over that period. There was no clear pattern among the unemployed or union members, though belief in education was weaker in those groups in two out of the three years of surveys. The percentage of Americans who said education should be "essential" or "very important" in deciding "how much people ought to earn" was 72.3 in 1992, 65.2 in 1999, and 62.7 in 2009. Among those with a high school degree or less, it rose from 64.1, to 64.6, to 72.9 over that period. The relationship between union membership and this belief was unclear; agreement appeared to be weaker among the unemployed, though again the relationship held up in only two out of three years. International Social Survey Programme (ISSP).

25 For the statement, "Differences in income in [the United States] are too large," the percentage who agreed or strongly agreed was 77.4 in 1992, 61.7 in 1996, and 64.6 in 2009. ISSP; McCall, *Undeserving Rich;* Katherine S. New-man and Elisabeth S. Jacobs, *Who Cares? Public Ambivalence and Government Activism from the New Deal to the Second Gilded Age* (Princeton, NJ: Prince-ton University Press, 2010).

26 When asked whether the government has a responsibility to reduce the income gap between "people with high incomes and those with low incomes," the percentage of Americans who agreed or strongly agreed was 39.2 in 1992,

32.6 in 1996, and 31.3 in 2009—a gradual decline. When asked about reducing the gap "between the rich and the poor," however, the percentage who said "definitely should be" or "probably should be" was 39.8 in 1985, 44.5 in 1990, 48.0 in 1996, and 51.0 in 2006—a gradual increase. Posed the question of whether government should provide a job for everyone who wants one, the percentage who said "definitely" or "probably should be" was 35.1 in 1985, 43.8 in 1990, 39.4 in 1996, and 39.7 in 2006. ISSP; Schlozman and Verba, *Injury to Insult,* 348.

27 According to the World Values Survey, the combined percentage of Canadians who believe that "hard work usually brings a better life"—specifically, those who gave answers 1 through 5 on the survey's ten-point scale—was 75.8 in 1990 and 73.9 in 2005, compared to U.S. percentages of 83.0 in 1990 and 75.0 in 2006, for gaps of 7.2 and 1.1, respectively. The other statistics come from the ISSP. In 1992, the percentages of the population who believe that education was "essential" or "very important" in getting ahead were 84.5 for Canadians and 87.1 for Americans. Between 1992 and 1999, the percentage who believed that education should affect pay fell from 56.7 to 53.4 in Canada, and from 72.3 to 65.2 in the United States; the gap fell from 15.6 points to 11.8 points. In Canada, the percentage saying that differences in income were too large was 71.1 in 1992 and 68.5 in 1999, compared to U.S. percentages of 77.4 in 1992 and 61.7 in 1996. The percentage of Canadians who agreed or agreed strongly that government should reduce income differences between rich and poor was 53.0 in 1996 and 66.4 in 2006—a substantial increase—while in the United States the proportion stayed fairly steady, at 48.0 percent in 1996 and 51.0 percent in 2006. In contrast, the percentage of Canadians who supported government responsibility for reducing the gap between high and low incomes fell slightly: from 48.2 in 1992 to 45.6 in 1999, compared to U.S. percentages of 39.2 in 1992 and 32.6 in 1996. In 2006, 38.8 percent of Canadians felt that it "definitely" or "probably" should be government's responsibility to provide a job, compared to 39.7 percent of Americans.

28 Karen Ho, *Liquidated: An Ethnography of Wall Street* (Durham, NC: Duke University Press, 2009); Robert N. Bellah, Richard Madsen, William M. Sullivan, Ann Swidler, and Steven M. Tipton, *Habits of the Heart: Individualism and Commitment in American Life* (Berkeley: University of California Press, 1985).

29 Lane's workers were less supportive of government solutions to the economy's problems than my workers. However, they criticized corporate executives and their high pay like my workers did. Lane, *A Company of One,* 152.

30 In other words, the hierarchy in society is largely justified, except when there are gross violations of the link between performance and reward. As research finds, arbitrary or unfair inequalities appearing at the level of one's reference group—the "lazy" workers that one worker rails against—are more heinous than inequalities resulting from high status "fairly earned" by elites. Daniel Bell, *The Coming of Post-Industrial Society: A Venture in Social Forecasting* (New York: Basic, 1973).

31 Chinoy, *Automobile Workers,* 129.

32 See MacLeod, *Ain't No Makin' It,* 219.

33 Between 2000 and 2014, union membership in America's private sector declined (from 9.0 to 6.6 percent), while public-sector membership was more stable (from 36.9 to 35.7 percent). Between 1999 and 2012, Canadian private-sector membership also fell (from 18.4 to 16.4 percent), while public-sector membership rose (from 70.8 to 71.4 percent). BLS, StatCan.

34 Asked whether they agreed more with the governors or unions on the question of curtailing

collective-bargaining rights for state workers, 48 percent said the unions (Gallup Poll, March 25–27, 2011). Paul Egan, "Poll Finds Michigan Voters Divided on Right-to-Work Laws," *Detroit Free Press,* December 5, 2012.

35 Katz, *Undeserving Poor,* 138.

36 Lawrence Richards, *Union-Free America: Workers and Antiunion Culture* (Urbana: University of Illinois Press, 2008), 13.

37 Frank Levy and Peter Temin, "Inequality and Institutions in 20th Century America," Working Paper No. 13106, NBER, Cambridge, MA, 2007; Jake Rosenfeld, *What Unions No Longer Do* (Cambridge, MA: Harvard University Press, 2014).

38 Richard B. Freeman and Joel Rogers, *What Workers Want* (Ithaca: Cornell, 1999/2006); Seymour Martin Lipset and Noah M. Meltz, *The Paradox of American Unionism: Why Americans Like Unions More Than Canadians Do but Join Much Less* (Ithaca, NY: ILR, 2004).

39 In 1957, 75 percent of Americans told Gallup they approved of unions; 14 percent said they disapproved. Over the next three decades, approval fell and disapproval rose, with approval stabilizing in the high 50s and disapproval in the low 30s. When the economy tanked, so did the approval rate, which hit a record low of 48 percent; disapproval soared to a record high of 45 percent. In 2014, 53 percent of Americans approved and 38 percent disapproved of unions.

In both countries, growing disapproval of unions may speak to a broader problem of political polarization, with conservatives in particular becoming more conservative and driving up overall rates of anti-union discontent. Jacob S. Hacker and Paul Pierson, *Winner-Take-All Politics: How Washington Made the Rich Richer—and Turned Its Back on the Middle Class* (New York: Simon & Schuster, 2010); Thomas E. Mann and Norman J. Ornstein, *It's Even Worse Than It Looks: How the American Constitutional System Collided with the New Politics of Extremism* (New York: Basic, 2012); Stuart Soroka, "Redistributive Preferences and Partisan Polarization: Canada in Comparative Perspective," presentation to the Canadian Studies Program and the Institute of Governmental Studies, University of California, Berkeley, May 9, 2014.

40 The problem with the Canadian data is that the questions and the polling firms vary across time. Gallup asked about union approval/disapproval in 1961–1975, but in other years it asked whether unions have been "a good thing or a bad thing for Canada." If we consider these to be the same question, the postwar years had the highest levels of approval, with a peak in 1956 (69 percent approval, 12 percent disapproval); approval largely stayed in the 50s in the decades that followed, while disapproval tripled by the 1970s and stayed largely in the 30s afterward. Gallup has not continued this line of questioning in more recent years, however, and to my knowledge no other national polls have asked comparable questions since a 2001 poll by Environics, which found that approval was 64 percent and disapproval 32 percent, compared to 57 percent and 39 percent in 1997. W. Craig Riddell, "Unionization in Canada and the United States," in *Small Differences That Matter: Labor Markets and Income Maintenance in Canada and the United States,* ed. David Card and Richard B. Freeman (Chicago, IL: University of Chicago Press, 1993), 139; Reginald W. Bibby, *Canadians and Unions: A National Reading at the Beginning of the New Century* (Mississauga, Ontario: Work Research Foundation, 2002).

The questions used in more recent years are significantly different in their wording and in their results. In 2007, Angus Reid asked Canadians whether they agreed that unions are "a necessary and important entity in our society"; 59 percent agreed, and 35 percent disagreed. In a 2013 Harris/Decima poll commissioned by the Canadian Association of University Teachers, a quarter of respondents said that unions were no longer needed; in contrast, polls commissioned by the employer-sponsored Canadian Labour-Watch Association found in both 2011 and 2013 that four in ten Canadians believed unions were no longer necessary.

41 According to Lipset and Meltz's 1996 survey, agreement with the statement "there is too much corruption in unions here" was 64 percent in the United States and 54 percent in Canada, and the percentage agreeing that the "union movement is getting weaker" was 73 percent in the U.S. and 62 percent in Canada. In 2011–14, 49 to 55 percent of Americans told Gallup that in the future unions will become "weaker than they are today"; in the previous decade, support for that view registered on average in the low 40s. Lipset and Meltz, *Paradox of American Unionism,* 87, 89.

42 James B. Jacobs, *Mobsters, Unions, and Feds: The Mafia and the American Labor Movement* (New York: New York University, 2006), 260–61, xi.

43 Jay Rosen, "Public Journalism: The Case for Public Scholarship," *Change* 27 (1995): 38.

44 One example is the ways that meritocracy leads to inequality even in the absence of corrupt elites—though it certainly has them, too.

45 Thanks to Katherine Newman for suggesting this term.

46 Robert D. Putnam, "E Pluribus Unum: Diversity and Community in the Twenty-first Century," *Scandinavian Political Studies* 30 (2007): 137–74; Ted Miguel, "Ethnic Diversity, Mobility, and School Funding: Theory and Evidence from Kenya," Development Economics Discussion Paper No. 14, Suntory Centre, London School of Economics, 1999; Cybelle Fox, Irene Bloemraad, and Christel Kesler, "Immigration and Redistributive Social Policy," in *Immigration, Poverty, and Socioeconomic Inequality,* ed. David Card and Steven Raphael (New York: Russell Sage, 2013), 381–420; Martin Gilens, *Why Americans Hate Welfare: Race, Media, and the Politics of Antipoverty Policy* (Chicago, IL: University of Chicago Press, 1999).

47 Lipset and Meltz, *Paradox of American Unionism,* 87.

48 Richards, *Union-Free America,* 13; Dudley, *End of the Line,* 59.

49 Howard Kimeldorf, *Battling for American Labor: Wobblies, Craft Workers, and the Making of the Union Movement* (Berkeley: University of California Press, 1999).

50 For an alternative view, see Freeman and Rogers, *What Workers Want.*

51 In 2011, 61.4 percent of Canadians agreed that unions "have too much power for the good of the country." This amounts to a ten-point drop from two decades earlier, according to Environics surveys. Lipset and Meltz cite older Canadian surveys that show a steady rise in this view: from 32 percent in 1950 to 62 percent in 1968, staying in the 60s in the early 1980s; their 1996 survey, however, found 47 percent sharing this view. In 1971, Lipset and Meltz note, 55 percent of Americans thought unions were too powerful, a proportion that had fallen to 30 percent in 1996; Gallup found the percentage in 2011 to be 43 percent. According to Gallup, the percentage of Americans who believe that unions should have "less influence" was in the low 30s from 1999 until 2008. In 2009, it shot up to 42 percent. Public opinion stayed roughly in the same place until 2013, when support for the anti-union view fell slightly, to 38 percent; the following year it dropped precipitously, reaching 27 percent. Interestingly, in another 2014 Gallup poll, 71 percent of Americans said they would vote for right-to-work laws, 82 percent agreed that no worker should be required to join unions or other private organizations, and

only 32 percent agreed that all workers should have to join and pay dues when they share in the gains won by a union. In contrast, Americans polled by Gallup in 1957 were more likely to take the unions' side in answering these same questions, with corresponding levels of agreement of 62 percent, 73 percent, and 44 percent, respectively. Environics Institute, *Focus Canada 2011* (Toronto: Environics, 2012); Lipset and Meltz, *Paradox of American Unionism;* Gallup.

52 The percentage of Americans belonging to unions was 31.8 in 1955, 28.9 in 1975, and 11.1 in 2014. The percentage in Canada fell from 37.5 in 1984 to 31.5 in 2012. BLS, StatCan; Riddell, "Unionization"; Bruce Western, *Between Class and Market: Postwar Unionization in the Capitalist Democracies* (Princeton, NJ: Princeton University Press, 1997), 195; Susan D. Phillips, "Restructuring Civil Society: Muting the Politics of Redistribution," in Banting and Myles, *Inequality and the Fading of Redistributive Politics.*

53 Schlozman and Verba, *Injury to Insult,* 349; Bruce Western and Jake Rosenfeld, "Unions, Norms, and the Rise in US Wage Inequality," *American Sociological Review* 76 (2011): 517–18.

54 Sandra Susan Smith, *Lone Pursuit: Distrust and Defensive Individualism among the Black Poor* (New York: Russell Sage, 2007).

55 Alford A. Young Jr., *The Minds of Marginalized Black Men: Making Sense of Mobility, Opportunity, and Future Life Chances* (Princeton, NJ: Princeton University Press, 2004); Hochschild, *Facing Up to the American Dream*; Lamont, *Dignity of Working Men.*

56 Daniel Bell, *The Cultural Contradictions of Capitalism* (New York: Basic, 1976/1996), 327.

■ CHAPTER 8

Theory of Politics

Editor's Introduction

This chapter discusses the differences between the *median voter theorem* and the *investment theory of politics*. Temin argues that the median voter theorem fails to produce accurate predictions because it does not recognize that America is a *dual economy* and that its history still affects its politics. He demonstrates how, even in the case of straightforward political issues, advertising dollars heavily influence the resulting political policy. The author continues with detailed information on the history of American politics: the original formation of the Constitution, the history of voter inequality, and the ongoing issues of voter suppression and how oppression is associated with the voter theorem. He contributes information on upper and elite classes and their continued growth, arguing that capitalism creates inequality in order to reward the capitalist class and allow them to dominate society. Moreover, Temin evaluates the structure of the political system by identifying limitations placed on the voters that create adversities to civic participation. In doing so, the author sheds light on the issue of voter education and just how much education, race, and the collective nature of inequality can affect behaviors in the political system. Finally, this chapter introduces the investment theory of politics, which Temin believes will better address questions concerning determinants of voting and political culture.

READING 8 The Investment Theory of Politics

Peter Temin

I now have shown how America is split in various ways. The first split is economically. Income inequality has progressed far enough to think of the United States as a dual economy. The second is racially. The relations between blacks and whites originated in early times in the New World, and they have taken many strange paths since then. Despite electing a black president twice in recent years, racism—that is to say, racecraft—has not disappeared. The third split is along gender lines [...]. are still not fully equal to men.

How does all this affect American politics? This is a difficult question and will take some effort to answer. I start with the Median Voter Theorem and work toward other approaches that are more illuminating.

The Median Voter Theorem is used widely in both professional and popular discussions. The theorem starts from a simple example. Assume there is to be a vote on a single issue, and everyone voting has a view ranging from absolutely yes to absolutely no with room for various positions in between. If everyone voting is selected for reasons other than their views on the issue in question, then it is likely that voters are spread out along a bell curve or one-humped camel. Technically, the distribution is very likely to follow a normal distribution, with more people in the center than at the extremes.

The Median Voter Theorem predicts that political candidates facing preferences like this gravitate to the center, to the median voter, the central figure in the distribution of voters. This view of politics is quite common and has spread from academia to public discussions. For example, Edward Luce, a journalist forecasting events in 2016 for the *Financial Times*, predicted the Republican presidential candidate in 2016 "will be too far to the right of the median voter to make it to the White House."[1]

This theorem appears to have strong predictions for politics in a dual economy. But it has serious problems. If the median person counted, American public policy would favor the low-wage sector. Since the low-wage sector contains over half the population, the median voter, if everyone voted, clearly is in the low-wage sector. But while the median voter would support, say, a higher minimum wage, it has not been raised in many years. Jamie Dimon, chairman of JPMorgan Chase, announced in mid-2016 that he was responding to the stagnation of wages by raising wages at JPMorgan Chase. This is laudable, but it is hardly the same as a raise in the national minimum wage.[2]

This paradox shows that the Median Voter Theorem is inconsistent with the dual economy. Lewis assumed that the lower sector of the dual economy had no influence over policy. Economic policy served the interest of the capitalist class; subsistence farmers had no political power. Lewis emphasized this point in the passages quoted in part I of this book to introduce his model by referring to the capitalists as imperialists, people who had little or no contact with the rest of society.

Many expositions of the Median Voter Theorem talk of people and voters as if they are the same people. But this approach is not appropriate in the United States. We have to go back to the origins of our Constitution to see why this

Peter Temin, "The Investment Theory of Politics," *Vanishing Middle Class: Prejudice and Power in a Dual Economy*, pp. 61-75, 197-198, 209-242.

is true and examine the history since then to understand how the Constitution was amended and reinterpreted.

The Constitutional Convention was convened in 1787 because the Articles of Confederation—the first written constitution of the United States, in effect from 1781—were not working. They had constructed a confederation of states that had no power to tax people; it could only bill states. It consequently lacked power to do much of anything else. The Convention was to propose a better alternative that would transfer some power to the federal government, but it had no power to enforce this change. Only if nine states of the Confederation ratified the Constitution would it go into effect. The Constitution therefore contained a series of compromises to persuade enough states to ratify it. Two differences among the states are relevant here: The states were (and are) of different sizes, and they were (and are) spread out from north to south.

The framers of the Constitution dealt with the different size of states by introducing a bicameral legislature. Representation in the House of Representatives was to be according to population, but each state was to have two senators, independent of the state's size. In addition, senators were to be elected by state legislatures rather than popular votes. This arrangement, adapted from England, both restricted the reach of democracy in the new country and helped convince small states like Rhode Island to ratify the Constitution.[3]

This arrangement helped the United States to come into being, but it restricted democracy in the new country. The Senate would temper the decisions of the House of Representatives, and the people's will was not directly linked to policy. The role of the Senate changed over time as the United States expanded westward and as agriculture was replaced by industrialization. People increasingly lived in cities, and cities were concentrated around ports. Atlantic ports were joined by ports on the Great Lakes and then on the Pacific Ocean. But while residents congregated in states with big ports and cities, senators came from states as they had been defined earlier. Democracy was limited by the contrast between the location of voters and the location of senators.

State legislatures had increasing difficulty appointing senators as the nineteenth century progressed. There were many gaps in the Senate in the late nineteenth century because the state legislatures could not agree who to appoint. The solution was to amend the Constitution to let the people elect senators. This was done in the Seventeenth Amendment, which took effect in 1913.

To the unequal counting of votes in the Senate, we must add the problems of redistricting the districts that elect U.S. representatives. This process has become politicized in the past several decades, and both parties have created safe districts for their members. As a result, ninety percent of representatives are in safe seats. The person wishing to influence public policy has the double burden of needing to live in a small state, for the Senate, with a competitive race for a representative. Very few American voters live in such locations.[4]

Despite this attention to the method of choosing senators, the Constitution makes no mention of eligibility to vote, instead turning the regulation of voting to the states. This was an odd way to write a constitution for a new democracy, but it was a result of the racial history of the American colonies. The Constitution needed to be ratified by both Northern and Southern states to take effect.

The assumption that voters are the entire adult population may be more or less accurate for Europe, where voting rates hover around 80 percent of the appropriate population for legislative elections, but the picture is very different for the United States. The mean voter turnout in presidential elections was 56 percent from 1976 through 2008. The mean turnout for off-year elections for the House of Representatives was only 38 percent.

An analysis of voter turnout by socioeconomic status in 1980 reveals who actually votes in the United States. Over half of the middle class, as it was then known, turned out to vote, while only 16 percent of the working class and unemployed voted. As can be seen in figure 1, the middle and upper groups comprised much of the population in 1980, and the lower group did not vote. Classification by location reveals the source of this result. Voter turnout in the North and West in off-year legislative elections was above 50 percent until 1970, falling to 40 percent since then. Voter turnout in the South, however, was only about 10 percent from 1918 to 1950, rising to around 30 percent more recently.[5]

The proposed new constitution of 1787 contained compromises to attract colonies that stretched up and down the Atlantic seaboard of the newly independent union. The most important of these concerned slavery. Southern colonies wanted their slaves to count in the allocation of representatives in the House of Representatives. As slaves were then considered property, not people, they clearly were not voters. The demand for representation therefore conflicted with the idea of a democratic union. Northern colonies were reluctant to agree to this inconsistent demand, but they could not insist on excluding slaves entirely and have the Southern colonies agree to ratify. The compromise, as every schoolchild knows, was to count slaves as three-fifths of a person and ban restrictions of the slave trade for twenty years.

Given this compromise on representation, it was impossible for the Constitutional Convention to define conditions for voting. In fact, most planners of the early republic did not think that universal suffrage was a healthy part of the government. They thought property owners would have a stake in the new constitution and would preserve it well. How much property would qualify a voter? Could free blacks vote? Could women vote? These questions were too difficult and too distracting for the Convention, which passed voting arrangements to the states.

The result was that voting was never a right of all Americans; it was a privilege of a prosperous portion of the population. States experimented with allowing free blacks and women to vote, but these outliers did not last. Free black men were excluded from militias in New York, but they voted if they met property requirements. Single women who met property requirements could vote in early New Jersey, where voting laws were generic. But when women's votes were thought to have affected the outcome of an election, the New Jersey legislature inserted gender specification in the voting law. During the Jacksonian period when property requirements for voting were lifted, race specification was inserted, and votes were reserved for white men. Keyssar calls it "partial" democracy, but it was an oligarchy in the South. Participation remained low as a result of these exclusions.[6]

The Civil War made surprising small alterations in this pattern. Voting in the South was more democratic during Reconstruction, but low turnout returned to the South due to Jim Crow laws and practices. Despite the Fourteenth and Fifteen Amendments, blacks were kept from registering to vote. The candidates in the general elections were chosen in primaries where far fewer people voted. These small gatherings of white people nominated sitting representatives and senators for reelection, and they were easily elected over and over. Their long tenure in Congress gave them enormous power because committee chairs were awarded by length of service. Due to the influence of these Southern lawmakers, the New Deal and the GI Bill delegated administration of benefits to the states. These benefits were confined to whites in the South, perpetuating this system.[7]

This pattern continues today. The Voting Rights Act of 1965 incorporated provisions to deal with the legacy of Jim Crow laws in the South. The Supreme Court ruled that its most effective provision was unconstitutional in *Shelby County v. Holder* in 2013. This provision required selected states and regions to preclear proposed voting arrangements with the federal government. In other words, the federal government would decide whether voting arrangements would violate the Voting Rights Act before they went into effect. The provision was ruled unconstitutional because the coverage formula was based on data over forty years old, making it no longer responsive to current needs and therefore an impermissible burden on the constitutional principles of federalism and equal sovereignty of the states.[8]

Despite the Supreme Court's assertion that all states are alike, the states that had been listed in the original bill immediately rushed to impose voting restrictions that otherwise would not have passed preclearance. While it seems clear that these restrictions are racially motivated, they can no longer be phrased in that way. The difficulties of voting therefore affect low-wage whites and blacks.

Southern states turned to poll taxes to keep blacks from voting when the Voting Rights Act prevented the South from legally restricting blacks from voting. When poll taxes were made illegal in 1964, the states turned to literacy tests and voter ID cards instead. These measures avoided the opprobrium of singling out blacks, but they also prevented low-wage whites from voting. What began as a race issue turned into a class discrimination. And politicians in 2016 were concerned about the effect of these new requirements on voting; voter IDs appeared to be a large barrier to voting by poor people.[9]

The old Southern practice has been transferred to the North by mass incarceration. As noted already, the number of imprisoned grew rapidly after 1970, making the United States an outlier in the proportion of its population in prison. Prisoners often come from center cities and are disproportionally black. Prisons typically are built in rural areas where private employment has decreased as government revenues increasingly are distributed to rural rather than urban areas. The Supreme Court ruled that prisoners should be counted as part of the population, although prisoners cannot vote. White Northerners in some rural areas now find themselves in the same voting position as white Southerners under Jim Crow rules.[10]

Another problem with translating the Median Voter Theorem into practice is that voters typically face two or more issues in a political choice. For example, racecraft and economics might figure in a single vote. Donald Trump, Republican candidate for president in 2016, said that federal district court judge Gonzalo P. Curiel, in charge of the lawsuit filed against him by people who had lost money at Trump University should not oversee the case because the judge "was a Mexican." When people noted that the judge hailed from Indiana, Trump still claimed he was unable to judge him because of his Mexican background. Paul Ryan, the Speaker of the House of Representatives, said that Trump's attack on the judge was racist, but that he supported him nonetheless. In this situation, therefore, a citizen's single vote ties together two issues: textbook racism and economics. The Median Voter Theorem does not tell the voter how to weigh this choice.[11]

Yet another way voting practices privilege the elites comes from the timing of votes. Tuesday voting restricts voting by low-wage workers who cannot get time off from their jobs. But there is no push to change this outdated practice. Tuesday voting began in the nineteenth century when most Americans were farmers and traveled by horse and buggy. They needed a day to get to the county seat, a day to vote, and a day to get home, without interfering with the three days of worship prevalent at that time. That left Tuesday and Wednesday, but Wednesday was market day. So, Tuesday it was. In 1875 Congress extended the Tuesday date for U.S. House of Representative elections and in 1914 for U.S. Senate elections.

Most Americans now live in cities, and it is hard to commute to jobs, take care of children, and get work done, let alone stand on lines to vote. This affects voters in the low-wage sector more than those in the FTE sector who typically have more control over their time. Census data indicate that the inconvenience of voting is the primary reason Americans are not participating in our elections. Some states have closed polling places in addition, leading to long lines and waits for potential voters. Early and absentee voting makes life easier for some voters, but states trying to limit poor voters cut funds for these activities, requiring more time and effort from voters. Columbus Day, Presidents' Day, and Martin Luther King Jr. Day are all scheduled on a Monday for the convenience of shoppers and travelers, but we have not adjusted to modern conditions to make voting more convenient for the sake of low-wage workers. There is little discussion of the timing of elections today, but one way to increase voting participation would be to change Election Day from Tuesday.[12]

Morgan Kausser and Alexander Keyssar remind us that the history of voting rights is not smooth and unidirectional. African Americans acquired voting rights in Reconstruction, but swiftly lost them again due to congressional and judicial decisions. They regained these rights in the Civil Rights era, but they are losing them again in "radical reinterpretations of the Voting Rights Act ... and the revolutionary reading of the equal protection clause introduced by the 'conservative' Supreme Court majority." This revolutionary reading became law in *Shaw v. Reno*, 509 US 630 (1993), when the Supreme Court subjected redistricting by race to strict scrutiny.[13]

Supporters of the Median Voter Theorem do not seem to notice these historical roots of voter participation variation. Perhaps they were reassured when women got the vote in the Nineteenth Amendment and nothing changed. The expansion of the vote came after the First World War when voting restrictions were lifted in several countries. The national organization of suffragettes distanced itself from black suffragettes, but "the South remained opposed, with the full-throated cry of states' rights giving tortured voice to the region's deep anxieties about race."[14]

Nevertheless, giving women the vote seemed not to affect national elections. Class rather than race had become central—at least outside the South—and women came from the same classes as men. They voted with men, and political scientists saw vindication of the Median Voter Theorem.

In addition to the problem of a partial democracy that restricts voting, the cost of getting information in order to vote does not play much part in the Median Voter Theorem. The theorem assumes that voters are spread out on a single line, caring only for one issue in any election, and that they all know their own preferences. Those assumptions go along with the way competition is taught, where consumers choose what kind of bread or tea to buy at the supermarket on the basis of freely available information. There is little mystery to consumer choices like these, and political theory here followed the economic presumption.

Within economics, the assumption of abundant free information has eroded in recent years.

In our complex civilization, people need to take time and sometimes spend money to get information to choose which product to buy. No one buys a smartphone, car, or house without getting some knowledge about what they intend to pay for. Workers seeking jobs often have to search to find one that fits their skills and needs. And it's a necessity for most adults to gather information about medical care, from finding a good doctor to choosing among various medications. Many economists have analyzed costs of information in diverse markets.

Information has costs, even if they are only the cost of time spent finding and absorbing the information. People with higher incomes can make more exhaustive searches for information about the goods and services they need. And the sellers of these goods and services invest vast amounts of resources in making information about their products available and accessible to potential customers. Advertising is the most obvious expenditure; consumers are surrounded with ads all around and in all forms, from the ads that line the subways to the ads on TV and the Internet. There are questions about the quality of information received through ads. The benefits of an advertised product often are exaggerated, and drawbacks or even dangers may be omitted. There are regulations for some kinds of ads, but there is a lot of room for unscrupulous businesses to take advantage of people.

Brand names provide one way to lower the cost of information to consumers. Many people rely on a familiar brand name as a signal to them that their purchase will provide the quality they seek. This lowers the cost of information to customers greatly. It is, however, costly for a company to establish and maintain a good brand name. Companies need to provide quality products for long enough for potential customers to know about and use and begin to trust their brands. And companies need to maintain the quality of their brand-name goods and services; even a temporary lapse can cause damage to the brand and subsequent sales.

Elections pose complex questions that rival the biggest purchases we make. For example, some candidates in recent political campaigns have made the claim that the Social Security program is about to run out of money. What does that mean? Is Social Security like your mortgage, so that running out of money means that you cease to get your pension—you are evicted from the system? Or that keeping people covered will mean benefits must fall across the board? It is hard to know from the many speeches that anticipate some kind of disaster what actually is going on.

There are problems with the current financing of Social Security that should be addressed in a calm fashion, but the strident tone of political rhetoric tends to obscure rather than explain them. A brief review of how Social Security works demonstrates how much information is needed to make an intelligent choice about the future of this program.

Social Security is not a pension plan where you pay in while young and collect when you reach a certain age. It is funded each year by taxes that workers pay to finance the expenditures due to current Social Security recipients. Since taxes in any year do not exactly equal the amounts needed for Social Security payments at that time, there is a buffer called the Social Security Trust Fund between the taxes and payments. This trust fund was built up in the last few decades to prepare for the enormous number of Baby Boomers born after the Second World War who would be collecting benefits.

Baby Boomers are now aging and have increased the number of Social Security recipients. The trust fund is now decreasing as the population ages. The Social Security administration is required to plan for seventy-five years in the future, which involves predictions about the changes in the relevant population. Current population projections indicate that the trust fund will be depleted within seventy-five years under current rules. The trust fund will be exhausted soon, and legislation is needed to deal with the problems this will raise.

Social Security is not about to collapse. It is the Social Security Trust Fund, not the whole system, which is running out of money. If the trust fund is exhausted and nothing is done, then benefits will be reduced. This will cause hardships for many Social Security recipients, but it does not mean the end of Social Security. The trust fund was close to being exhausted in 1982, and Congress took action to revise the system.

Social Security taxes are collected on wages only up to $118,500; the limit could be raised or even eliminated to balance the system. This cap on earnings subject to Social Security tax was set before inequality rose, and it now stands close to the boundary between the FTE and low-wage sectors. Raising the limit of wages subject to tax therefore would extend the funding of Social Security into the FTE sector. But the FTE sector is not interested in helping the low-wage sector, and nothing has been done.[15]

There are problems with Social Security, but people need information to understand the choices on how to address them. There is no imminent disaster. Instead there are problems that come up as conditions change and have been dealt with periodically. The latest major revision was instituted thirty years ago when inequality was not as severe as it is now, and there is a need to revise the taxes or benefits for the longer run again. These measures normally were taken by bipartisan actions and commissions set up for the long-run plans. If nothing is done at the moment, Social Security benefits will fall, and there will be administrative problems with intergovernmental payments.

How are voters to understand all this? Unfunded benefits like Social Security have almost disappeared for most workers. The history of Social Security also is unfamiliar. The choices have only appeared as occasional talking points; they have not been calmly compared to alternatives. The cost of information is high, as ordinary people need to find out where to get the relevant information and then how to access and understand it. Without that information, voter attitudes will be based more on emotion than reason.

Social Security is a relatively simple issue. Questions of government deficits or debt are far more complex. There are no simple rules or simple corrections that are needed. There are instead many separate parts that go into both the causes and the effects of these aggregate measures. Voters have very little access to this information and very little background in the reasoning used to produce plans. It is extremely hard if not impossible at times for them to have enough information to make reasonable voting choices.

Many voters in the low-wage sector want to know why their wages have not grown in the past thirty years, as shown in figure 2. Why are their wages disconnected from their productivity? Why has the American dream been denied to them? This is a complex problem with many parts. It is inconceivable that many members of the low-wage sector could find the information needed to put this picture together. Voters therefore have to rely on others to give them help. But who will provide the information?

As with complex goods for sale in our economy, people with money are advertising solutions to these problems. Just as large businesses dominate the information for consumer choices, large political organizations dominate the information for political choices. And brand names—party names in this case—summarize the information for voters. The problem is that there are only a few brand names in the political sphere, and there is no separate information available on the many issues voters need to take into account when voting. Voters need to know not only what they think about a variety of issues, but also how important these disparate choices are in casting a single vote.

The absence of political knowledge makes the Median Voter Theorem problematical. For example, Larry Bartels, a prominent political scientist working with the Median Voter Theorem, considered voters' opinions about the Bush tax cuts in 2001 and 2003. Finding that many ordinary people favored them, he asked incredulously: "How did ordinary people, ignorant and uncertain as they were in this domain, formulate any views at all about such a complex matter of public policy?"[16]

Similar questions arise in considering the invasion of Iraq in 2003. This invasion may have been a logical consequence of Nixon's Project Independence. It also was the consequence of George H. W. Bush's advisers: "Washington developed an Ahab-like mania regarding Saddam [Hussein]" in the 1990s. The invasion of Iraq was decided on by the Bush administration and then sold to the country, mostly by Secretary of State Condoleezza Rice and Vice President Dick Cheney. Not only was the military exempt from the desire for small government favored by the new conservatives, the war also was to be sold to the American public, not decided by them.[17]

There is no consideration of the barriers preventing some people from voting, and no consideration of the costs of information required to make choices in the Median Voter Theorem. These important aspects of the electoral process need to be brought from the periphery to the center of analysis.

An alternate approach starts from the cost of information discussed here. Just as business firms invest in providing information to consumers, political groups invest in providing information to voters. They make investments to convince people to vote just as business people make investments to convince others to buy. And large political organizations have the resources to make big investments in political education, just as large businesses have the resources to produce many ads and maintain many brands. This theory is known as the Investment Theory of Politics.[18]

This theory argues that the effects of voting are determined by entities—businesses, rich individuals, PACs—that are able to make large investments in political contests by various means. One way is to control who can vote, allowing only those people who will vote the way the investing entity wants. Another way is to advertise these entities' views heavily—on TV and on electronic billboards—and with powerful impact because voters have trouble getting other information about the effects of their votes. Voters typically need costly information for any single issue. Lacking the time or energy to get this information, they rely on advertising and party identification. They also have to vote on a small number of candidates. Each candidate represents positions on a bundle of decisions, and voters have to choose between these packages.

In the Investment Theory of Politics, in contrast to the Median Voter Theorem, voters are spread around a multi-dimensional space with scarce information needed to determine their position in each dimension. Faced with a small number of candidates, voters rely on the signals they receive from rich and powerful entities that invest in making their bundle of preferences attractive. Who can doubt the Investment Theory of Politics when politicians spend so much of their time and effort raising money?

The result is that voters have less influence on political outcomes than the investing entities.

Elections become contests between several oligarchic parties whose major public policy proposals reflect the interests of large investors. The Investment Theory of Politics focuses attention on investors' interests, rather than those of candidates or voters. The expectation is that investors will not be responsive to public desires, particularly if they conflict with their interests, and they will be responsive to their own concerns. They will try to adjust the public to their views, rather than altering their views to accommodate voters. In other words, the Bush administration's policy of selling the Iraq War to the American people was the norm, not the exception.[19]

Bartels analyzed roll-call votes on the minimum wage, civil rights, budget waiver, and cloture. He found that "senators attached no weight at all to the views of constituents in the bottom third of the income distribution. … The views of middle-income constituents seem to have been only slightly more influential." He found in an analysis of social issues that "even on abortion—a social issue with little or no specifically economic content—economic inequality produced substantial inequality in political representation." Bartels concluded from the analysis of many examples "that the specific policy views of citizens, whether rich or poor, have less impact on the policy-making process than the ideological convictions of elected officials." This is what the Investment Theory of Politics predicts. Bartels's amazement confirms both the power of the Median Voter Theorem among academics and its great limitations in the analysis of American policy formation.[20]

The public appears more aware than political scientists of what is going on. Two-thirds of people interviewed in a recent Gallup Poll thought that major donors had a lot of influence over congressional votes. When Gallup arranged survey results by the extent to which respondents knew about the structure of the American government, the more knowledgeable people were more likely to say that major donors had a lot of influence—while people in the district electing Congress members had almost no influence.[21]

The source of these findings can be seen in the 2012 congressional elections. The proportion of votes cast for Democratic representatives was closely related to the amount of money spent on their behalf as shown in figure 8.1. In fact, the observations are so tightly clustered around a straight line that the figure suggests that the expenditure of political funds is the most important determinant of party votes. The figure also reveals that the relation is linear: more money yields more votes. Personalities, issues, and campaign events are the focus of newspaper stories, but money is the prime determinant of the electoral outcome. Voter views captured by interviews may appear decisive, but they are in fact the mechanism by which the money spent affects votes. A more dramatic confirmation of the Investment Theory of Politics is hard to imagine.[22]

A new working paper by the same authors extends figure 8.1 to congressional elections since 1980. With the exception of one or two elections at the beginning, all the graphs—for both senators and representatives—look exactly like figure 8.1. The Investment Theory of Politics explains congressional votes well for the past thirty-five years. While there is more money in politics now and the role of dark money has mushroomed in recent years, money has been driving American congressional elections for many years.[23]

Anecdotal information suggests that figure 8.1 applies to local elections also, but the information is not available to make a formal test. The problem is the growth of dark money, that is, money from unidentified sources. The Brennan Center for Justice studied local elections in several states after 2010 and found that almost forty times as much dark money was in use in 2014

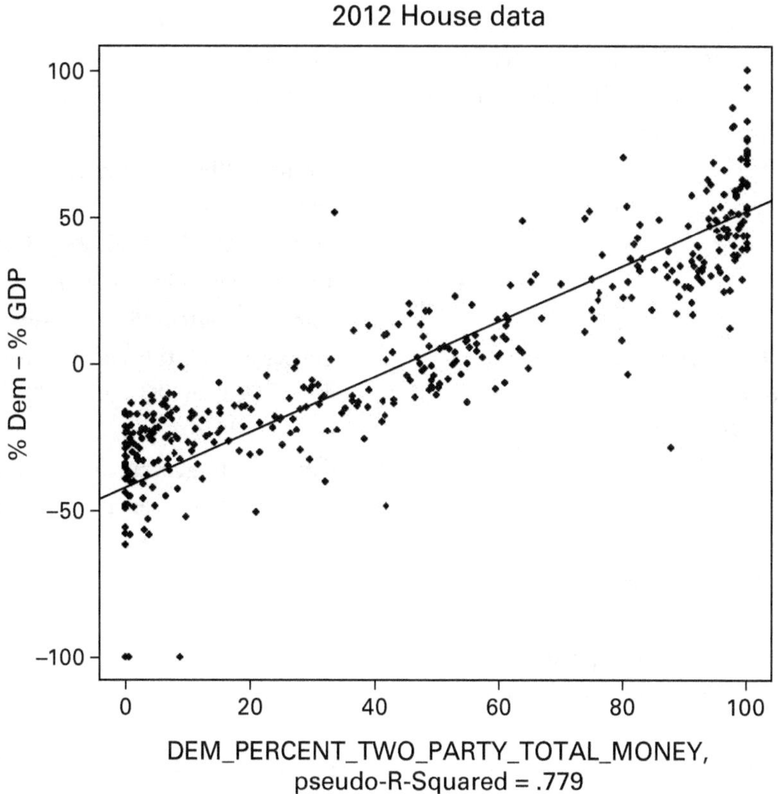

FIGURE 8.1 Money and Congressional Elections, 2012

Source: Ferguson, Jorgensen, and Chen 2013

as in 2006. Three-quarters of outside spending in 2006 was fully identifiable, but only about a quarter was transparent in 2014. This growth of political spending without oversight facilitates corruption, and it is best understood through the Investment Theory of Politics.[24]

A study of almost two thousand policy decisions made in the past twenty years extends this result on voting to policy decisions. The authors distinguished two kinds of interests: majoritarian interests reflecting the views of median voters and elite preferences typified by the 90th percentile of income distribution, that is, by the top half of the FTE sector. They found that the interests of the elites were very different and sometimes opposed to those of the median voters. The policy outcomes did not reflect the median voters' views, seen as the majoritarian views. When the interests of the majority opposed those of the elites, they almost always lost out in political contests. The strong status quo bias built into American politics also made it hard for the majority to change policies they disagreed with. In short, the Investment Theory of Politics is a far better predictor of political contests than the Median Voter Theorem.[25]

The Investment Theory of Politics reveals how politics works in a dual economy. The FTE sector dominates decision making, and the low-wage sector is shut out of this process. This exclusion is preserved in a supposedly democratic society by maintaining that voting is a privilege, not a right, restricting access to voting by the low-wage sector, and by the promulgation of information by the businesses and rich individuals who want to steer policy toward the FTE sector. In short, we are living by "the Golden Rule—whoever has the gold rules."[26]

Notes

1 Luce 2015.
2 Dimon 2016.
3 Levinson 2006; Maier 2011.
4 Overton 2006.
5 Burnham 2015, 29, 35, 46.
6 Keyssar 2000, part I; Burnham 2010.
7 Katznelson 2013.
8 570 US __ (2013); Overton 2006.
9 Hasen 2012; Wines and Fernandez 2016.
10 Thompson 2010.
11 Herszenhorn 2016. Trump speedily said his remarks had been misconstrued (Rappeport 2016).
12 http://www.whytuesday.org/.
13 Keyssar 2000; Kousser 1999, 2.
14 Keyssar 2000, 175.
15 Two kinds of actions are needed now. For the long run: adjustments in either the payments to recipients or the taxes that finance them, and possibly changes in both. For the short run: the government needs to loan Social Security funds to deal with immediate problems. The latter issue is straightforward. Just as the federal government loaned money to banks in the financial crash of 2008, one branch of the government needs to loan money to another to assure continuity of actions. The former, long-run issue is a question of public policy. Conservative politicians want to reduce benefits to restore a balance between taxes and payments for the next seventy-five years. Increasing the age at which recipients get Social Security benefits is one way to reduce benefits. Liberal politicians want to increase taxes to balance the system (Diamond and Orszag 2005; Hill 2016).
16 Bartels 2008, 177.
17 Bacevich 2016, 194, 244. Tony Blair sold the war to the British public in the same way (Ross 2016).
18 Ferguson 1995, chapter 1.
19 Ibid.
20 Bartels 2008, 265, 267, 289. Bartels reaffirmed this conclusion in a more recent book, saying, "Election outcomes are essentially random choices among the available parties—musical chairs" (Achen and Bartels 2016, 312).
21 Traugott 2016.
22 Ferguson, Jorgensen, and Chen 2013.
23 Ferguson, Jorgensen and Chen 2016.
24 Lee and Norden 2016.
25 Gilens and Page 2014.
26 Mayer 2016, 90.

References

Achen, Christopher H., and Larry M. Bartells. 2016. *Democracy for Realists: Why Elections Do Not Produce Responsible Government.* Princeton: Princeton University Press.

Bacevich, Andrew J. 2016. *America's War for the Great Middle East: A Military History.* New York: Random House.

Bartels, Larry M. 2008. *Unequal Democracy: The Political Economy of the New Gilded Age.* New York: Russell Sage Foundation.

Burnham, Walter Dean. 2010. *Voting in American Elections: The Shaping of the American Political Universe since 1788.* Bethesda, MD: Academic Press.

Burnham, Walter Dean. 2015. "Voter Turnout and the Path to Plutocracy." In *Polarized Politics; The Impact of Divisiveness in the US Political System*, ed. William Crotty, 27–69. Boulder, CO: Lynne Rienner.

Diamond, Peter A., and Peter R. Orszag. 2005. *Saving Social Security: A Balanced Approach.* Washington, DC: Brookings Institution Press.

Dimon, Jamie. 2016. "Why We're Giving Our Employees a Raise." *New York Times*, July 12.

Ferguson, Thomas. 1995. *Golden Rule: The Investment Theory of Party Competition and the Logic of Money-Driven Political Systems*. Chicago: University of Chicago Press.

Ferguson, Thomas, Paul Jorgensen, and Jie Chen. 2013. "Party Competition and Industrial Structure in the 2012 Elections: Who's Really Driving the Taxi to the Dark Side?" *International Journal of Political Economy* 42 (2) (Summer): 3–41.

Ferguson, Thomas, Paul Jorgensen, and Jie Chen. 2016. "How Money Drives US Congressional Elections." Institute of New Economic Thinking Working Paper No. 48 (August 1). https://www.ineteconomics.org/ideas-papers/research-papers/how-money-drives-us-congressional-elections?p=ideas-papers/research-papers/how-money-drives-us-congressional-elections. Accessed September 20, 2016.

Gilens, Martin, and Benjamin I. Page. 2014. "Testing Theories of American Politics: Elites, Interest Groups, and Average Citizens." *Perspectives on Politics* 12 (3) (September): 564–581.

Hasen, Richard L. 2012. *The Voting Wars: From Florida 2000 to the Next Election Meltdown*. New Haven: Yale University Press.

Herszenhorn, David M. 2016a. "G.O.P. Senators Say Obama Supreme Court Pic Will Be Rejected." *New York Times*, February 23.

Herszenhorn, David M. 2016b. "Wisconsin Race Frames Dispute over Supreme Court." *New York Times*, March 24.

Hill, Steven. 2016. *Expand Social Security Now!* Boston: Beacon Press.

Katznelson, Ira. 2013. *Fear Itself: The New Deal and the Origins of Our Time*. New York: Norton.

Keyssar, Alexander. 2000. *The Right to Vote: The Contested History of Democracy in the United States*. Revised edition. New York: Basic Books.

Kousser, J. Morgan. 1999. *Colorblind Injustice: Minority Voting Rights and the Undoing of the Second Reconstruction*. Chapel Hill: University of North Carolina Press.

Lee, Chisun, and Lawrence Norden. 2016. "The Secret Power Behind Local Elections." *New York Times*, June 25.

Levinson, Sanford. 2006. *Our Undemocratic Constitution: Where the Constitution Goes Wrong (and How We the People Can Correct It)*. New York: Oxford University Press.

Luce, Edward. 2015. "Forecasting the World in 2016." *Financial Times*, December 31.

Maier, Pauline. 2011. *Ratification: The People Debate the Constitution, 1787–1788*. New York: Simon and Shuster.

Mayer, Jane. 2016. *Dark Money: The Hidden History of the Billionaires behind the Rise of the Radical Right*. New York: Doubleday.

Overton, Spencer. 2006. *Stealing Democracy: The New Politics of Voter Suppression*. New York: Norton.

Rappeport, Alan. 2016. "Donald Trump Says His Remarks on Judge Were 'Misconstrued.'" *New York Times*, June 7.

Ross, Carne. 2016. "Chilcot Report: How Tony Blair Sold the War." *New York Times*, July 6.

Thompson, Heather Ann. 2010. "Why Mass Incarceration Matters: Rethinking Crisis, Decline, and Transformation in Postwar American History." *Journal of American History* 97 (3) (December): 703–734.

Traugott, Michael W. 2016. "Americans: Major Donors Sway Congress More than Constituents." Gallup, June 1–5. http://www.gallup.com/poll/193484/americans-major-donors-sway-congress-constituents.aspx?g_source=Politics&g_medium=newsfeed&g_campaign=tiles. Accessed September 22, 2016.

Wines, Michael, and Manny Fernandez. 2016. "Stricter Rules for Voter IDs Reshape Races." *New York Times*, May 1.

CPSIA information can be obtained
at www.ICGtesting.com
Printed in the USA
LVHW060136110321
681116LV00002B/7